PENGUINS STOPPED PLAY

It seemed a simple enough idea at the outset: to assemble a team of eleven men to play cricket on each of the seven continents of the globe.

Except—hold on a minute—that's not a simple idea at all. And when you throw in incompetent airline officials, amorous Argentine colonels' wives, cunning Bajan drug dealers, gay Australian waiters, overzealous American anti-terrorist police, idiotic Welshmen dressed as Santa Claus, Archbishop Desmond Tutu and whole armies of pitch-invading Antarctic penguins, you quickly arrive at a lot more than you bargained for.

Harry Thompson's hilarious book tells the story of one of those great madcap enterprises that only an Englishman could have dreamed up, and only a bunch of Englishmen could possibly have wished to carry out.

PENGUINS STOPPED PLAY

Eleven Village Cricketers Take on the World

Harry Thompson

WINDSOR
PARAGON

First published 2006
by
John Murray
This Large Print edition published 2007
by
BBC Audiobooks Ltd by arrangement with
Hodder & Stoughton

Hardcover ISBN: 978 1 405 61636 2
Softcover ISBN: 978 1 405 61637 9

British Library Cataloguing in Publication Data available

Printed and bound in Great Britain by
Antony Rowe Ltd., Chippenham, Wiltshire

For Lisa, Gordon, Betty and Bill Thompson, with much love—and for Scotties everywhere

Contents

Acknowledgements

Profound thanks to Bill Hamilton, Roland Philipps, Rowan Yapp, Pippa Brown, Katie Hurley, a succession of Brasenose College groundsmen, and every team who has ever played us.

1

Antarctica

I am in Antarctica. I am standing at Cape Evans, a promontory on the western side of Ross Island, a rugged, solitary slab of rock that thrusts through the clean lines of the Ross Ice Shelf. Or, to be more precise, I am standing nine miles out to sea from Cape Evans, on the iced-over surface of the ocean. My weight is supported only by a membrane of frozen sea water. It is a gorgeous, windless day, the sky an impossibly perfect cornflower blue. Or, to be more precise, it is a gorgeous, windless night, for, despite the sunshine, the time is half past three in the morning.

The scene that presents itself is one that instinctively commands hushed respect. Behind me tower the massive, smoking bulk of Mount Erebus, a 13,000-foot active volcano smothered from top to toe in creamy snow, and the harder black wedge of its lieutenant, Mount Terror. Ahead, the Olympus range of the Transantarctic Mountains stretches to the northern horizon, the serried peaks riven only by gigantic frozen waterfalls of ice: the Wilson Glacier, the Oates-Piedmont Glacier, the Nordenskjöld Ice Tongue. This is an almost entirely white world. Even through my sunglasses, the brilliant glare of sun on snow lances effortlessly into my streaming pupils. The silence is absolute.

In the distance, a man in a bright vermilion cagoule is running towards me, picking up pace as his thermal boots grip the ice. He is a teacher from New Zealand, and his name is Craig. I blink my eyes dry and try to focus intently on the tightly gripped fingers of his right hand. When he arrives at a spot approximately twenty-two yards away from me, he leaps high into the air and releases the object in his hand at speed in my direction. It is a cricket ball. I am holding a bat. I am doing what any right-thinking Englishman should be doing at times of hardship and adversity: I am playing cricket. The silence is absolute because, of course, it is rank bad manners to carry on chattering once the bowler has begun his run-up.

Well, of course, it wasn't a real cricket bat. It was an oar. And the wicket was really a purple rucksack. But the ball was real enough—trust a Kiwi to pack a cricket ball in his luggage on a trip to Antarctica. The match was New Zealand v. The Rest of the World, and I was opening the batting for The Rest of the World—the only time in my life that's ever going to happen. Craig's first ball kept low and skidded harmlessly past the purple nylon of my off stump. Cricket balls don't actually bounce a great deal on ice, in case you're interested. No? Oh, very well then. Back to the match. His second ball did much the same; but the third was on target. I jabbed hastily down on it, and it squirted down to long leg for what looked like an easy two. As I turned for the second run, however, I beheld an extraordinary sight: the long-leg fielder was being attacked by a gigantic seabird. It was an enormous skua, all beak and talons, and it had evidently arrived at the erroneous conclusion that the ball was a big, succulent red egg. Fielder and ball were locked in a whirling dance of brown feathers and Day-Glo nylon.

Now, there are those who would argue that sport should always follow a clear-cut moral code. In the late eighties, for instance, the football team I support, Everton, were banned from European competition because of the violent activities of certain Liverpool supporters. Nick Hornby, a better man than I, delivered a well-argued homily in *Fever Pitch* to the effect that any decent, upstanding member of the human race could only concur with the decision. I, on the other hand, couldn't help feeling that it was a monstrous injustice. And so it is with no little embarrassment that I must confess, here and now, that whereas others saw a man being attacked by a giant bird—a fellow human being in distress, let's face it—I saw only the opportunity to steal a third run. And what's more, what was even better, to turn a streaky inside edge into an all-run four.

By the time the bird had finally been driven away using various nautical-looking pieces of wood, and I was several runs to the good, it was clear that our hushed and deserted white world was about to undergo a profound change. Some fifty yards away was the ice edge, where our tour vessel, a robust little Russian scientific ship that had been tossed about like a cork on the way down, now lay moored. Behind was the deep, cerulean mirror of the Ross Sea itself. Suddenly the surface was broken, the light scattered like stars, by a pod of killer whales which porpoised the length of the jagged ice edge. Next, rearing out of the water, a glistening humpback whale followed suit. Thunderstruck with excitement, we stopped to watch. Then, when the whales looked as if they would porpoise off into the distance, they all performed an about-turn, and back they came, bounding in and out of the water as they passed by a second time. The humpback, I swear, even cocked its head to one side, to get a better view of us. They were watching us watching them. It was quite incredible. Never before had I seen this many spectators at an amateur cricket match.

It wasn't just the whales. A leopard seal, perhaps the most fearsome predator of the southern ocean, hauled itself up on an ice floe to take a gander. Ignore the 'seal' bit—think 'leopard' here. These creatures are twelve feet long, with evil little heads and wicked jaws. Imagine the head of Ridley Scott's Alien atop the body of Mike Gatting after a particularly hefty tea. One of them recently killed and ate a wetsuited British research scientist who was swimming in the Ross Sea. Luckily for us, the leopard seal has a top speed of about 2 m.p.h. on dry land (the Mike Gatting comparison becomes ever more relevant). If it was indeed eyeing us up with a view to a tasty snack, it was clearly out of luck. That is, as long as the ice beneath our feet held firm.

Clearly, our thundering footsteps on the ice sheet had echoed into the very depths of the Ross Sea below, and had brought a whole David Attenborough-documentary's worth of wildlife up to take a look. It was not long before the first penguin hopped out of the water, wandered across, and stood there on a length, facing me down as I brandished my oar. The game halted. We gazed at each other, our eyes locked. Hell, I wasn't scared. He was eighteen inches high. I knew everything there was to know about his breeding habits, gestation period, feeding habits and moulting timetable. The fact was, I knew a hell of a lot about penguins. He, on the other hand, was a relative novice when it came to cricket. I had the advantage, both physical and intellectual, and I think he could sense that.

I should explain at this juncture that if you choose to holiday in the Antarctic you have to spend five days on a boat, being battered by gales for the first two of them, then grinding slowly and agonizingly through hundreds of miles of pack ice for the remainder of the trip. The daylight being constant, you soon stop going to bed, and resort to catnaps instead. You are up for nearly twenty-four hours a day, with nothing to do but eat, read, play cards or listen to music on headphones. To fill your time, the expedition naturalists lecture you constantly about penguins. By the time you get within spitting distance of the South Pole, you have learned more about penguins than the entire staff of London Zoo. I knew everything there was to know about the king penguin (the one on the biscuit wrapper—coloured chest), the gentoo (red feet), the rockhopper (Denis Healey eyebrows), the emperor (fat bastard), the royal (looks like Michael Winner after a few drinks) and many, many more. So I knew by its black face and white staring eyes that the penguin now before me was an Adélie, named by the early French explorer Dumont d'Urville after his wife. As to what had prompted that romantic gesture—whether his wife had an especially beak-shaped nose, or had smelt of fish—history sheds no light. Suffice to say that the Adélie, being named after a French *girl*, is one of the more effeminate penguin species. So, in strict defiance of the Antarctic convention that prohibits the disturbing of wildlife, I hustled the little fellow away.

The game lurched on. The next ball was fast, short and wide—the bowler was a Kiwi, not an Aussie—so I had a speculative welly at it. For once, I connected. As so often when I've hit a ball as hard as I can, the ball didn't actually go anywhere, as all the power seemed to flow backwards from the impact, into the bat. In this case the oar actually shattered, into a trillion pieces. It had spent the night out on deck, and was frozen solid: wicketkeeper and slips alike were showered with tiny, glassy shards of frozen wood. Again the game had to be halted, while another oar was fetched.

The delay was an open invitation to the penguins. They came in waves, hundreds of them, crowding across the outfield, mingling with the slips, poking around at silly mid-off, blocking the bowlers' run-up, and invading the wicket itself. Antarctica is famous for its immense penguin colonies, million-strong bird cities that reassemble every spring in the same spot, year after year. Here it appeared that we were about to found a brand-new colony. Naturalists would one day be confounded as to its origin. One penguin on its own I could bully, but against wave after wave of inquisitive little monochrome invaders we were all helpless. Before long there was a vast crowd of them, filling the space between myself and the bowler, peering up in confusion. Waving the splintered handle of the oar to keep back the dinner-jacketed hordes, I felt like the conductor of the LSO at a particularly drunken staff party. Already, many of the outfielders had run back to the ship to grab their cameras. There was only one option open to us. For the first time—surely—in history, a cricket match would have to be cancelled because penguins had stopped play.

*   *   *

So what the hell was I doing there, in Antarctica, facing up to two hundred untamed Adélie penguins with only the handle of a frozen oar to defend myself? Why had I travelled fourteen thousand miles to play this game? Why had I braved the heaving seas of the Roaring Forties, the Furious Fifties and Screaming Sixties? (I didn't name the latitudes in question—that really is what they're called—but, believe me, there's nothing camp about a forty-foot wave.) Well, it was all the fault of Captain Robert Falcon Scott, RN, leader of the failed Antarctic expedition of 1911–12. Cape Evans was his base, and Shackleton's before him. A long, long time ago—more than a quarter of a century ago, in fact—I and a few friends had begun a cricket team, which we named after Captain Scott, that most splendid of runners-up. Inevitably, books and videos about the Captain had followed, presents from well-meaning relatives. I had stored up a modicum of useless knowledge about polar exploration as a result. Many years later, when I developed an enjoyable sideline as an occasional travel writer, it seemed entirely logical for a national newspaper to suggest that I travel a mere fourteen thousand miles to see a hut—the hut where Scott, Oates, Evans, Bowers,

Wilson and Co. had overwintered before their last, fatal journey.

We'd already stopped at Shackleton's hut on the way down: it was an incredible place, freeze-dried by the Antarctic cold at the exact moment that Shackleton and his men had abandoned it, running down to the shore to board their relief ship. Here was a veritable polar *Marie Celeste*: Shackleton's own filth-encrusted socks hung rigid above his reindeer-skin sleeping bag; his boots stood to attention on the floor below. A half-read copy of the *Gentleman's Magazine*, offering discounted Eton collars, lay unfurled on a half-made bunk; uneaten hams hung from roof-hooks; the shelves groaned with tins of tripe and onions, Bird's egg powder and Heinz India Relish. Scott's hut promised more of the same on a grander scale, tinged with the desperately sad knowledge that—unlike Shackleton, who was to survive a series of remarkable escapades—Scott and his men had walked out of there to their deaths, beaten to the Pole by Amundsen and caught by ill chance in one of the worst blizzards in Antarctic history on the return journey.

As our little vessel headed south in glorious sunshine, nosing optimistically around Cape Evans, we were met with an unpleasant sight: sea ice, nine miles of it, thick and unseasonal, clogging the shore. Our ship was not an icebreaker. It seemed we had reached the end of the road: 13,991 miles was to be our limit. There was nothing we could do to force a passage. I was utterly downcast: after all those years of being bombarded with polar literature, Scott's hut had taken on an almost spiritual significance. It had become the Kaaba at the heart of my own personal Mecca. (That, and the awkward fact that I was being paid to write an article about it.) Refusing to be beaten, I bearded Rodney Russ, the expedition leader, in his den. Russ was a genial Kiwi who put me in mind of Sir Les Paterson, if Sir Les had gone three years without cutting or combing his hair. Such setbacks were part and parcel of Antarctic life for an experienced old campaigner like Rodney, but, incredibly, moved by my predicament, he agreed to my suggestion that we mount a ground assault. Why, it was only an eighteen-mile round trip. We could actually see Scott's hut in the distance, taunting us, a little wooden rectangle on the tip of Cape Evans: it didn't look that far away.

We set out across the sea ice in the small hours—not that the Antarctic summer makes any distinction between the small hours and the middle of the afternoon. The slippery surface and the extraordinary glare aside, it was easy going. Bravely, Rodney decided that he should forge ahead, ten yards out in front of everyone else. We fell in behind. After five miles of pleasant Sunday stroll, reality kicked in when Rodney suddenly disappeared. A small dark hole in the ice marked the spot where he had last been seen. Milliseconds of utter panic followed, then waves of relief as he spluttered to the surface, shivering fit to burst but otherwise all right. Thankfully, it appeared that there had been no leopard seals in the vicinity. He was fished out, and items of dry clothing were donated. Ruefully—and very gingerly—we made our way back to the ship.

A pall of disappointment hung over our little

camp. The whole day had been set aside for the visit to Scott's hut. There was nothing else on the menu, nothing to do.

'I've got a cricket ball in my bag,' said Craig the teacher.

A score of faces—Australian, New Zealand and English—lit up.

*   *   *

But why Captain Scott, I hear you ask? Why a turn-of-the-century failed explorer, who to my knowledge played a great many games of polar football, but never even dreamed of a game of Antarctic cricket? The answer to that lies in another snowy landscape and a cold college room warmed by a single spluttering gas fire in the deep, icy winter of 1978.

2

Oxford

The whole Captain Scott obsession was down, in the first place, to Robert. Marcus, an old school friend whom I'd known since I was ten, had arrived at the same university at the same time as me, and had fetched up on a landing in Worcester College with two other first-years, Terry and Robert. Marcus, Terry and I had experienced roughly similar north-London upbringings of an almost sublime uneventfulness: reciting passages from the previous night's *Monty Python* or discovering that there was arctic roll for lunch had usually been the highlights of our school day. Robert, however, was different. His life had been *exotic*.

Robert was dapper and good-looking, with the clipped tones of Empire. He had grown up in Penang, in northern Malaysia, and had boarded at Repton. His father had been an executive with Standard Chartered Bank, but had also served as Belgian consul in his spare time—which was something of a mystery, as there was by all accounts nothing remotely Belgian about him. The family had also briefly been posted to Iran, where Robert's beloved brother 'Pickaxe' had been conceived. The nickname derived from his sibling's majestic aquiline nose, the result, Robert assured us darkly, of an illicit liaison between his mother and a high-ranking Persian. Robert and Pickaxe's had been a thoroughly colonial childhood, cosseted by servants and swathed in luxury. Their garden was so huge, Robert informed us, that David Attenborough had once filmed part of a wildlife documentary there. His family's life was straitjacketed by the unwritten laws of colonial society. His father, said Robert, would never even contemplate going to work without first breakfasting on Frank Cooper's Oxford Marmalade. On one occasion the great man had presented himself at the breakfast table at six o'clock sharp, as was his custom, only to discover a different marmalade before him, which he had refused to touch. Upon being informed that the house, and indeed the whole town, had run out of Frank Cooper's, he had simply sat at the breakfast table, unmoving, while the servants were dispatched to neighbouring houses in search of a jar. Not until roughly midday had any Frank Cooper's been located, enabling breakfast finally to proceed.

All Robert's heroes were like this: inflexible Empire eccentrics, men whose code of conduct took priority over any hardships, real or perceived. He absolutely adored Captain Scott, whose clipped refusal to surrender his manners or his dignity in the face of an icy death thrilled him to the core. Another hero was Cecil Rhodes, simply for the words of advice he had given: 'Remember only this, that you are British, and in the lottery of life you have won first prize.' Then there was R. C. Edwards, who had entered the record books as the only first-class wicketkeeper to lose all his luggage, including a full set of *Wisdens*, on an expedition to Uzbekistan. Robert found it hilarious, as we all did, that anyone should consider a full set of *Wisdens* to be vital expedition luggage. Of course Robert possessed his own set of *Wisdens*, and had practically memorized every statistic therein. He loved cricket, and was himself a graceful and elegant batsman in the Ranjitsinhji mould.

Robert's personality was both intoxicating and a little mad. His relationship with cricket, particularly, verged on the erotic. He frequently went to bed wearing cricket equipment, and had mysteriously managed to wear out the thumb and index finger of his right-hand wicketkeeping inner. He had changed his middle name to Viv, after Viv Richards. At school, he had once accepted a bet which involved tiptoeing into his housemaster's living room, past the armchair in which said housemaster slumbered, across to the fridge, and stealing there from a six-pack of beer. All of which had to be accomplished—and was—stark naked, except for cricket pads, gloves, spikes, a bat and his first-eleven cap. Alcohol, incidentally, was to Robert as prayer is to a Muslim. It would not have surprised me to see him genuflect in the direction of Thresher's. He could easily knock back a whole bottle of gin or vodka at one sitting, without—apparently—suffering the slightest effect, although as an impecunious student he had earmarked Martini as the most economical pence-per-proof option.

One of the first things that Robert did at Oxford was to rebrand Terry. Neither of his two Christian names—Terry or Darren—would do, so he was renamed Terence. He was a Young Conservative—bizarrely, he became William Hague's running mate in the student elections, where he did spectacularly badly—but that too was discouraged. Robert did not approve of the Young Conservatives. Sartorially, however, Terence was deliberately left to tread his own extraordinary path. He had giant Hank Marvin spectacles (he was amazingly short-sighted) perched above an enormous nose. He had bought a job lot of fluorescent-orange synthetic shirts with vast aeroplane collars and brown, flapping flared trousers from Wembley Market in 1973, and was grimly determined to wear them all out before buying any more. Unfortunately, they were utterly indestructible, being made of that stuff they insulate the Space Shuttle with, and I believe he still has them. In the heyday of punk and new wave, while the rest of us struggled into drainpipe trousers and jackets with impossibly tiny lapels, Robert and Terence made the oddest pair, the one dressed like a 1930s bank manager in a suit, tie, waistcoat and watch chain, the other looking like a reject from a Slade audition.

No matter how much ridicule any garment aroused, however, Terence would never part with it until he actually needed to buy a replacement, for he was quite staggeringly mean. He always claimed to have no money, and never bought a drink. On one occasion he was manhandled to the ground in a pub, and his wallet was extracted. It contained £70. It was, he squawked, 'all accounted for'.

Robert found Terence endlessly amusing, and played constant tricks on him. He would sneak into his room while he was in the shower, and sellotape his bottle glasses to the ceiling. He decided that Terence was a Russian spy (he was of Russian-Jewish extraction), and left little messages 'from Mr Brezhnev' hidden throughout his room; they were still turning up amid his belongings several years later. On the night before Terence's exams, Robert woke him up at 3 a.m. and refused to let him go back to sleep until he had 'spoken to the Kremlin' via his tormentor's umbrella handle. But, just as Robert's regard for the heroes of Empire was tempered with ridicule, so his constant ridiculing of Terence was indisputably founded on mutual regard. These strange friends of Marcus seemed a lot more entertaining than my own fellow students at Brasenose College, who for the most part spent their days toiling in the lab and their evenings vomiting up lager, so I found myself spending increasing amounts of time with them.

The third member of the trio, Marcus, was weedy, fastidious and amusing—and, it goes without saying, far more normal than the other two. Marcus and I had attended Highgate School, which was run at that time by a headmaster named Roy Giles, a man with all the charisma of a cereal packet. We were both keen on cricket, in theory at least, but the chances of our ever getting a game were nil. Highgate liked to hold back its slower pupils for a year or two, which meant that sport was invariably dominated by bigger boys. Worse still, Giles had put those bigger boys (most of whom bore a disturbing resemblance to Bruce Foxton of the Jam) in charge of their fellows, and therefore in charge of who did what. On any given summer afternoon's games, the slow-witted elite relaxed at cricket while the smaller, weedier, more academic kids—in a kind of bizarre revenge for their classroom performances—were forced to plough for mile after mile across Hampstead Heath, splashing through bogs, being stung by nettles and scratched by brambles. After seven years there, I had never been allowed even to pick up a cricket bat. It was beginning to rankle.

Consequently, one of the things both Marcus and I had been looking forward to at university was the chance to play a bit of cricket. Unfortunately, we ran into rather similar obstacles. Upon arrival at Brasenose College, I immediately sought out the cricket captain, a burly northerner called Phil Hanley, and made my keenness clear.

'What do you do?' he asked. 'Bat or bowl?'

I was forced to confess that I had never actually played the game. I just wanted to try it. It looked like fun on the telly—it seemed pretty easy, in point of fact. Somebody lobbed a ball in your direction, and you whacked it for miles and miles. Piece of piss.

It was, Hanley explained tartly, out of the question that I be allowed to play. Cricket at Brasenose was an extremely serious matter. Unlike other colleges, Brasenose did not even possess a second eleven, lest their second-rate endeavours scuff up the hallowed turf of the college square.

'I could practise,' I offered, 'and try to learn the game.'

'Look,' said Hanley, 'I'll tell you what I'll do, as a concession. Every year we have a one-off novelty game, where we wheel out a barrel of beer and everyone gets blind drunk, until the players can barely stand up. It's a right laugh. I'll let you play in that if you like.'

'But I want to play cricket, not get drunk,' I protested. 'I can get drunk any time I want.'

'In that case,' Hanley elaborated, 'you can piss off.'

The die was cast. Marcus and I had not been allowed to play cricket by our colleges. Robert was good enough to play for his college, but couldn't be arsed to get up early enough for the practice sessions. Terence—well, Terence couldn't play cricket either, but he'd happily tag along with the rest of us if we felt like doing something about it. There was only one option open to us. We would start our own cricket team. We would play fantasy village-green cricket against horny-handed blacksmiths, not spotty, serious-minded student cricket. And we would name our team after Captain Scott, because he came second, and because he did so in the right spirit. We would call it the Captain Scott Invitation XI, because anybody—absolutely *anybody*—could invite themselves to play. It didn't matter if they'd never played before, or if they were complete rubbish—just as long as they did their best.

*   *   *

Our first task was to recruit some more players, which we did by means of a classified ad. None of the motley bunch that assembled in my college room that wintry night had ever played the game before, except Tom Cairns, a would-be actor in impossibly tight leather trousers, who assured us that he was a rather nifty bowler. Now, when somebody tells you that they're rather good at any sport, it means they're either (a) a five times Olympic gold medallist or (b) utterly useless. We took Cairns at face value—none of us had ever seen trousers that tight before—and it was only when his bowling average sailed past the 100 mark in mid-season that we realized he too was a member of the latter category.

Our first game, against the village of Bladon, north of Oxford, could not have conformed to the pictured idyll more closely: a blazing mid-May day of the kind that comes around once every hundred years or so, a gorgeous wooden-railed pitch at the bottom of a hill beneath the stately bulk of Blenheim Palace, sheep grazing along the boundary, a pond glittering between the trees, and an opposition comprised entirely of gnarled Mummerset yokels. One of our players asked for ice in the pub. 'Oice? For the Captain Scott XI? Har! Har! Har!' The entire pub rocked with laughter. 'No, I really would like some ice,' he explained, whereupon the pub fell about again, a procedure that was to be repeated several times before he retreated in disarray.

It was only when the game began that it finally dawned on us that we didn't have the slightest idea what we were doing. I made the deeply humiliating personal discovery that my own cricketing ability roughly approximated to that of Mother Teresa of Calcutta. I couldn't bat, bowl or field, let alone captain. Batting, for instance, bore no resemblance whatsoever to the childishly easy activity portrayed on television. If you've never tried it, imagine trying to hit a swerving cherry tomato travelling at 100 m.p.h, wielding a broom handle. After Bladon had declared on a comfortable 250–4 (a huge score for a village match, had we but known it), we proceeded serenely enough to 58, courtesy of Robert and Tom Cairns, who could bat a bit even if he couldn't bowl. Thereafter Robert was given out lbw by Terence (incorrectly, as it turned out, for he hadn't read the rules) and the whole thing fell to pieces. Robert chased Terence into the trees with a cricket stump. The next eight men scored five runs between them. Five of us made 0. I did indeed manage to whack my first ball for miles and miles: unfortunately I did so vertically, and was caught when it finally returned earthward, having disturbed several Russian satellites. We were all out for 63, and lost by 187 runs.

And so the newborn Captain Scott XI went about its business. We quickly became known as the worst team in Oxfordshire, utterly inept in every department. In one match we were all out for 7, in another for 8. I hit every ball I received vertically upward, and by the end of the season had mustered the princely total of one run. My only consolation was that Marcus had accumulated 0. Even our wicketkeeping—this was Robert's job—was a hopeless mess, because Robert refused to collect any ball travelling down the leg side of the wicket, lest the need to scurry across compromised his dignity. Such leg byes frequently accounted for a quarter of the opposition total, usually more than our whole team had managed between them. Robert was discreetly replaced behind the stumps by Terence, who was no better; indeed, Lot's wife would have been more agile. Terence did however, afford us all some amusement when he took a particularly fast delivery in the testicles, after which it was discovered that he had not been wearing a box. Once he had finished writhing around in agony he was offered one, but declined, as there was only one ball left in the innings, and such a thing was hardly likely to happen twice in two balls. You've guessed it: that is, of course, precisely what happened next. The first time, he had received some rudimentary medical attention. The second time, he was left to roll around in agony by himself, as the rest of us were rolling around alongside him, helpless with laughter.

The Captain Scott XI may have been rubbish, but it did not lack for members. There were plenty of misfits willing to throw in their lot with us over the ensuing years. There was the oddly nicknamed Greenbum, who appeared to be about twelve, and insisted on playing in a tie and brogues, essaying a variety of impressions of famous Test bowlers. There was Bob, a fat northern piss-artist, who stood in the general election as Oxford's Monster

Raving Loony Party candidate. Some of the new recruits could even play cricket. One player, by the name of Roly, had even been in the Magdalen College first team, but was now unable to go back. A terrible sufferer from piles, he had been advised by the college doctor that a woman's sanitary towel placed in his underwear would prevent blood spots from seeping through the seat of his cricket whites. The next day, opening the batting for Magdalen, he had set off for a quick single, only to find the field frozen in attitudes of confusion and horror as he ran his bat in. There, in the middle of the wicket, having made its escape via the ankle of his trousers, was a bloodied woman's sanitary towel. He walked over, calmly replaced it in his underwear, allowed himself to be clean bowled at the next opportunity, marched back in the direction of the pavilion, straight past it and on to a passing bus, never to return.

Other new recruits were to become famous in due course, notably Ian Hislop and Hugh Grant. Grant was a foppish and elegant bat who never scored any runs. Hislop was a violently aggressive, indiscriminate slogger, who for ever endeared himself to the team one day at the bizarrely named village of Marsh Gibbon. He vaulted a fence to retrieve a six-hit, only to discover that the dried mud surface on to which he had jumped was in fact a thin crust covering a deep pool of liquid cowshit. He emerged a glistening brown from the waist down, occasioning yet more uncontrollable and hysterical laughter from his team-mates. Fame always takes its toll in the end, though. We last saw Hislop batting with a black cab waiting at square leg, the meter running, ready to take him somewhere more important. We never saw Grant again after the release of *Four Weddings and a Funeral*, when he was besieged in the showers at Ardley-with-Fewcott by a horde of heavily made-up fourteen-year-old girls, all of whom claimed to have 'just popped down to watch the cricket' in miniskirts and six-inch heels. His subsequent encounter with the hooker Divine Brown on Sunset Boulevard occasioned us much glee, however—not for reasons of *schadenfreude*, but because Ms Brown told police that she recognized Grant, from his voice, as 'that guy who played Captain Peacock in *Are You Being Served?*'.

But if nobody in our side minded that we were hopeless, the problem was that other teams did. There was a limited appetite among the villages of Oxfordshire for crushingly one-sided contests against a bunch of larky students who insisted on dipping themselves in cowshit. It was my job to find our fixtures, by sticking a pin into a map of the county, then writing a blind letter to 'The Cricket Captain, X village', but so many teams didn't want us back that the map soon began to resemble a colander. The team would have to improve, I saw—starting with myself.

Painstakingly, I taught myself to become a mediocre medium-pace bowler. I also learned one shot: the forward defensive. In so doing, I transformed myself from the runless slogger of our first season into a runless limpet, adhesion now my only virtue. If they can't get us all out, ran the thinking, we might at least get a draw. This theory was most famously vindicated in a match at Queen's College (we had started to play one or two student games), where only nine of us turned up. They scored 107. We had scored 48 when our last wicket fell, leaving me on 0 not out with nearly an hour and a half still to play. The Queen's skipper, bored by the one-sided nature of the contest, testily gave us 120 seconds to find a tenth man or he would declare a home victory. A beefy rower, walking by on the towpath, was pressed into service, blasted a huge four to loud cheers, then was out next ball. With 120 seconds to find an eleventh and last man, in desperation I located a tramp rummaging in the bins behind the pavilion.

'Do you know how to play cricket?' I asked him.

'Well, sir, I ain't played in twenty-five years.'

'Do you remember how to play a forward defensive?'

'I think I sort of remember, sir.'

'Excellent. Put these on, would you?'

The tramp obliged, and together he and I negotiated the remaining eighty minutes, blocking every delivery, refusing to run, and elevating the home side to new heights of fury. Only on the last ball, when the tension got too much, did he finally lose his cool, and balloon a catch up to the nearest fielder. The student in question was so surprised that he dropped it. I was so surprised that I literally fell over backwards. So did many of the fielders. We had our draw.

* * *

Our university years ended in a blaze of irresponsibility. Irrevocably hooked, we played eight games in the eleven days leading up to our final exams. Almost all of us got third-class degrees as a result. Only Marcus refused to play, saying we were mad to throw aside our academic futures like that. He sat in his room all year, swotting hard, and got a third-class degree like everyone else. The exception was Robert, who didn't get a degree at all. He was sent down just before finals, when the college finally spotted the size of his unpaid bar bill. But that didn't stop him: he returned disguised as W. G. Grace, wearing a huge, waist-length red beard that he and I had purchased in the Covered Market, and walked straight past several of his unsuspecting tutors.

I found a job back in London with the BBC, but I missed the camaraderie of the Captain Scott XI. I tried playing cricket for the BBC, where I discovered what it was like to be a stranger in someone else's team: roundly ignored, not allowed to bat or bowl, and invariably posted, alone, to the furthest boundary. Never, I vowed, would this happen to any new Captain Scott players. I switched to an actors' team, but this was alien territory indeed. Whereas the Scotties had assembled in the pub, and staggered down to the ground approximately ten minutes after the appointed start time, the actors made their rendezvous in the changing room ninety minutes beforehand, where they would all strip naked and stand around with their hands on their hips, shouting 'So, how's Chichester going?' at each other, in voices trained to dazzle Row Z. The only other non-actor in the side was the director Sam Mendes, a brilliant cricketer. On one occasion when he'd hit 50, and all the actors were shouting 'Ra! Ra!' (the actors never cheered; they always shouted 'Ra! Ra!'), I happened to be standing behind one such enthusiastic soul, and could hear him muttering to himself between 'Ra's. 'Give us a job, Sam,' he repeated endlessly between clenched teeth. 'Give us a fucking job, Sam.'

It was one of my earliest glimpses of the solipsistic reality behind the myth of leather upon willow, of crisp whites and manicured grass. I wasn't entirely naive of course: Bladon apart, I was aware that—more often than not—the village greens of England were overrun with bad-tempered, competitive stockbrokers in Gucci pads. And for every jolly old man with a Captain Birdseye beard, six or seven snarling hair-gelled youths with gold chains yapped and swore. Every time we lost a fixture, the reason given—true or not—was that Upper Snodbury would be eschewing friendlies in future to concentrate on Division 5 (South) of the Heinz Toast Toppers Relegation League. But Captain Scott, I felt, somehow rose above all this mundanity, even if said mundanity invariably kicked our arses on the cricket field. If we could only take back the team (which was still going on without us in Oxford) and transfer it to London, we could have a lot of fun.

And so (without much difficulty) we wrested back what had in any case become a faltering enterprise, and even succeeded in persuading Sir Peter Scott, Captain Scott's son, to become our president. We had violent blue-and-yellow caps made, with Captain Oates's famous last words, 'I'm just going outside', translated (probably inaccurately) into Latin as 'Modo Egredior' on the peak. I arranged fixtures across the whole of south-east England, in a green swath stretching from Essex to Hampshire. We spent our weekends in gloriously named hamlets like Steep and Over

Wallop, all picked from the AA book of splendid villages. I particularly liked the paired villages (Upper and Lower) of Gloucestershire, and always tried to imagine a missing third village. There were, for example, the Lavers (Upper, Lower, and Rod) and the Barringtons (Upper, Lower and Ken). Another favourite was the Suffolk duo of Nedging and Norton, which we decided provided the perfect description for a particular shot to a particular ball. A 'Norton' became one of those looping, innocuous deliveries that describes a gentle parabola, is imbued with no guile or skill whatsoever by its maker, but which by its very inviting plainness is tricky to play; a 'Nedge', meanwhile, became one of those thick edges that squirts in entirely the opposite direction from that intended.

Such whimsy aside, the plain reality is that we were utterly mashed by all and sundry. In the 1984 season we lost 22 out of 24 matches. More often than not we were beaten well before the tea interval. At Evenley in Northamptonshire a baked-potato seller set up a pitchside stall: we were beaten and on our way home in our cars before a single potato had baked. Our own players invariably found it hilarious; other teams rarely did. In particular, certain players seemed to specialize in enraging the opposition. Bob, for instance, once appeared at the crease barely able to focus, wearing no shirt, no pads and no batting gloves. The opposition fast bowler, the then Chancellor of the Exchequer's son, Dominic Lawson, was so incensed at this evident challenge to his masculinity that he bowled a series of rapid and vicious bouncers at Bob's head. In fact Bob was so drunk that, even if he'd had an hour, he would have been unable to don any of the above items. Our captaincy tended to rotate at this time, so Bob even got a go at the tiller. He insisted on placing all our fielders in a ten-degree arc, and switching bowler every over. Not surprisingly, the results were disastrous. Once again, opposition teams queued up in droves for the chance never to play us again.

In a panic, I started to recruit one or two half-decent cricketers. More often than not, they fled in horror at what they saw. When they batted, they were given out lbw by their new team-mates at the first available excuse. If they stuck around, they were invariably ostracized by the hard core of the side, who regarded talented players (Robert aside) as the very spawn of hell. Those that stayed were permitted to do so either because they were entertaining characters in their own right or because they were especially thick-skinned, or both. One such was Francis, a pink, seal-headed banker, who emerged from several years of open detestation to become a pillar of the old guard. Francis was a Zen master of mischief: on business trips, he enjoyed having the luggage of his commercial rivals rerouted from Helsinki to Manila, or demanding that small children be ejected from the first-class compartment. He forged a letter to Bob from a mythical official of his golf club, Mr C. Lyon, threatening him with disciplinary action if he did not call immediately to explain his drunken behaviour on the greens. An abject Bob rang the number on the letter, and found himself on the phone to the sea-lion enclosure at London Zoo, asking a weary keeper if he could speak to 'Mr C. Lyon'. Invariably, Francis expressed the most right-wing opinion he could think of on any subject, in an attempt to shock. Fascinated by death and serial killing, he even travelled to China in the hope of witnessing a public execution. On the cricket field he was a law unto himself: sometimes he would go in to bat in a position of his own choosing, ignoring the wishes of his captain or of whoever was meant to be batting there. Overcoming their initial reluctance, the old guard of the team—or 'the layabouts' as they had come to call themselves—accepted this immensely entertaining character with open arms.

The layabout ethic was simple. We always had to bat first, to get the game over quickly; there was no point hanging around, bowling all day—the idea was to lose fast, then drive off to a pub. There was only one way to bat, and that was to take a huge mow at every ball, a shot of which Coco the Clown (or Ronnie Irani) would have been proud. Catches were there to be dropped—invariably occasioning much hilarity—which was, of course, agonizing for any bowler who had spent the last three overs teasing the batsman, waiting for the attempted big hit before slipping him the vital slower delivery. If the batsman went on to score a century, so much the better—it would serve the bowler right for taking it all so seriously. Seriousness, in any form, was anathema. Anybody who batted 'seriously' was to be deliberately run out by a comrade, or dispatched lbw by the umpire, as quickly as possible. Bob even devised a system of making umpiring decisions on a rota basis: he simply gave his team-mates out on every second appeal from the opposing team. It did not take long, of course, for opposing teams to spot this, and to appeal at every delivery. A lot of the time it was fun. Sometimes, though, I found the constant hilarity slightly dispiriting. I felt as if I had surfaced in Phil Hanley's drunken beer-barrel game.

Marcus, although a 'layabout' by social inclination, was as furiously determined as I was to overcome his natural lack of ability and to bat properly. Together, we started opening the batting, partly because nobody else would do it, partly in an attempt to defuse the menace of the opposition opening bowlers and protect the team's 'recognized' batsmen (though I'm not sure who had ever recognized them, apart from their own mothers). Together, the pair of us accounted for nearly all of the team's lbw dismissals (and yes, he was usually as cross as I was, for a few minutes at least). Of course we did our best to keep our legs out of the way, to give our comrades no chance to whip out the finger, but this only made them more determined to get rid of us. Playing against the very same actors' team I had once turned out for, I was physically attacked at the crease by a sozzled Francis, wielding an upraised cricket bat. It was a very hot day, and he had imbibed several pints of beer. Our score was 41–5 (all five wickets had gone down at the other end, to the usual wild heaves). I was still there on 18 not out, and was deemed by my very continued presence to have failed to 'get on with it'. The actors' team beat us by teatime, and declined to play us again, muttering 'I say' loudly to each other as they left.

Meanwhile, the original source of all this hilarity, Robert, had moved into a house with me in Shepherd's Bush, having secured a job on the *Spectator* magazine. All was sweetness and light at first, but when I was sent on a film-directing course, finding it easier to source music from my own record collection than through the cumbersome bureaucracy of the BBC Gramophone Library, I took to nipping home at odd times of day. Bizarrely, Robert was always there, drink in hand. Even more bizarrely, many of my records seemed to have vanished. The first time, he told an entirely plausible story about feeling unwell at work. The second time, he told an equally plausible story about his boss going home sick, and as he, Robert, was still learning the ropes, there had been no point in him loitering meaninglessly about the office. The third time, whatever the cock-and-bull story was, I wasn't listening. I went to a phonebox and called the *Spectator*. There was, I quickly ascertained, nobody of Robert's name working there. I asked to speak to his supposed boss. Robert, it transpired, had been interviewed for the post, but unsuccessfully. He had no job.

This put me in a terrible quandary. What to do? Feeling rather ashamed, I searched his room when he went out. His jacket pockets were stuffed with receipts from the Record and Tape Exchange, Goldhawk Road branch. He had been selling my record collection to make ends meet. Under his mattress was a huge mound—and I mean a *huge* mound—of empty Martini bottles. Upon his return, I confronted him. At once he flew into an incredible rage, his face contorted and crimson with fury, stoutly denying the evidence placed before his own eyes. Waving the breadknife at me, his eyes flashing, he called me every name under the sun, all trace of the dapper and amusing companion of my university years boiling away like steam from a kettle. And then, with a slam of the front door, he was gone.

Feeling rather frightened by now, I found the number of Pickaxe, the beloved brother, telephoned him, and unburdened myself of the whole sorry tale.

'I think Robert's not very well,' I concluded lamely.

'Oh, so he's doing it to you now, is he? Well, he's been doing it to me for years. I can't stand the c**t. I won't have anything to do with him.'

So I called Robert's parents, whose sighs told me that this was not a new problem. The next day they came to collect him, not in a vintage Bentley but in an ordinary family car. Robert's father was no moustachioed colonel but a kind, rather sad, beaten-down man, with a pronounced Lancashire accent. They took him to see a psychiatrist, but Robert—who was very plausible indeed—managed to convince the therapist that it was his parents, not him, who were the fantasists. One of our team-mates (most of whom refused to believe a word of my story) found him a real job, as an estate agent. A few weeks later he was arrested at work. He had been stealing alcohol from the houses he was supposed to be selling.

* * *

When Robert returned from a prolonged psychiatric incarceration, he was welcomed like a long-lost son by the layabouts. I, on the other hand, had the vague feeling that I was being blamed for vandalizing something rather beautiful. I had pulled the wings off a butterfly. There were no hard feelings between Robert and me, of course, but this was not the same Robert as before. He was cured now, sober and rehabilitated, with a sensible civil-service job. He looked entirely different. He seemed to have shrunk during his ordeal, to have lost a lot of his physical strength. Samson-like, all his hair had fallen out, and he had taken to sporting little round wire-rimmed glasses and a clipped 1930s moustache. He was the living spit of Dr Crippen with the voice of Lord Haw-Haw, a refugee from one of Mr Cholmondeley-Warner's public information films.

Summers came and went, and gradually, in the face of moral resistance from the core of the team, practice made us better players. After eight years, we finally lasted the full forty overs of a forty-over match. On our tenth anniversary, on a lumpy and sloping artificial wicket apparently made from dried school porridge, Marcus and I returned to our alma mater to defeat a Highgate School eleven. It drizzled continuously, and the school guillemots looked on laconically from the many puddles saturating the outfield. The tea, which seemed to consist of waste radioactive materials dyed a violent pink or fluorescent green, would surely have been condemned by the Health and Safety Executive, had they been aware of its existence. I didn't care. We'd beaten rotten old Highgate School. We'd killed our parents. Our team—if there weren't too many layabouts there to sabotage things—was now good enough to engineer one or two close finishes, which was all

I'd ever wanted from a game of cricket.

The real enemy, of course, was not the opposition. The enemy was always within. An invisible divide had arisen between those who wanted to do their best and those who wanted to lose in a certain style. (I say an invisible divide, but many of the latter had taken to wearing brightly patterned waistcoats and bootlace ties. Well, it was the end of the 1980s.) To begin with, the division was only one of attitude. Opening the batting in a game at Queen's College, finally, after ten years of trying, and extremely inelegantly, I managed to prod my way to 50. The batsman at the other end, Charlie by name, whose previous highest score was a mere 3 but who had been coached pre-season, managed the same improbable feat from the very next ball. We congratulated each other, then both thought we had better retire to give someone else a bat. As we expected, we walked off the field to a deafening silence from our team-mates. But it was worse than that: no one would speak to us. The entire team had sent us to Coventry. Robert had even amended the scorebook: the other nine players had the word 'Mr' and their initials before their names, in the style used to denote an amateur in the old days; we had our initials after our names, implying that we were professionals. It was meant as the ultimate insult. Curiously, I didn't remember the same treatment being meted out when Robert had scored fifties in the past; but then Robert didn't tend to make big scores any more.

Other players fell victim to the same tactics at moments of success. A dramatic and exciting last-ball win, which I enjoyed from the umpire's vantage point, was greeted—or rather, not greeted—by the rest of the team positioning themselves in the pavilion, backs to the game, pointedly watching a wildlife documentary. Even Marcus, a diehard layabout, was sent to Coventry when he achieved a new personal best of 35. Increasingly thereafter, games were openly sabotaged. Half the team would bust a gut to get us into a good position, whereupon the other half would deliberately relinquish the advantage. It was easily done, and could be achieved with bat, ball or umpiring finger. Robert, needing 3 to win from the last over with five men still to come, simply patted all six balls back to the bowler. Greenbum, who liked to wear a Sony Walkman while fielding, developed the technique of kicking the ball all the way to (and over) the boundary for four, instead of picking it up and returning it to the keeper. Another layabout, umpiring, simply refused to call 'over' until—on the eleventh ball of the last over—we had lost the game. On the frankly homicidal wicket at Charlton-on-Otmoor, where balls can easily leap off a good length and behead the unwary batsman, we managed to restrict the home side to a hard-fought 50 all out. In reply, we inched our way to a hairy 44–2. We too finished on 50 all out. Our last three wickets fell with the score on 50, going down because Robert and two others simply stood aside and let the ball hit the stumps. For them it was a hilarious and honourable tie. For us, bruised black and blue from hours of defiance, it was a bitter pill. For the opposition, it was simply mystifying. I had never minded when we'd been out for 7 and 8 because that had been the best we could do. But this was different. This was deliberate sabotage.

Was it really unsporting to win, as they contended? Or was it unsporting not to try, which was how it felt to me? There were times when I could see both points of view. It's not as if we hadn't enjoyed many a jolly afternoon out in the country playing the old way. And I understood exactly what it was like to be a useless cricketer: the occasional big score notwithstanding, I was as likely as any of the layabouts to make a big fat 0. Like them, I agreed absolutely that the batting and bowling should be shared around: I just felt that our worst bowlers should be allocated a discreet over or two in the middle of the innings, not ten overs with the new ball against some bloke who used to play for the Transvaal. I had wanted a team where it didn't matter if you were rubbish, as long as you tried your best: not a team where it mattered that you were rubbish and that you did your worst. The pursuit of hilarity was too studied for me, too forced, and seemed to conceal an unwillingness to confront one's own limitations. How much easier to pretend, loudly, that you didn't care about your own or the team's performance because none of it mattered in the slightest? But they did care, for they put so much effort into competing with their team-mates, into restricting and curtailing the efforts of their own friends. In its way, it was behaviour just as uniquely British as leaving a complete set of *Wisdens* behind in Uzbekistan. Personally, I preferred to face up to my own considerable limitations, and relished any microscopic improvement in my own or the side's performance. I could always have given the whole thing up, I suppose, or stood around naked in a different changing room at midday, hands on hips, bitching about the voice-over on the Honeynut Loops commercial. The trouble was, I just cared too much for this stupid bloody team to walk away.

* * *

What really crystallized my disillusionment was the arrival of Cie. We'd faced Cie for years—he was a member of a Crouch End side called the Railway Taverners, but they mainly played on Sundays, whereas we had a huge number of Saturday games too. Cie would do absolutely anything for a game of cricket—he was an out-and-out cricket whore—so he became a Saturday regular. In midweek he would turn out for a raft of other teams. Cie would play cricket seven days a week if he could. He utterly worshipped the game. He even refused to get a job (he was paid a small retainer by his family to sleep in a flat above their fruit-machine business), in order to keep his days free. Cie never knew when a match might come up. Anywhere. With anyone.

Cie (it was pronounced 'C') had been introduced to cricket at the unexpectedly late age of thirty, by Mick Jagger's brother, Chris. A Kenyan Asian by birth (hence the unusual name), he had joined the forced exodus from that country as a teenager, just in time to catch the tail end of the 1960s. He'd passed those formative years in north London, in a haze of dope smoke and Jimi Hendrix records, had left school without a qualification, and had fallen into a job manning the pavement display at a greengrocer's. One

Saturday Chris Jagger, who lived locally, walked past and demanded to know what he was doing the next day. 'Nothing,' said Cie.

'Then you're playing cricket for us,' said Jagger. 'You're Indian—you must be able to spin the ball.'

Cie had to explain that he was African, not Indian, and that he'd never played cricket in his life before.

'It doesn't matter,' retorted the wily Jagger. 'They won't know that. We'll tell them you're a brilliant Indian spin bowler, and that we're about to bring you on any minute. That'll panic them into throwing away their wickets.'

The ruse worked, and the bogus Indian became hooked on cricket as no one before or since.

Cie was quite simply the nicest person that any of us had ever met. He didn't have an ounce of malice, or rudeness, or bitchiness, or jealousy, in his body. Everyone loved him. He was thoroughly, genuinely delighted if you did well. Before every game he was full of encouragement—'You're going to score 50 today, Harry, I can feel it in my bones, man'—and when you actually scored 0 he was the first, and indeed the only, team-mate to put an arm round your shoulders and offer words of solace. 'I can't believe it, man, you were looking so great out there,' he would lie. 'Hey, you're going to get 50 tomorrow on that form, man, I just know it.' Cie called everybody 'man'. He always had a smile, whatever the circumstances. He was a living embodiment of just where we had gone wrong. He may not have been the intellectual equal of some of his new team-mates— navigating a carload of players to Holkham Hall in Norfolk once, he managed to send them up the wrong side of the

Wash, and arrived at the tea interval—but he put them to shame in so many other important ways.

Cie would certainly have passed Norman Tebbit's cricket test. He was a mad-keen England fan, and was so thrilled when Robin Smith finally got a much-deserved century at Lord's that he ran on to the pitch to shake the batsman by the hand. Commentators who rail against pitch invaders as hooligans or drunks cannot have encountered anyone like Cie, who simply wanted to share some of his own overwhelming happiness with the successful batsman. As it happened, the members of Cie's Sunday team, the Railway Taverners, usually monopolized the jobs as temporary Test-match stewards at Lord's, so he was subsequently chased around the ground by a gaggle of his own Day-Glo-jacketed team-mates, who finally captured and ejected him.

On the field, Cie had indeed (ironically, in the light of Chris Jagger's original surmise) metamorphosed into a devilish spin bowler. His performances, though, could be erratic. Finally, we discovered his secret: dope. Without it, his bowling was no more than ordinary. But give him several oak-tree-sized spliffs behind the pavilion during the tea interval and he could make the ball fizz, swirl, bite and spit. 'Yeah, man,' he would exult as he bamboozled his way through the opposition. The ball, it seemed, was as stoned as he was. Unfortunately, all this dope-smoking brought with it an attendant problem, apart from the M40 police patrols: namely that, after a joint or two, he couldn't bat for toffee. It didn't matter. We were glad to sacrifice the one for the other. He was just great to watch. I would pick Cie up every Saturday morning from the Hanger Lane roundabout, where he would be waiting with one of the huge, greasy sausage sandwiches he always bought me for breakfast—for Cie would have nothing to do with vegetables, or fruit, or any newfangled nonsense like that. In the car, he would complain boisterously about any music recorded after 1974. He was convinced, I'm sure, that Harold Wilson was still prime minister and that Hendrix was still alive.

In Cie's first game, at the weirdly named Nomansland in Wiltshire (a place with no visible trench lines or artillery positions), one of the layabouts—who had been going in at number three—was half an hour late, so I put the new man in there instead. By the time the old lag arrived, Cie was already batting. Outraged, the latecomer made a racist remark, got back in his car and drove straight back to London. Thereafter he stuck mainly to playing on Sundays, when Marcus was captain. The contrast in approach between the old stager and the new man said it all for me.

And that was how the eleven divided by tacit agreement during the 1990s. On Saturdays I would captain, and we'd aim for a competitive game with a close finish. On Sundays Marcus would captain, and we'd see a more light-hearted approach from a 'good-tune team', as the layabouts liked to refer to a Sunday side full of their own kind. Assembled in such concentrated numbers like wildebeest at a Serengeti watering hole, they were easy meat for any opposition, but I encouraged the teams that didn't mind stuffing us to play us on Sundays, and the ones that liked us to fight back to meet us on Saturdays. One Saturday we faced Brasenose

College and squeaked past them in a thriller. As I sat with Cie on the bench before the red-brick pavilion, drinking a beer while the sun sank below the treeline, I wondered what had ever become of Phil Hanley, and told Cie the story of Hanley's inadvertent role in the founding of the team. Then, as we got up, something made me look round, and for the first time I noticed the inscription carved along the back of the bench: 'In Memory of Phil Hanley—a Great Brasenose Sportsman'. He had seemed so huge, so unassailable. I felt strangely awful, having sat on his bench and taken his name in vain.

The relationship between the two halves of the Captain Scott XI was not so much symbiotic as uneasy, like an Arab–Israeli truce. Only a few of us—Terence and myself, mainly—were idiotically keen enough to play twice every weekend. Some solution, surely, would have to be found. But then, like a couple whose marriage is failing but who unwisely decide they should hold it together by having another child, someone had the bright idea that the whole team should pack their bags and go on holiday together. We should go and play cricket, ran the theory, on the other side of the world. Englishmen abroad always stick together. It sounded like a great idea, and also like a terrible mistake. It turned out to be both.

3

Delhi

The British colonial legacy in India is an increasingly tenuous one. First-time British visitors to the subcontinent schooled in the films of Merchant–Ivory, Michael Bates's dodgy accent in *It Ain't Half Hot Mum* or Sir Alec Guinness's even dodgier one in *A Passage to India* are usually surprised to find the English language less widely spoken than in most Third World countries, and the pound sterling about as useful as a bag of chocolate coins. There are, however, still one or two familiar beacons from Old England to light the way. An obsession with queuing and needless bureaucracy. A comprehensive network of unpunctual and unsafe trains. And, of course, the spectacularly pointless sport of cricket.

Cricketers are the rock stars of India. As soon as an Indian male ascertains that a tourist is from a cricket-playing nation, he will almost certainly bring his encyclopaedic knowledge of world cricket to bear by shouting out the names of relevant test cricketers. 'Marcus Trescothick! Ashley Giles!' will echo after you as you walk down the street. 'Freddie Flintoff!' will follow you into your hotel. As the lift doors hiss shut, you will hear a muffled exclamation that may or may not have been 'Paul Collingwood!' When I was young I spent six weeks travelling around India, and was invited to bat in a scratch game on Cochin village green. My first ball was a gentle leg-spinner, which

I creamed for four. 'Ian Botham! Ian Botham!' shouted the dhoti-clad locals, rather knowledgeably I thought. The next ball looked identical, but wasn't. As I shaped to hit it, it came back unexpectedly and removed my middle stump. 'Derek Pringle! Derek Pringle!' shouted the locals, equally knowledgeably I thought.

Exhausted from my travels, I took refuge from the heat for a couple of hours in the TV room of the Umaid Bhawan Hotel in Jodhpur, a former maharaja's palace which still belonged to the dignitary in question. I say 'TV room', but that is something of a misnomer. From my vantage point on the sofa before the TV, were I to have craned round, I would have needed binoculars to see the back wall; and, were I to have gazed upward, a telescope would have been helpful to pick out the rafters. This was a fully fledged ancestral hall. There were two other sofas at right angles to mine, each with an elderly Indian gentleman ensconced. Each addressed his fellow in English, in a perfect cut-glass accent: here, at least, the Raj was alive and well.

'I say, old boy,' one said to the other. 'I do believe our chaps are going to win this one.'

We were watching a Test match: India v. Australia, from the Chidambaram Stadium in Madras.

'Nonsense, old man,' said the other. 'I dare say the Aussies will have the edge over our fellows.'

'My dear chap, just because you're a maharaja doesn't mean you know the first thing about cricket. I say India will come out on top.'

'Now look here, old boy, just because *you're* a maharaja doesn't mean *you* know the first thing about cricket. Australia will win.'

'Well, if you're so damned sure, old man, how about a little wager? Shall we make it . . . *interesting*?'

'A capital idea, old fellow, a capital idea indeed. Let's make it . . . *interesting*.'

My head whirled. What would the wager be? What would two fully fledged maharajas bet? Two thousand head of camel? The palace we were sitting in? Three or four wives?

'How about . . . *a bar of chocolate*?'

The chocolate bars in question were on sale in the hotel gift shop. They cost 2p each.

'Capital idea. *Now* we'll see who knows the most about cricket.'

The 1986 encounter between India and Australia at Madras became only the second Test match in world history to finish as a tie.

* * *

The idea of returning to India to play a proper cricket match there, or even two, came about because a real Indian player had joined our side: a lawyer from Delhi called Anuj. Just how good a lawyer he was remained open to interpretation. On one occasion we were supposed to rendezvous with our fellow players at a pub in Harrow, but arrived at the place to find it shut down. Standing in the doorway, a women in a quite staggeringly bad mood told me it had been closed for 'redecorations'.

'You should have told me we were meeting at this pub,' said Anuj.

'It's in the fixture list,' I pointed out, as wearily

as ever. Anuj liked to have even the smallest task done for him.

'I could have told you it would be closed down.'

'Yeah?'

'The landlord is in prison for sexually assaulting a barmaid.'

'How do you know?'

'I'm his lawyer.'

Despite being short and spherical, Anuj was a useful cricketer—that's if he turned up at all. He had a tendency to regard cricket as a business opportunity, which meant that if a better business opportunity came up he was liable to pack his bat and vanish unexpectedly. Getting fed up with this, I told him that if there were any more no-shows I would put him down as having scored a duck (always hit a cricketer where it hurts—in the batting average). The following Sunday he didn't turn up again, insisting that he had been ordered by the Indian High Commission to go to Heathrow Airport, to consult with a passing dignitary who was changing planes on his way to the USA. The next weekend, still annoyed, I moved him down the order to number eleven. He exploded with anger, almost taking a bite out of the pavilion. 'You cannot do that! You cannot do that, do you hear? Last Sunday I scored 61 not out! . . . Oops.'

Anuj was also the laziest player on earth. The rotund princeling would never scamper a single hit by another bat, and if forced to run by his partner was frequently in danger of being lapped. Off his own bowling he fielded like Jonty Rhodes, but if someone else was bowling he fielded like Thora Hird. He refused to go for any ball that passed by more than a yard on either side of him, on the grounds that he had been 'put in the wrong place'. It was his proud boast that he had never dropped a catch—but this was only because he had never gone for one. A cricket tour to Delhi? 'Leave everything to me,' said Anuj. 'I'll organize everything.' Not without trepidation, I left everything to him.

We had, after all, been away on a number of European weekends, all of them characterized by a lead-in period of foolish optimism. We had dreamed of idyllic sundrenched afternoons, of picnics on the grass and bottles of white wine cooling in ice buckets, while in the background our dream selves languidly squashed a rabble of confused Frenchmen/Italians/Spaniards. The reality, of course, had been entirely different. Invariably we'd found ourselves shivering in driving rain, of the kind that would have put even the British summer to shame, in grim suburban municipal sports grounds, being murdered by gigantic expats from the various Test-playing countries. In Paris a team of huge Caribbean fast bowlers (eight of whom played for the French national side) had unrolled a plastic mat in that part of the Bois de Boulogne where prostitutes normally go to pick up their clients. The scrub-strewn outfield had resembled a wide-shot from a spaghetti western; the playing surface had been worse. One man short, we had asked for a substitute player. They had given us Imran Khan. Unfortunately it had turned out to be a different Imran Khan. Apparently there are thousands of them.

Our only scenic game had been at the Château de Thoiry, south of Paris, where a bunch of

Pakistanis (most of them on a par with the real Imran Khan) had scored 244 against us, to which we had replied gamely with 48 and an interesting selection of cranial injuries. The only game where it hadn't rained had been in Madrid (it had been freezing cold instead), where a team of Australians had put us to the sword to the tune of 277 runs. Granted, one of them had been called Luis Rivero, but he'd still said 'G'day, mate' before taking 26 off his first over, finally depositing the match ball clean out of the ground and into the back of a Burgos-bound truck on the adjacent motorway. In the Dordogne we had been powdered to a pulp, in a howling gale in the middle of August, by a team of middle-class Englishmen. (Admittedly, this had been less of a surprise than the other expat-dominated teams, as there are no actual Frenchmen remaining in the Dordogne.) Finally, in Rome, we had arranged fixtures against Lazio and Roma—yes, *the* Lazio and Roma: the big football teams are all multi-sport clubs—on a weekend when, the home-fixtures secretary had assured me, it never ever rained in central Italy. It had in fact rained so hard that the Roma match had been washed away, while the bar where we'd ended the evening had filled with black, icy water to a depth of eighteen inches. Amazingly, we'd got a game in against Lazio the following day, their pitch an island of concrete in a shimmering lagoon. With thumping tour hangovers (one of our number had even been sick at the wicket), we'd been smashed into a million tiny pieces. Sri Lankans, in case you're interested.

Professional weathermen, with their vast array of satellites, computers and other modern technology, would do well to consult those who waste their summer weekends playing cricket. The same goes for the sunspot-observers and the elderly, wizened countrymen who claim to be able to predict good weather from the movements of moles and hedgehogs: even if I saw a mole wearing a Hawaiian shirt and tiny sunglasses, I wouldn't trust the little bastard to predict the weekend weather accurately. Cricketers, on the other hand, know perfectly well that there will be a misleadingly nice spell at the start of May, a bucketing thunderstorm at the end of July, and that the last bank holiday in August will be so hellish as to bring forth the four horsemen of the apocalypse by mistake. In the Captain Scott XI, we also know that it will pour with rain on the weekend—whichever weekend that may be—when we're due to play Charlton-on-Otmoor. This otherwise inoffensive village in north Oxfordshire attracts driving rain like a lovelorn admirer. To go out to bat at Charlton is to know what it's like to slip off a duckboard on day 43 of the Somme. Often, when the cloak of mist and rain descends there, unwary outfielders changing position between overs miss the safe, marked paths and are never seen again. One year, a huge, churning, Arkansas-style twister appeared in a neighbouring field. 'It's going round by Bicester,' said several gnarled old men, in a knowledgeable, mole-watching sort of way. Instead it turned at right angles and ploughed straight through the middle of the wicket, carrying uprooted tree stumps, outhouses and small children with it. And in the deep pools left in its wake floated the drowned bodies of several Hawaiian-shirted moles, wearing tiny Ray-Bans.

* * *

The Delhi trip was fixed for January—midwinter in India too, but the only time we could be sure of blue skies. It was to be prefaced by a week in Hong Kong organized by Francis, who'd just been posted there for a year by his bank. By some miracle we even managed to find eleven people to make the trip, encapsulating a whole range of ability, from Marcus and me at the bottom to Jonathan at the top end. Jonathan was an MCC member I'd borrowed from the actors' team, whose professional highlight to date was doing the voice-over for the Ferrero Rocher 'ambassador's reception' TV ads, and who appeared less interested than his fellows in exposing himself. There was no Robert (he'd decided, apparently, never to leave the country again), but we had a good bowler in the comedian Hugh Dennis, whom I'd borrowed from work: he'd been one of the stars of *The Mary Whitehouse Experience*, and now had his own show, entitled *Punt and Dennis* (known in the team as *Shunt and Vanished*, on account of its frequent moves to increasingly less mainstream transmission slots). There was also an unexpected addition to the party, in the shape of Marcus's fiancée. Unexpected, in that none of us had known he was getting married. Or had a girlfriend.

In my experience, the girlfriend of a regular cricketer, or 'cricket widow' to use the technical term, routinely goes through four stages, usually lasting about a year each. Stage one, characterized by feelings of deep and soulful affection, pictures the loved one striding across the greensward in athletic fashion, looking awfully manly in freshly creased whites, a picture of sturdy English resilience. It is important for any cricketer not to let his stage-one girlfriend actually come to a match, lest she see him swish pathetically over a two-bouncing long hop for nought, or hear the extremely vocal derision of his team-mates, thus shattering the illusion. In stage one, cricket = love. Stage two, the following summer, is characterized more by resigned acceptance. Go on then, play cricket, she thinks. As least I know where he is. At least he's not shagging my best friend. Stage three, another year on, is when she begins to compete with the sport itself. The phrase 'You and your bloody cricket' will recur constantly, especially if Angela's barbecue happens to clash with the vital fixture at Great Yieldham. 'I'm not stopping you going,' the cricketer defends himself gamely, diplomatically keeping secret the knowledge that he's never been able to stand Angela or any of her ghastly friends. 'Anyway, I'll be along later.' Yes, at midnight. Stage four is a variant of stage three. The oft-repeated phrase now is 'You and your *fucking* cricket.' When Angela has another barbecue, the cricketer's girlfriend gets off with Angela's friend Roger, who's a lawyer with an open-top car who hates sport, and never comes back.

To be fair, I have encountered one or two rather more persistent and long-suffering girlfriends. One of them even wanted to marry me, and was determined to catch the bridal bouquet at a friend's wedding, an event for which I had stupidly failed to find a clashing fixture. In a moment of bizarre coincidence, the bride hurled the bouquet not at any women, but straight at me. It was tricky dilemma indeed. How to get rid of the thing? I thought, as it sailed towards me. Straight drive? Pull shot? Leg glance? In the event I played down the wrong line, flailing lamely at it, and succeeded only in edging it. There, waiting at the equivalent of first slip to gobble it up, was my girlfriend. Of course, she pouched it like an Australian.

Another determined lady was going out with one of our better batsmen, a fat, phlegmatic Lancastrian. Upon reaching stage four, she screamed, 'Ian, it's cricket or *me*!' into his face. 'All right,' he said ruminatively, after a thoughtful pause. 'Cricket.' She fled into the night in tears. But a few months later she was back, smiling sweetly like one of those deep-sea fish that have a toothsome grin and a light on the end of a fishing rod, promising him he could play cricket whenever he liked. He took the bait like a patsy, and walked up the aisle. Now he puts up shelves on Sundays, cricket completely *verboten*, his house arrest as effective as any al-Qaeda terrorist's. Marcus's fiancée was dreamily rooted at the very base of stage one. But he wasn't just bringing her to a single five-hour match. He was bringing her on a two-week cricket tour of Asia—384 hours of solid cricket/cricketers. Not since the charge of the Light Brigade had anyone taken such a foolhardy decision.

We found colonial Hong Kong in something approaching a state of panic about the approaching handover to mainland China. The older hands, in particular, had to make the difficult choice between staying in a dictatorship or returning to a Britain which—in the words of one member of the Kowloon Cricket Club—now amounted to little more than 'a load of poofs'. (The speaker, I was pleased to note, was the possessor of a gloriously anachronistic moustache, giving him an unwitting resemblance to Freddie Mercury that would probably see him arrested on his first innocent visit to a British public lavatory.) The Hong Kong cricketers were uncomfortably aware that their pitches—immaculate green islands in a threatening sea of tower blocks—were candidates for the title of Most Valuable Sporting Real Estate in the World, each one worth something in the region of a billion Hong Kong dollars. In some cases they had frantically courted members from the ranks of the local Chinese, in order to lose the dangerous tag of expat exclusivity. One club, Craigengower CC, had gone too far, recruiting so many Chinese that the new members had been able to call a special meeting at which they'd voted to rip up the cricket pitch and replace it with tennis courts. The horrified cricketers had been powerless to stop the destruction. All the other clubs had hastily brought in new rules giving their cricketing members five votes each.

The city itself, I thought, looked fabulous by night, especially from Victoria Park looking down towards the Happy Valley racecourse, or approaching the road tunnel through Hong Kong Island, where the lines of glowing headlights both above and below put me in mind of a scene from *Blade Runner*. But by day, perhaps because of the persistent blanket of clammy drizzle, it felt cold and impersonal and—its neon extinguished—

slightly tatty. Francis treated us all royally, hiring a junk to take us to Aberdeen Harbour and a private yacht, no less, to take us to the Hilton Seafood Café on Lamma Island. Ten of us did the tourist rounds, while Marcus's fiancée familiarized herself with the inside of Versace, Fendi, Donna Karan, Giorgio Armani and her intended's wallet. But, despite all the fun, Hong Kong was one of the least welcoming places I had ever visited. The Chinese, it was clear, did not care much for the Europeans, or their stupid sports, even if they had been grateful for the 150-year opportunity to make a shedload of cash. This became clearest on a day trip to Macau, the equivalent Portuguese colony, a world of rotting Mediterranean shutters now given over mainly to gambling—a place altogether more charismatic than Hong Kong's high-rise corduroy. In the taxi queue at Macau's ferry terminal, the cabbies simply refused to stop for anyone who wasn't Chinese: no smelly whiteys were getting into *their* nice clean vehicles. It was no more than amusing to find ourselves on the wrong end of racism, for Macau taxi drivers are in the main very small, and there were ten of us, enabling us to make our cab requirements physically very clear indeed. But as we relaxed over plateloads of giant prawns, spread across the red-and-white chequered tablecloths of Fernando's Portuguese restaurant, a lazy little oasis amid all the moneymaking, the episode gave pause for thought: how soul-destroying to have to go through that every day of one's entire life.

The day of our first game, against Kowloon, was a real three-jumper affair, dawning colder and more dispiritingly gloomy than a spring morning in the Thames valley. I was nervous, no question. I had spent a minute or two at the crease before I got my first vaguely dangerous-looking ball. Gingerly I thrust my bat and pad as far down the wicket as I could (I had taken to batting two yards outside the crease, to minimize lbws), and heard the disquieting thud of ball on canvas. I looked up. Terence was umpiring. Surely, I thought, having come all this way, I'll get the benefit of the doubt, even if there isn't any. But no. Not a bit of it. Terence had been watching me trotting out that tiresome defensive stuff for fifteen years, and was no more inclined to put up with it now than he'd ever been. Out came his oft-used digit. Any London cricketer who's travelled twenty-seven miles down the A3 to Englefield Green to be given dubiously lbw for nought will know the sinking feeling in the pit of the stomach that accompanies the moment. To envisage how bad that feels when you've just travelled seven *thousand* miles to be given lbw, simply multiply the experience by 260. I trailed back to the pavilion. The expected routine drubbing followed. Nobody made any runs at all. Appropriately enough for the Far East, we committed hara-kiri.

The second game, against a team of bankers (no rhyming slang intended), took place at the Hong Kong Cricket Club, which nestles in a hillside cleft high above Happy Valley. The sun took pity on us for once, as our ringer Jonathan bashed a quickfire century, enabling us to post a meaty-looking total of 215. The bowling side of things did not begin well, though, when Hugh Dennis lost his radar. It's a curious thing, a bowler's radar. There he is one minute, Mr Reliable, putting the ball on the spot again and again with the accuracy of a Swiss watch; then, a moment later, for no apparent reason, he'll be spraying it around like the US Marines on a precision hostage-rescue mission. On this occasion Dennis, who was meant (obviously) to be aiming at the batsman's stumps, bowled ball after ball straight at his own feet. Nothing, it seemed, could prevent this happening. Finally he threw in the towel, dejected, and walked off the pitch in disgust. A small boy who'd been watching the game recognized him from the television. 'Do some more of the funny bowling! Do some more of the funny bowling!' he begged. Dennis decided there and then that he would never bowl again.

The game was a thriller, and came down to the last over, which I had to bowl, with the home side's last pair needing 12 to win. These arrears were considerably reduced when the first ball departed for a towering six. The next ball was pushed for a single: they needed 5 to win off four balls, with the last man on strike. Then an incredible thing happened, an event that none of us could possibly have foreseen. Terence actually took a stumping. Let me put this into a historical perspective. Terence had taken only one stumping that I could remember in fifteen years, and that was when the batsman had been so sure he was about to be stumped that he had set off for the pavilion without bothering to look round. In fact he could have made it to the pavilion and strolled back to the wicket before Terence had the ball under control; indeed, it was probably not until later that evening as he drove home that our keeper finally accomplished the feat. It would have been quicker, ran the team joke, for Terence to have posted the ball back to the stumps than to attempt to whip off the bails himself. We had simply never legislated for Terence to pull off a stumping. And now he'd done it. We'd done it. We'd won a match abroad, by four runs. We mobbed our delighted wicketkeeper.

*   *   *

With a grim First-World-meets-Third-World inevitability, things first started to go wrong soon after we touched down at New Delhi's airport. There we were greeted by a sweetly smiling Indian woman sporting a pink angora cardigan and a name badge reading 'Anita', who placed a garland of scented blooms about each of our necks and led us to a battered tour bus upon which was painted the legend, in capital letters, 'MEET-U ENTERPRISES'.

'And now', said Anita, 'the bus will take you to your team hotel.'

'Fine,' said Francis, 'and after that, we'd like it to drop us off at *our* hotel.'

'*Your* hotel?' A few jaws dropped.

'Absolutely. I've booked into the Hyatt. If you think I'm spending the night in a £10-a-night rat-hole with you lot, you've got another think coming.'

All round Hong Kong, Anuj had been loudly proclaiming the low cost of life in New Delhi and the accommodation he had fixed up there. Some of the more impecunious players, like Cie, had struggled badly to afford the £130-a-night Hong Kong hotel rooms Francis had booked, and had been looking forward to an easing of financial pressures in India. Francis, whose wages were roughly equivalent to the annual GDP of the Philippines, obviously shared no such concerns. The Hyatt cost a cool £160 a night. Marcus's fiancée, who had run through plenty of Marcus's money in Hong Kong's marbled shopping malls, was another who wasn't going to slum it in a £10-a-night hotel, which meant he was going with her. In an atmosphere of deathly hush, the bus dropped most of us at the team hotel, then rattled off to the Hyatt.

Irritatingly, Francis and Co. turned out to be right, in their judgement of cheap Indian hotels if not their moral stance. The team hotel was, quite literally, a rat-hole. There were rat droppings on the pillows, on the blankets, even *in between* the sheets. Rats trotted happily in and out of the kitchen bearing large chunks of food. The place was entirely alive with rats. It wouldn't have surprised me if the manager had turned out to be a large rat.

'That's it,' said Terence and Jonathan. 'We're off to the Hyatt.'

'I can't afford to stay at the Hyatt,' said Cie quietly, a sentiment echoed by a few of the other players. In vain, I argued for a compromise. Clearly we would have to find another hotel anyway: why not aim for, say, a three-star place? But the Hyatt party wasn't budging. The team would henceforth be split into two parties, and, with one or two exceptions, it was the layabouts who were going to stay at the Hyatt and the Saturday players who were not.

This first crack in the façade of team unity was swiftly papered over the following morning, however, when we beheld the magnificent setting for our first match, the Roshanara Club in Old Delhi. The most venerable cricket club in India, a pre-war Test-match ground and a location for the film *Gandhi*, it was a remarkably prestigious venue in which to entertain a useless bunch of British no-hopers. Here we were to play no less an institution than the Delhi High Court, with a second game to follow later in the week at the Wankhede Stadium, the city's current Test match venue (a place much loved by infantile cricket fans the world over for its vernacular pronunciation: 'Wank-a-day'). Anuj had really done us proud.

The Roshanara Club, although in Old Delhi, was of the same Anglo–Indian vintage and grandeur as Sir Edwin Lutyens's imperial city of New Delhi. A massive arched stone pavilion, curlicue-tipped and painted a delicate saffron yellow (more Indian than Anglo), overlooked a wide green field lined with swaying palms. Great hawks and vultures wheeled high above the square, turbaned waiters glided past bearing trays loaded with gin-and-tonics, while a mildewed portrait of the club's Scottish founder looked down on the faded inscription 'Work is the curse of the drinking classes'. The pitch itself was like marble: no grass was visible, but the packed earth had been rolled and beaten, and rolled and beaten again, until its surface had attained—literally—a mirror sheen. It was a cricket pitch you could see your face in.

This being India, there were important pre-match rituals to be gone through. The inauguration ceremony was presided over by the chief of Delhi's secret police, a fat, sinister-looking individual with hair dyed bright ginger, who looked as if he'd just popped over from the torture cells: Graham Greene would have been proud of such a creation. As we lined up to be presented to this gentleman, he said not a word, but instead gravely presented each of us with a Pyrex cooking dish in Christmas wrapping. Mysterious. The scene was made even more surreal by Terence, who had bought some white zinc cream of the kind favoured at the time by Australian Test cricketers; but instead of daubing it in warlike stripes, in the professionally approved Adam Ant style, he had covered his whole face in the stuff. Thus we were treated to the interesting spectacle of a confused secret policeman handing a Pyrex cooking dish to an equally bewildered-looking Marcel Marceau.

And, this being India, the home team was—in keeping with every Commonwealth cricket team we have ever encountered—desperate to get one over on the old country. Wherever we have been around the world, I have stressed until I am blue in the face that we are an amateur team, that we are a village side, that we are—not to put too fine a point on it—a crock of shit. And wherever we have been we have arrived to face the opposition bursting with top-notch ringers. Amid the charming young lawyers of the Delhi High Court were several serious-looking pros, including one recognizable face, the Indian Test cricketer Surinder Khanna. The man was an *international* for heaven's sake. Did they not *know* that Terence had not ascended to the giddy heights of double figures since the decade before last? There appeared to be only one chink in the home side's armour: their captain, an overweight, middle-aged dignitary, who, it was clear from the warm-up, was such a terrible cricketer that he would have been right at home in our team. But what he lacked on the physical side he made up for in low animal cunning. I won the toss and, as we had already agreed upon a thirty-five-over match, opted to bat first. The pitch being immaculate, it would normally have been more sensible to chase, but it gets dark early in Delhi in winter: if we were playing thirty-five overs, whoever batted second would have serious problems with the light. As soon as I had made my decision, however, the fat scoundrel turned and said, 'In that case we shall play thirty overs. Otherwise we shall be batting in the dark.'

I have often found myself wondering if such amateur skulduggery might not be transferred by England captains to the international arena. How wonderful if Michael Waughan, upon losing the toss to the Australians, could simply unilaterally alter the parameters of the match. 'OK, Ricky old chap, you bat for fifty overs, then we'll have twenty overs from 6.30, and if you don't get us all out we'll call it a draw—OK?'

Another handy ploy, much loved by village captains, is the forgotten ball. Inserted on a grassy cart track, all Waughan would have to say would be, 'Sorry, Ricky—I appear to have left the match ball in my wife's car.' Then he could hand the Australians a ball some 400 overs old, with the consistency of an undercooked meringue, knowing full well that when they came to bat they would be unable to get it off the square. Of course, if Ricky Ponting has ever played at Guiting Power in Gloucestershire, he will know that the correct response is to smile like a Boy Scout and remark cheerily, 'That's OK. I brought a new ball along with me just in case. I'll go and get it, shall I?'

Perhaps the most ingenious method of swinging a game your way, much employed across the village greens of England, is the timely introduction of a small boy. When batting out for a draw, the small boy (who is usually about fourteen) is generally sent in at about number nine. The umpire, who is quite often the boy's father, then explains to the visiting captain that the poor lamb cannot possibly be expected to face anything but the mildest bowling. The fast bowlers have to be removed, and left to gnash their teeth and beat their chests in the outfield, while the fourteen-year-old flays the team's occasional off-spinner to all corners of the ground with a series of scorching drives. Any attempt to bowl properly is met with a look of wounded bewilderment from the batsman and a stern lecture on sportsmanship from the umpire. It later transpires that the boy is captain of Lancashire Under-19s. This has happened to the Captain Scott XI innumerable times. At Lurgashall in Sussex, for instance, a fifteen-year-old (who later turned out to be a Sussex junior) pulled our medium-pacer for a series of towering sixes over square leg. When he took a ball on the glove, however, he promptly burst into tears. The umpire announced he would call any ball that was too fast or difficult for the lad a wide. The resulting total of wides (32 in all) won them the game. The boy top-scored, and finished not out. Surely England have a spare small boy whom they could include in the one-day squad? He couldn't do worse than Ian Bell.

Frankly, though, I was surprised that the captain

of the Delhi High Court team had felt the need to pull a fast one at all. I could feel another ghastly mismatch coming as I walked out to open the batting. After a minute or two at the crease, along came my first vaguely dangerous-looking ball (going at quite a lick), so I thrust the usual nervous bat-and-pad as far down the wicket as I could. Once again I heard the disquieting thud of ball on canvas. I looked up. The vultures circled above, licking their beaks. But there, standing behind the stumps at the far end, was *a professional umpire.* 'Howzat?' asked the bowler. Said umpire gave him a look of derision. Not out. The vultures squawked away in disappointment. For the next ten minutes I was in a state of shock. I had never been hit on the leg and not given out lbw before. I felt quite light-headed. I was even tempted to try this wonderful new sensation over and over again.

A second, immediate, surprise was provided by the presence of a match commentator, an urbane Sikh in a blue turban, who sat next to the scorer, broadcasting over loudspeakers to the sparse crowd. 'A confident appeal, but the umpire's having none of it,' he announced suavely. 'Thompson looks surprised. Almost dazed. He's prodding the pitch.'

I was indeed prodding the pitch. Only to gain time, as it was like prodding stainless steel. But this was a novel sensation, having everything I did announced to the waiting world. I flexed my knees.

'And Thompson's flexing his knees.'

I lifted one leg and waggled it a bit.

'And Thompson's lifted one leg, and is . . . sort of . . . waggling it a bit.'

I began to feel almost godlike.

The other marvellous surprise was the pitch. I had spent years up to my knees in English spring mud, my feeble, desk-bound physique woefully inadequate for the task of hefting balls which had almost stopped dead over puddles, bracken and distant hedges. But this was different, utterly different. Just angling the bat face sent the ball flashing away to the boundary, like a marble on a sheet of glass. Freed from the shackles of fear, protected from the enemy within by the two stout guardians in their white coats, elevated above mere mortal status by the commentary wafting down from the loudspeakers, and barely needing to lift the bat to send the ball careening to all corners, I suddenly felt strangely unbeatable. Was this odd feeling confidence, I wondered? The first wicket didn't go down until ten overs had passed, by which time the score was already 70. I was soon able to retire on 50, as was Jonathan. A huge score looked on the cards, especially as—when Cie passed me on the way to the wicket—we could both see the rotund figure of the dignitary warming up, ready to toss down a few. 'Yeah, man,' said Cie, who sometimes put me in mind of an Asian Austin Powers.

As soon as Cie reached the crease, the dignitary put himself on to bowl. Cie left the first ball alone, a rank long hop down the leg side, but as it passed him it brushed his bum. 'Howzthaat!' yelled the dignitary. Quick as a flash, the umpire whipped out his finger. Cie—who as far as I know had never disputed a decision in his life—stood rooted to the spot in disbelief. Whether he had been singled out for this treatment as a fellow Asian, or whether he had simply arrived at the crease at the wrong moment, it was just about the most blatant sawing-off I had ever seen. My newfound, dreamlike confidence in the professional umpires shattered, like Edith Piaf's shaving mirror during a high note. Poor Cie was distraught. He almost limped back to the pavilion. He had been looking forward to batting in India for a whole year.

It is, as every cricketer knows, almost an impossibility to remain at the crease if you have been given out, even if you have been clearly and disgracefully cheated. I did once see it happen, though, in a match between BBC Radio Comedy and a London listings magazine. In pursuit of cheap humour, I'd persuaded one of our radio producers, who actually *was* blind, to come along and umpire, white stick and all. The very first ball produced a thick edge from the journalists' opening bat, which was well held at third slip. Ted, the blind umpire, raised his finger, and we ran to congratulate the fielder. Then somebody noticed that the batsman was still there.

'You're out, mate. You were caught,' he was rudely informed.

'Yes, but *he* doesn't know that,' protested the batsman, pointing at Ted.

'Yes I do,' said Ted. 'You hit it. I heard the edge. I'm not deaf you know.'

But the journalist utterly refused to leave. He should have walked, of course, as anybody who knows he is out should always walk, for there is a difference between a referee (who is there to decide what happened) and an umpire (who is there to adjudicate between disputes if appealed to by either side). If there is no dispute as to what happened, there is no need to involve the umpire.

That is, unless the umpire is in the employ of the Delhi High Court, in which case certain proprieties have to be observed vis-à-vis the professional and social status of the bowler. Actually, I'm not at all sure why the dignitary in question felt himself in need of bogus lbws anyway, for in all the next day's papers his bowling figures had been wildly inflated. To add insult to injury, Cie's surname (Malde) had been rendered by the Indian match reporters as 'Mouldy'.

Cie's dismissal sowed fatal seeds of doubt, and our middle order wobbled, but we recovered well to finish on 196-7. It was a competitive total, but we still had (among others) Mr Surinder Khanna, the opposition's Test batsman, to worry about. After tea—not platefuls of cucumber sandwiches with the crusts off, but platefuls of laceratingly hot curry—the Indians set off after the runs like a train (an overcrowded train, obviously, in these parts), Khanna to the fore. He didn't just flick the ball around as we had done. He rifled the thing. To field one of his drives, even on such a perfect surface, was to risk a whole rack of broken fingers. We medium pacers were proving easy meat. It was time to bring on the spinners, of which we had two: Cie and Cliff, the charming Australian proprietor of the Grape Street Wine Bar in Shaftesbury Avenue. Not being English, and therefore able to field, Cliff had been known for many years as the team's panther (although why the term 'panther' is invariably used to describe somebody who can catch a ball is rather a mystery—I've never seen a large cat with no fingers catch a ball, especially not a 5½ oz cricket ball travelling at speed). In Cliff's case, his glory days were generally thought to be behind him, and one or two 'stuffed panther' jibes had already been trotted out.

Surinder Khanna simply larruped Cliff's first ball with the speed and ferocity of an armour-piercing bullet, horizontally, straight back into the bowler's gonads. Totally unaware that he was clutching three large red spheres and not two, the unfortunate Antipodean leaped about the field like a scalded cat, both hands jammed between his legs. The commentator, genuinely bemused, assumed he was watching some kind of Australian victory dance. It was a good thirty seconds before Cliff could be sufficiently calmed down to take in the fact that he had dismissed a Test batsman.

Now it was the Indians' turn to wobble. Cie took three further wickets: Cliff, hurtling about the field with renewed vigour, like a, well, special kind of big-handed panther with fingers, caught the lot. But, sadly, the breakthrough had come just a little too late. A missed run-out and a dropped catch from Marcus, and the Indians squeaked home with a few balls to spare. It had, though, been a tremendous day, and the evening promised to be no less entertaining, for the High Court team had arranged a banquet in our honour at a nearby restaurant, to which various dignitaries and members of the Indian government had been invited.

The match over, however, one or two familiar problems began to surface. The layabouts took one look at the showers and responded in predictably Lady Bracknellish fashion. They were not showering and changing there, they announced, amid the juddering water pipes of Empire, but would return to the luxurious surroundings of the Hyatt to do so. The rest of us headed off to the restaurant, relaxed with a drink, chatted to our hosts, and waited. And waited. Seven o'clock, the appointed time for the start of the banquet, came and went. After half an hour I telephoned the Hyatt and managed to locate Terence.

'We've only just got here,' he said. 'The rush-hour traffic was terrible.'

Only then, for the first time, did I discover exactly where the Hyatt was. It was out near the airport, several miles away in the distant southern suburbs of New Delhi. We were to the north of Old Delhi, itself well to the north of central New Delhi. In London terms, it was like playing cricket in Hampstead, then popping back to your hotel in Gatwick to put on some clean trousers.

'For fuck's sake, get a shirt and tie on and get everybody here quick,' I said. 'There's a whole banquet laid out for us, and half the Indian government.'

'We'll be there by nine,' promised Terence.

The rest of us piled on the excuses: terrible traffic, the impossibility of finding a cab, an accident blocking the carriageway, Martians landing and cordoning off the city centre, anything really to while away the time. The brother of the Indian Chancellor of the Exchequer was sympathetic. He knew the back roads, he said, and would go to fetch them himself, in some comfort: he commandeered a pair of limousines and set off. I called the Hyatt to let them know he was coming, but no one was answering their phones.

At nine o'clock we took our places at the table, but the food was placed on hold. The five empty places seemed to dominate the room. Indeed, they could hardly have been more conspicuous if Elvis, Marilyn and the Rat Pack had been sat there, injecting themselves with heroin. The dignitaries were, understandably, beginning to get restless.

They'll be here any second,' I said, irritatingly brightly, for the zillionth time.

Nine thirty came and went. Then ten o'clock. Finally the brother of the Indian Chancellor of the Exchequer returned, bearing Terence and Jonathan.

'Where are the others?' I asked.

'Er . . . they've gone to bed,' said Terence.

'Gone to *bed*?'

'They said they were tired. They've been playing cricket all day.'

I wanted the ground to swallow me up. Our embarrassment was absolute. Anuj, his legal career dissolving before his eyes, was almost apoplectic. Again the lesson was borne in on me that to wallow amid the fine buildings, the traditions and the trappings of Empire is all very well, but one must do so with humility, and with respect to the local inheritors of the colonial apparatus. To turn up and treat the natives as if it were still 1932 is out of the question. Those of us who had waited at the restaurant felt tarnished by association. One of the best days of my life had turned into one of the worst evenings I had ever experienced.

* * *

Most of the rest of the week passed peaceably, even enjoyably. By tacit agreement, in a British manner, we simply did not mention the disaster of the banquet. There was another match in the diary, and there seemed to be an unspoken pact that any recriminations should wait until after this second encounter had taken place. But the Indians are master diplomats, and they too made no mention either of the banquet or of the second game, which began to assume a worryingly chimeric aspect. There was nothing we could do but wait. So we went on the tourist trail.

Delhi was the magnificent capital of the Moguls when Bombay and Madras were mere trading posts and Calcutta a village of mud flats; it still possesses over a thousand monuments. But, like many a continuously occupied capital city, it has been somehow rendered anonymous, and has been comprehensively ruined in the process, by the forces of economic necessity, greed and downright philistinism. Most of the world's most beautiful cities enjoyed a limited heyday, then suddenly withered intact, to be gratefully resurrected by a later generation: Jaisalmer in north-west Rajasthan is one such, Parati in Brazil another. Those that have continuously thrived, conversely, are usually the least interesting. Neither Mogul Old Delhi nor Lutyens's grand imperial New Delhi, in the absence of a Parisian-style preservation order, has been able to preserve its integrity. Misspelt neon signs, tacky market stalls selling fake sunglasses, concrete office fronts, branches of McDonalds, and those odd bits of twisted metal that always seem to stick out of concrete paving stones across the Third World have all made their depredations. There are one or two oddities of genuine interest in Delhi: a fifth-century iron pillar by the Qutab Minar, for instance, twenty-four feet high, inscribed with six lines of Sanskrit, and of such a density that it has never rusted. Its origin remains a mystery. By all orthodox historical reckoning, its manufacture should have been an impossibility. A more modern curiosity is the sexologists' ghetto in the Chandni Chowk market, stall after stall of glitzy neon offering the medical expertise of seedy middle-aged 'sexperts'. The most sinister, for me, was Dr Sablok, who sounded like a minor-league Bond villain.

After Delhi, we were shuttled round the tourist triangle of northern India by Anita of MEET-U ENTERPRISES, who proved herself both resolutely determined to stay on the beaten track at all costs and a consummate liar. Wanting to visit the Iron Fort, a sprawling, crumbling castle that featured on few tourist itineraries, I bearded her as she stood sweating gently in the hotel lobby in her (presumably surgically attached) pink angora cardigan.

'I'm sorry,' she smiled brightly. 'The Iron Fort is sixty-five kilometres from here. It is too far to visit.'

'Excuse me,' I asked the hotel receptionist. 'How far is the Iron Fort from here?'

'Two kilometres,' he replied laconically.

'I'm sorry,' countered Anita, smiling so brightly now that I began to worry whether she was really a Stepfordistan wife. 'The Iron Fort is closed to the public.'

'Excuse me,' I bothered the receptionist again. 'Is the Iron Fort closed to the public?'

'No,' he replied, even more laconically than

before. 'There's a village inside it.'

Anita ran out of excuses, her teeth clamped together in an attitude of rock-hard merriment.

This of course was tourist India, which bears little relation to the rest of the country, and principally involves shuttling Westerners from one opportunity-to-buy to another. But there were no shops at the Iron Fort. Everyone you meet in tourist India—*everyone*—will, sooner or later, no matter how friendly they appear, attempt to sell you something. The only person I met who didn't attempt to sell me anything turned out to be a Christian priest, and he was—in a way—trying to sell me God. Curiously, it was our semi-Anglicized Indian (Anuj) and our Anglicized-Africanized Asian (Cie) who proved the most naive purchasers, swept away on a cloud of spiritual sentimentality at the opportunity to make contact with their roots. Cie bought a 'marble' model of the Taj Mahal which crumbled to dust when the bus engine started. Anuj, with great reverence, unveiled a cloth bag full of 'magic' stones that he had bought from an elderly man in a dhoti at considerable expense.

'But, Anuj,' somebody pointed out, 'these stones are identical to the ones at the old man's feet. Look, there are thousands of them.'

It was true. Anuj had, essentially, shelled out for a bag of roadside gravel.

'No, but these are special *magic* stones,' he intoned, sounding remarkably like Lord Percy in *Blackadder*.

To be fair to the Indians who flog all this nonsense, for many of them it is the only way to make a living. Most taxis, for instance, belong to souvenir-shop owners, who command the drivers to divert their fares to the owners' premises. Mindful of this scam, I took a cab to the palace at Fatehpur Sikri, another Mogul extravaganza, studded with monster bees' nests, and offered the driver double the fare if he would take me there and back without diverting to a souvenir shop. If, on the other hand, he went anywhere near a shop of any kind he would get nothing. Quite cunning I thought, and the man accepted with alacrity. On the return journey I fell asleep, and woke to find the taxi parked in the yard of a souvenir shop.

'It is the best souvenir shop in all Rajasthan, sir,' he beamed.

'You know what we agreed,' I did my best to growl. 'If you don't start this cab in ten seconds and drive away, you'll get nothing.' I began counting down.

'Please,' he begged. 'I will lose my job if you do not go into the shop.'

'You accepted the deal. That's your problem. Four . . . three . . . two . . .'

When I reached 'one' he fired the ignition and the taxi began to move off. Immediately, the shop-owner hurtled frothing and outraged from his premises, yanked open the cab door, wrenched the driver out into the dust, and started beating him up. So it was that I found myself in the back of a driverless cab, rolling gently out on to the Delhi road, growing more and more worried until—luckily—the camber acted as a brake.

For all the talk of heat and dust, it is the salesmen that make India hard work. The place is no hotter or dustier or poorer than any number of Third World countries, but buying and selling is ingrained in the national culture, and inextricably entwined with such areas of life (sacrosanct enclaves to us in the West) as friendships and family relationships. Anuj was always trying to sell the layabouts shares in Europa foods. It didn't go down too well.

By the time we'd climbed to the Amber Fort on elephant-back, craned our necks at the Palace of Winds in Jaipur, sat on the seat before the Taj Mahal where Lady Di had once simpered, and bicycled each other on rickshaws around the Bharatpur bird sanctuary at dawn, the week was more or less at an end, and it had become clear that the final game was not going to take place at all. Not that (this being India) we were going to get any straight answers on that score. Nor, frankly, did we deserve any. The recriminations began in earnest at the airport, when Anita presented us with our mysteriously rounded (but, to be honest, hardly very substantial) bills. Half the team blamed the other half for the cancellation of the final match. The other half insisted that it had never really existed, that it was another Indian lie, and that the banquet no-show was merely being trotted out as an excuse. Francis refused to pay Anita a penny, because she had been caught fibbing so often. Unfortunately, another player had already helpfully paid Francis's bill for him when he was in the loo. Francis refused to pay *him* a penny either, which kicked off another row. The whole tour descended into undignified finger-jabbing, shouting and mutual recriminations.

Keeping any touring side together is a bit like upending a bucket of mice and hoping that they'll all head in the same direction in an orderly fashion; but this was ridiculous. I'd done my best to keep them together, and it hadn't been good enough. By prior arrangement, I and Andy, one of my team-mates, had agreed to hire a venerable Ambassador saloon and head south to some of the country's less touristed areas. So, I'm ashamed to say, we simply slipped away and left the warring parties to it. It felt like catching the last helicopter off the US Embassy roof in Saigon, hours before the Vietcong arrived. Andy and I had a fabulous time, taking in such incredible wonders as the deserted city of Mandu, said to be the original inspiration for Xanadu, an extraordinary cliff top complex of exquisite palaces, ornamental pools, graceful baths and pavilions, with nary a souvenir stall in sight. We were the first visitors for a month, and the caretaker kindly fed us a couple of chicken breasts, cooked in a pot of yoghurt and (I'm not kidding) half a pound of hot chilli each. It was an amazing place (what we saw of it when we weren't doubled up in the lavatory), which dwarfed the Taj Mahal, the Red Fort and all the monuments of Old Delhi put together. It wasn't hard to get to either: it just wasn't near any major cities or airports. There's a lesson there, I suppose.

I heard, when we got back, that Marcus's fiancée had dumped him at Heathrow, anger etched into her face, a score of shopping bags jammed under each arm. 'You and your *fucking* cricket!' she had screamed at him across the carousel. She had reached stage four in the space of just two short weeks.

4

Pietermaritzburg

After a catalogue of disasters like the one we'd compiled for ourselves in India, our natural response, at the time, was to go and do it all again. I stress, *at the time*. Reading this (if you haven't already tossed the book aside in disbelief), you're probably feeling like a parent confronted by a small boy who's admitting that, yes, he *knows* he was told not to put the cat in the tumble-dryer, but he thought it could still do with fluffing up a bit. I'm afraid it's true, though. We did all go to South Africa. Yes, I know, *I know*. I'm *sorry*. But we did only go to Pietermaritzburg. That's all. Only there. OK, all right, and Durban. And Cape Town. But nowhere else.

The South African trip came about through a fairly astonishing coincidence. I'd been there before, on holiday, and, after being thoroughly impressed by the vaulting extravagance of Table Mountain, had been slightly less thrilled by the 'garden route' to Port Elizabeth. I suppose that four hundred miles of grass and trees are not so exciting if you've arrived from Britain, where grass and trees are rather the default setting—although the road did seem tiresomely popular with coachloads of bobbing heads in that familiar Weybridge blue-grey. In search of more stimulating sensations I'd headed north, to the many wonders of Namibia: giant copper-coloured sand dunes, petrified oases, two-thousand-year-old plants that drink fog, a canyon the size of the Grand Canyon with no visitors, deserted German towns half-buried in sand containing perfectly preserved pre-war cinemas and bowling alleys, gigantic colonies of seals, penguins, pelicans and flamingos (as well as all the usual African game in abundance), prehistoric cave paintings, and, on the Skeleton Coast, lines of shattered, rusting fishing boats and freighters, thrown up on to the beach like children's toys by the world's fiercest ocean currents. Namibia, as you‘ve probably guessed from the above scattering of terms such as 'deserted' and 'no visitors', is one of the least densely populated countries on the planet, so it came as something of a surprise, on the Skeleton Coast, (a) to bump into another human being, and (b) to discover that the said human being was my old friend Simon from university, a former Captain Scott player who'd emigrated to France on graduation. He even had a friend with him, Willie by name, who ran the Pietermaritzburg inter-city cricket team. They too had headed north from South Africa in search of a more unusual vacation. Oh, but we must come and tour South Africa, said Willie. We could even stay on his farm. He'd even fix up a day–night match, under floodlights. My eyes did a Tom and Jerry fruit-machine act. I'd said yes before I'd realized what I was signing us—and him—up for. Poor Willie.

The idea of touring South Africa appeared to fire the entire team with enthusiasm, especially as I'd glued a week in Cape Town, with a visit to the Test match and a game against a local side (fixed up by an aunt who lived locally), on to the front of the Pietermaritzburg trip. In fact a good twenty or so players threw their hats into the ring, about half of them saying they were definitely coming, the rest announcing that they were '99.9% certain'. The average reader will no doubt regard this as, on the face of it, a pretty solid mandate to proceed. Anyone who's ever organized a cricket tour, on the other hand, will know that these are worrying statistics indeed. For no one is ever *definitely* coming on any sort of tour until their cash is firmly in your bank account (and even then you may have to take evasive action to avoid having to give it back). Indeed, the whole range of responses to the question 'Are you *definitely* coming on tour?' constitutes a vocabulary in itself, one which—for the uninitiated—may require translation:

Tourese
I'm *definitely* coming on tour.
English
I might well come on tour. Then again, I might not. I'll be letting you know the night before we're due to leave.

Tourese
I'm 99.9% certain to come on tour.
English
I'm 0.1% certain to come on tour.

Tourese
Fabulous! I'd love to come. Of course, I'll need to clear it with the wife.
English
My wife won't let me go on tour. She won't even let me go to the pub.

Tourese
I'll definitely come if I can get the money together.
English
I'll definitely come if you pay for my air ticket, my hotel, all my meals and unlimited free drinks.

Tourese
I'm very interested. Put me down provisionally.
English
I wouldn't come if the alternative was having my face chewed off by a swarm of locusts.

In the event, of the eleven 'definites', only three dropped out a fortnight before we were due to leave Heathrow—quite a reasonable result, given my earlier fears. In only a mild panic, I contacted the Surrey League, and wrote a letter to every member club, canvassing for players. Exactly three replied in the affirmative. This was rather a cunning plan, I thought: Surrey League, just below county level—why, we might even avoid getting utterly pasted for once. I had of course informed Willie that we were only a rubbish village team, but foreigners never seemed to get just *how* rubbish English village teams are. In countries where everyone grows up in the sunshine, eats half an ox a week, and can fire a cricket ball in horizontally from the boundary at 90 m.p.h. by the age of eleven, the whole concept of rubbish cricket is entirely alien. It's not that they are aware of it and are mystified by it: they have simply never encountered it. There actually aren't any white people in Australia, New Zealand or South Africa who are not well nourished, reasonably athletic and good at sport. In Britain, on the other hand, the Labour governments of the 1960s and '70s made competition in school sport a dirty word, while the Conservative governments of the 1980s and '90s flogged off all the school playing fields to be turned into sausage factories. And the only protein in our kids' school food would seem to be ingested via the dreaded Turkey Twizzler. As true-born Englishmen we had a lot of ground to make up on our South African counterparts, but hopefully our Surrey League men would help us over the hurdles.

* * *

Cape Town, I must confess, was a blast. Our week there could not have gone better. The first South Africa v. England Test series following decades of isolation was taking place, and the whole of England seemed to have decamped to the sun. We bumped into Allan Lamb in Hout Bay, and had a drink with him. We bumped into David Gower at Newlands, and had a drink with him. We bumped into Griff Rhys Jones, who invited the whole team to a barbecue in the garden of a mansion he had rented in Constantia. His next-door neighbour? One N. Mandela. (What they talked about, and whether or not the conversations were carried out nose to nose, is a question too mind-boggling even to consider.) We enjoyed a spectacularly drunken New Year's Eve at the freshly tarted-up Victoria and Alfred waterfront (no, it's not a mistake—Alfred was one of her sons, apparently). That very night, one of our ringers even managed to get off with a girl (well, one of our regular players was hardly likely to have achieved such a feat). I know this because I came upon his fellows disconsolately passing a cigarette back and forth as they spent the night on the step of their shared room. Ah, the joys of male bonhomie.

It wasn't just the English tourists who were in party mood. A genuine feeling of mass exultation attended the unshackling of an entire people and the birth of a new nation. The restoration of sporting contacts with the rest of the world seemed symbolic of so much more. Cape Town, of course, is South Africa's most liberal city. I'd made a brief foray into rural Transvaal on my previous trip, and, although I hadn't actually seen any puce Dutchmen with ZZ Top beards sat astride horses, using high-powered rifles to shoot watermelons with black faces painted on them, the atmosphere had been strained to say the least. The various races, let's say, had not been in a hurry to serve each other in shops. But here in Cape Town, black and white were doing their best to make up for lost time. Black people poured me glasses of champagne from their magnum on New Year's Eve. When he learned my nationality, a black guy wearing a 'Niggaz with Attitude' lapel badge even mock-berated me for the paucity of English tourists visiting the country during the apartheid years. 'Where were you all? Why didn't you visit us? Don't you English *like* black people?' A whole host of complicated explanations involving Barclay's Bank and Cape fruit whirred uselessly in my head. He had a point. If someone didn't come to visit *me* because of an antipathy to Tony Blair, I'd find it equally hard to make the mental connection. I settled for making a humble apology instead.

Down at the Test match, mixed-race crowds broke open the Castle lagers and floated aimlessly on a sea of good-humoured tolerance. On the unshaded grassy banks, where we sat slowly broiling like lobsters, the chants and Mexican waves were marshalled by 'Craig the Waveman', a rake-thin, extrovert white paramedic, whose day job involved risking death on a regular basis, bringing medical help to the sick of the Crossroads township. We did our bit, I hope, painting tricolour South African flags on to the children's faces and holding mock 'Speak English Properly' classes for the Afrikaners, the correct pronunciations (it's 'Smith' not 'Smuth') written out on a giant Union flag. The Test match itself was largely irrelevant—merely an excuse for the fiesta—but for the record it was low-scoring and hard-fought, at least for the first two and a half days. Then, on the afternoon of the third day, Devon Malcolm started bowling like a drain, and England's grip on the game relaxed like that of a dying man. South Africa were winners by sundown. None of the England fans cared a hoot. We simply rode the wave of euphoria while it lasted, relishing the collision of a moment of enormous historical significance with a dirty-great party. I'd been there when the Brandenburg Gate had opened and the Berlin Wall was starting to look like a Swiss cheese, and the atmosphere had been nothing like this. As the winning runs were struck, Cie, Anuj and I vaulted the barrier and hurtled on to the pitch, along with approximately ten thousand others. As we reached the edge of the square, another pitch invader, a small elderly black man in a nautical-looking peaked cap and neat tie, launched himself wildly into my arms. As we whirled in giddy celebration, me holding him clear of the ground like a small boy, I caught my first glimpse of his face. It was Archbishop Desmond Tutu.

England's capitulation, one sensed, had been in the way of a gentleman's obligation. Whether they needed to be so obliging the following day, when they were hammered by a local state reserve side in a hastily arranged time-filling fixture, is open to debate. But we in the Captain Scott XI felt suitably obliging the day after that, when we duly capitulated to Rygersdal 3rd XI on their magnificent ground immediately beneath Table Mountain. We'd started well enough, reaching 50–0 (of which, I confess, I hadn't contributed very many at all), but it had taken fifteen overs to get there, and the boos and catcalls had started. The middle order were impatient to slash and mow. And slash and mow they did. The next five men made eight runs between them, in double-quick time, and we were duly rolled over. Cie bagged a few wickets in reply, but the poor mite was utterly exhausted. He was so excited to be playing cricket in South Africa, he'd got up every day at 6 a.m. (no matter how punishing the night before) in order to put himself through a rigorous exercise routine. Invariably, by 8 a.m. he was so bushwhacked that he had to go back to bed until lunchtime.

One interesting discovery to emerge from the defeat was that our three ringers were as useless as the rest of us. In fact they were to contribute just fourteen runs between them on the entire tour.

'So . . . the Surrey League,' I ventured. 'That's the one just below county level, isn't it?'

'No. You're thinking of the Surrey Championship. We're in the Surrey League.'

'Ah. Of course. What's that then?'

'Well, we work for an insurance firm. And they've got a team. And no one else in our office wanted to play.'

'Ah. Right. Got it. Thank you.'

So much for cunning plans.

*   *   *

If India had taught us anything, it was that the second week of a tour rarely resembles the first. So it was with South Africa. Willie's farm turned out to be in the rather scenic middle of nowhere, close to the main road between Pietermaritzburg and Durban, about an hour from the former. Just how rural an area it was can be gauged by the fact that anyone filling up at the local petrol station was automatically entered in a free draw to win a live sheep (yes, all right, we went through every permutation of *those* jokes at the time, thank you very much). Natal was a world away from the multiracial festivities of Cape Town, as evinced by the twelve-foot fence and armed guards surrounding Willie's property. Farmers were routinely murdered in these parts. The black population of Natal seemed more interested in payback than party time.

Within the encircling defences, however, Willie was munificence itself. He had agreed, for a start, to put up eleven cricketers and provide them with three meals each for the hardly cost-covering sum of £7 per head per day. We had the run of his tennis court and swimming pool. We even had a team van with driver, to take us anywhere we wanted within Natal. Accommodation-wise, there were four single rooms on offer, with the rest of the team billeted in multi-share bedrooms. As soon as these arrangements were announced, there was a scene of near-carnage, as the Hyatt-dwellers (Francis, Marcus, Terence and Jonathan) grabbed their suitcases and, claws bared, scrambled over each other in a frantic race for the four single rooms. Nobody had actually followed them, as nobody else had wanted to be killed in the rush; but they were not to know that.

Our opposition, we soon discovered, were partly to be found staying in the very same building. South African cricket is structured somewhat differently from English cricket, and rather closer to the Australian model. There are a handful of big state sides, any of which would crush an English county eleven. Below that comes inter-city cricket, rather like Australian 'A'-grade cricket, which is where English pros working abroad tend to fetch up; their accommodation and a small wage are provided for them, whereas their local team-mates tend to be amateurs. The Pietermaritzburg side, it transpired, contained no fewer than five English pros, all first-class county players, all in the side to play us, and all staying on Willie's farm. Our hearts sank.

'Willie,' I breathed. 'I told you. We're a rubbish village team. These people play for Essex, Kent and Surrey. We'll be utterly demolished.'

'Oh, come on,' he said. 'The gap can't be *that* big. Besides, I'm sure they won't take it terribly seriously.'

From where I was standing, the gap made the

Grand Canyon look like a hairline crack.

Naively, perhaps, Willie had thought that a houseful of Englishmen would naturally hit it off, as, say, a houseful of South Africans might; whereas I got the distinct impression that the English pros, who had come all this way to test themselves at the highest level and improve their game, were mightily unimpressed at the prospect of taking a few days out to entertain a bunch of complete no-hopers. Certainly—with the exception of Robert Rollins, Essex's charming wicketkeeper-batsman—they kept themselves to themselves and studiously ignored us. Our attempts at making polite conversation about first-class cricket were met with the kind of withering scorn normally reserved for the enquiries of tabloid journalists. Frankly, I can't blame them. In their position, I'd be the last person I'd want to meet in a farmhouse in South Africa.

Of course, given a minivan and the run of Natal, keeping ourselves to ourselves should not have been a problem. But we had reckoned without the rain. It rained and it rained and it rained. Whenever we tried to go anywhere, either the road had been washed away or the bridges were down, or—in the case of a day trip to the Drakensberg Mountains—our van became so embedded in thick mud that we had to manhaul it out. Such apocalyptic weather had our Rome floods beaten all ends up: in all, a total of eighteen people actually drowned in the area during our stay. This was Boer War country, and a number of us had wanted to explore the historical sites remaining from that conflict. After all, one of our founding inspirations had been Captain Valentine Todd, who had insisted on continuing to play cricket during the siege of Ladysmith, and had been killed by a shell while running in to bowl; the umpires being unable to prize the ball from his lifeless grasp, they had declared both ball and bowler 'dead'. In my head, though, such Boer War dramas had been played out in searing heat—not floods and driving rain. Had Todd been killed scuba-diving it would undoubtedly have peeled a layer of glamour from the story. As it was, our outings were confined to the tarmac highway that ran inland from Durban through the deluge, passing Pietermaritzburg on the way.

We settled on Durban first—all of us except Anuj, who'd been told by an Indian he'd met in Cape Town to avoid the place at all costs, as it was a dump. I'm surprised that an Indian should have expressed such sentiments, as Durban's town centre was filled, wall to wall, with Indians. It was like a cross between Blackpool beach and Calcutta, relocated to the steamy tropics: mile after mile of fairground rides, big dippers, candyfloss stalls and amusement arcades, all packed with sari-clad trippers. The air hung heavy like hot soup. It had been easy to forget, amid the simplicities of Cape Town (where only a few Malays in the colourful Bo-Kaap district muddy what appears to be a simple racial dichotomy) that South Africa is an extremely complex immigrant society. With extraordinary ignorance, the post-colonial government lumped together anyone between the two extremes of colour into a single, nebulous subgroup. In reality, however, South African bloodstock is one of the hottest soups of all, awash with rich ingredients. The country has seen waves of immigrants not just from England, Holland, Germany and France, but also from India, Sri Lanka, Malaysia, Indonesia and Madagascar. Even the resident black tribes are descended from immigrant forebears, who (along with the whites) ruthlessly exterminated the indigenous population of Bushmen and Khoikhoi. Indeed, it was at Pietermaritzburg in 1906 that an immigrant, Mahatma Gandhi, having been thrown off a train for refusing to leave a carriage full of whites, began the first serious anti-racist movement in the country.

Natal is where most of the pure-bred Indians have settled, and we met more the following day, when we headed in the other direction to check out the spectacular Howick Falls, made all the more spectacular by a river in spate. As we gazed in awe at the sight of millions of tons of water plummeting several hundred feet into the abyss below us, Anuj fell deep into conversation with a fellow-Indian. The man was from Durban, it transpired, and within a few minutes not only had convinced Anuj that Durban was a veritable paradise on earth, but had also persuaded him to come to dinner there the following night. This, inevitably, presented problems twenty-four hours later, when Anuj demanded that the team bus return to Durban so that he could fulfil his dinner engagement. Ten voices chorused no.

'We've already been to Durban, Anuj. We're not going again. You said you didn't want to come.'

'Today is different. Today I must go to Durban.'

'That's your problem.'

Willie came to the rescue, by graciously diverting one of his farm Land Rovers and another driver for Anuj's use. But, come the appointed time, Anuj lay ensconced in a swing seat with a glass and a drink, watching the rain pound the surface of the pool. The driver stood expectantly to attention in the downpour, the vehicle door open.

'Come on, Anuj,' I chivvied. 'Your car's here.'

'I do not think I shall go,' he yawned. 'I am too comfortable.'

'But this guy's invited you to dinner, Anuj. You've accepted. He'll have bought all the food. And Willie's arranged a Land Rover.'

'I do not want to go.'

I gestured to the driver that the trip appeared to be off. Anuj reclined further back into his seat.

'Well? Aren't you going to call this bloke, to tell him you're not coming? You don't want him to start cooking your dinner.'

'I can't be bothered.'

'You *can't be bothered*? It's just one phone call! The guy's expecting you for dinner!'

'You do not understand,' said Anuj wearily. 'I do not need to call him. *This man is lower caste.*'

Jesus. And I thought we had a class system. All of it, too, after Anuj had been so seriously embarrassed by our various lapses in manners in Delhi. It was around this time that Jonathan demanded to be moved to a better single room, on the grounds that he had only managed to secure the single room nearest the loo, and did not wish to be disturbed by the noise of chain-flushes. He did not feel that he was getting full value for his £7. Had it been Gielgud making the request, I might have at least taken achievement into consideration. But I rather doubted that the ambassador's-reception voice-over merited such preferential treatment. Willie, though, kindly relented once again, and turfed an uncomplaining relative out of a room in a neighbouring building.

I, meanwhile, began to yearn to be part of a normal cricket team.

* * *

Pietermaritzburg itself, although founded by Boer settlers, stands now as a little English colonial island, hemmed in by prosperous Indian suburbs and sprawling black townships, and disfigured at intervals by fast-sporing concrete shopping centres. Perhaps its most beautiful building is its cricket pavilion, which overlooks the city's tree-lined former Test ground. Close inspection revealed an elegant, two-tiered red-and-white structure with spindly wrought-iron pillars and gingerbreaded wood, flanked at either end by a pair of domed, almost Islamic, cylindrical towers. I say 'close inspection' because, from the square, it was hard to make out the pavilion behind the sheeting curtain of rain. How on earth we had been allowed to play in such conditions was beyond me. God knows what damage we were doing to the square. In fact, by the end of the game, I could swear we were playing at a level about a foot below the surrounding grass. Cricket in rain is one of the more pointless pastimes available on God's earth. It goes against the whole ethos of the game. But, if you've come 5,600 miles to play, you get out there and you play.

The pattern of our innings mirrored that of its predecessor in Cape Town: a long, dogged and dull opening partnership, followed by a job lot of incoherent swishing, a middle-order collapse and a mini-revival from the tail. The result was a total of 134—inadequate in the context of the game, but a fair effort given the quality of the opposition. Anuj, being a proper bowler (he'd once been the Delhi University equivalent of a blue, before unwisely eating several thousand doughnuts), caused a few scares in the home ranks with an artful slow- slow- medium spell of 5–19, but then Darren Cousins of Essex came in and put us out of our misery, wellying a series of straight sixes into the pavilion. We had lost—for the third overseas match in a row—by three wickets.

Our final game, a day–nighter at the modern Noodsberg Oval, with accompanying barbecue (swiftly extinguished by the rain, of course), was to be the pièce de résistance of our trip. I'd even gone to the trouble of buying eleven pairs of polyester day–night pyjamas (£2.99 a head from Goldhawk Road market) on which our surnames had been stencilled. This had not been a simple task (although our only Polish-descended player, a thin person called Momtchiloff, had thankfully not made the trip—he wasn't nearly fat enough to get his whole name on his back), but the effort was worth it, we thought, for the joke. The looks of utter contempt we received from the home side when we took the field—even worse than those cast our way when we'd showed up in whites—made it clear how they felt about our little gag in Pietermaritzburg. Not that we cared what *they* thought. Far more worrisome was the sheeting rain, stronger than ever, that cut through the flimsy polyester and iced us to the bone.

Jonathan, who as an MCC batsman didn't like not being taken seriously as a cricketer, gave me a little lecture on professionalism as we set out to open the batting. 'We're playing against pros,' he told me with deep, ambassador's-reception-style gravitas, 'so we have to play like pros too. Sharp, crisp calling. If it goes in front of me it's my call. Behind me it's yours. And if one of us calls, the other runs—no hesitation, no debate about it. OK?' 'OK.'

He Chinese-cut his first ball to deep fine leg.

'Yes!' I shouted, put my head down, and charged like a bull. Twenty-two yards later I found myself face to face with Jonathan in his crease.

'What are you *doing*?' I asked his face loudly. 'I said yes!'

'Never a run there.'

'What are you *talking* about? The fielder's not even picked it up yet!'

'He's about to pick it up. Look, he's picking it up now.'

'He might be picking it up *now*, but when I said yes there was an easy run there.'

'Nope. Never a run there.'

'It was my call anyway. You said we had to run if the other one called. You've *got* to run.'

'I'll never make it. Look, the ball's on its way back.'

'You said we had to play like pros!'

'I am playing like a pro. Any pro would know there was never a run there.'

So I set off back to my own end, in that futile, angry sprint, culminating in a wretched, pointless, full-length dive, that every cricketer knows so well. At the exact moment that the bails were whipped off before my despairing eyes, I had covered 43.9 yards at top speed and had had time to engage in a lively debate at the halfway stage.

'Never a run there,' muttered Jonathan, as I passed him on the way to the pavilion.

'*You* are a selfish c**t,' I riposted, finally losing my temper and my dignity. The English county pros grinned at last. It was the culmination not just of a fraught week, but of nigh on two decades of frustration. Jonathan refused to speak to me for the rest of the trip. He also went on to make a quite brilliant 83 not out.

It's happened to all of us, of course. Some cricketers have turned the act of running their fellows out into an art form. (I'm not bad at it myself, in point of fact.) One team-mate, who shall remain nameless, once did me up like a kipper with an almost surreal piece of genius—a veritable work of art. Having patted yet another forward defensive harmlessly on to the turf, I looked up to see him standing before me, wraith-like, in the exact centre of the wicket. 'Do you?' he said cryptically. Confused and unsure what to do, I set off for the other end. He didn't even flicker, but simply raised a priestly palm when I drew level with him. I froze. Suddenly he turned and scampered back to the other end like a startled squirrel, leaving me alone in the middle of the wicket. I heard the click of the bails being removed behind me. I had been utterly, thoroughly and completely outwitted, and to what purpose I still have no idea to this day.

Without question the finest run-out I ever witnessed, however, occurred in a Captain Scott game against Tusmore House, a country-estate side in Oxfordshire. I mention it now merely for entertainment purposes. The bowler, who was on our side, was stung by a wasp that had flown down his shirt at the exact moment of delivery. The resulting ball (a gentle full toss) being even less deadly than the one intended, the gleeful batsman stepped forward to pulverize it. Like a cannon shell it shot from the bat, straight into the testicles of the non-striker, who had already set off for a run, poleaxing him on the spot. The ball looped directly from there into the hands of the bowler, who—still distracted by the presence of an angry wasp inside his shirt—dropped it. Both men, rolling on the ground in pain, became aware of the loose ball, and of the possibilities inherent in the situation. Their eyes locked in simultaneous realization. It was a race. The bowler grabbed the ball as the non-striker raced for the crease, and managed a direct hit, thus running his opponent out by inches. I'd like to see Simon Hughes in his little caravan analyse *that.*

Back at the Noodsberg Oval, meanwhile, Jonathan—unhampered by his turgid opening partner (perhaps he had done the team a service after all)—put on a century stand with the number three before the inevitable middle-order swish-and-collapse brought us up short at a final total of 161. Not bad. In reply, in the levelling conditions, the Pietermaritzburg XI stuttered somewhat. Their best bat and skipper, Paul Atkins of Surrey, edged to first slip on 17. I had brought along a video camera to record the game—somewhat uselessly, as the only thing visible in the viewfinder were the floodlights, which resembled distant cars on a torrential night on the M25, so I discarded it on a table under the rain-soaked awning of the pavilion. As it turned out, however, in doing so I'd inadvertently failed to switch it off, so when we returned to England I came across a two-hour video of a tabletop, together with a perfect audio recording of the home side arguing with each other. The atmosphere in the Pietermaritzburg side was, if anything, even less harmonious than that in our own. Atkins, furious at his own dismissal, could be heard swearing at and berating his team, making it abundantly clear to each and every one of them that they were *not* going to lose to a bunch of useless, crap, rubbish, shit village cricketers on holiday from England.

They didn't. But it went to the wire. The defining moment came when the best remaining home batsman, with only three wickets in hand, attempted a huge hit, but succeeded only in lofting the ball into the lower stratosphere. Eventually it came down, far into the outfield, upon one of the Surrey League boys. He caught it. Then, like a bar of wet soap, it squirmed out of his hands and into his face, smashing several bones therein. He went to hospital. We held our heads. All, that is, except one of the other ringers, who'd taken a violent dislike to his fellow during the trip, and could barely suppress his glee at the accident. The next day he was even happier, when his comrade returned to Willie's farm with a face like a giant red football. We sat in silence, watching England get crushed by South Africa for the sixth one-day game in succession. The rain beat against the windows. Cape Town seemed a lifetime away. It must, I thought, be something endemic to cricket tours. I made a quiet little promise to myself: I would never, ever, personally organize a tour again, as long as I lived.

* * *

Things had to change, and they did. But by accident. What altered the Captain Scott XI, profoundly and irrevocably, so that it became quite unrecognizable as its former self, was the arrival of four lawyers. Obviously, any lawyers reading this book will have thought to themselves, 'Oh, good! Lawyers.' Obviously, anyone else will have immediately rushed off to shower themselves in Dettol. But bear with me: these were no ordinary lawyers. In fact they were the least lawyerly lawyers one could possibly imagine. Three of them were brothers, brought along by Cie from his Muswell Hill stamping ground: the O'Herlihys, as they were called, were the unusual offspring of a hulking Irish father and a slim, elegant Malaysian mother. They were gobby and confident and optimistic. They sported shoulder-length ponytails and shades. They were hopelessly unpunctual, and would usually arrive an hour late for matches, their spluttering vehicle knee-deep in the wrappers of hastily consumed Burger Kings. They were quite unlike anything we'd seen before. Sean, the eldest, was even bigger than his dad. He earned himself the nickname The Chairminator at one game, after a white plastic chair in the pavilion disintegrated rather than take his weight. He liked to moonlight as a nightclub bouncer, and his vast frame was a mass of scars and dislocated bits sticking out at odd angles. He also enjoyed fielding close to the bat—*very* close to the bat—an experience which, under the right conditions, was not unlike a solar eclipse for the unfortunate batsman. To say that he was physically confident would be an understatement. Sean being a keen Arsenal fan, I went with two of the O'Herlihy brothers and a huge black bouncer colleague called Andy to see Arsenal win the Premiership at Old Trafford. Our tickets, bought off a tout, turned out to be slap bang in the middle of the Stretford End. When Arsenal clinched the championship, Sean went bananas with delight, shouting and dancing. Twenty thousand narrowed Mancunian eyes turned on him.

'I don't know what you're all looking at *me* for,' he exulted. '*You're* the ones who support the shit team. You were rubbish tonight, just like you've been all season! You got a problem with that, mate? No? Then I'd shut up about it if I were you!' And so on, and so on.

'I'm getting out of here,' whispered Andy, who was six foot six and twenty stone. He made his way hastily towards the exit—no easy matter, as the hostile crowds had thickened, and I had climbed into his underwear for safekeeping. We last saw Sean's brother tugging loyally but fruitlessly at his arm, as his sibling let rip with various 'Woohoo!'s and cries of 'Champions!' Needless to say, he emerged half an hour later totally unscathed.

I've never seen Sean O'Herlihy actually start trouble, but boy he knows how to finish it. One Scott game on Richmond Green, attended by quite a large crowd on account of the hot weather, was invaded by a gang of skinheads, who yelled abuse, hurled beer cans, and pulled out all the boundary markers. Showing a surprising turn of speed, Sean hurtled after the ringleader and rugby-tackled him, squashing his nose as he fell. The others fled, and the assault crumbled to dust. The ringleader, however, bright crimson trickling from his nostrils, pointedly marched on to the middle of the wicket, sat cross-legged there, and telephoned the police to report that his 'human rights had been infringed'. A police van turned up soon after, and Sean scarpered.

'Surely', I remonstrated with him, 'we can just explain that *they* attacked us? This is a bunch of skinheads disrupting a reputable cricket match. Surely the police will take our side?'

'In 1935, maybe. Today? No chance. I'm a lawyer, remember. I know.'

He was right, of course. The police turned up, halted play for an hour, concurred that the skinheads' human right to wreck a cricket match had indeed been infringed, and—in the absence of Sean—arrested his brother, on the unanswerable grounds that he looked like the guilty party. No matter that twenty-one cricketers insisted they were making a mistake. The description had been clear: the police were seeking a dark-skinned bloke with sunglasses and a ponytail, and that's what they'd got.

That particular legal pickle was solved to our satisfaction, because the police had in fact arrested half of a pair of identical twins (it's always tricky, making a case against one of a pair of identical twins, neither of whom had anything to do with the alleged offence in the first place). James and Eiran O'Herlihy looked like half-sized versions of Sean, a pair of Russian dolls from inside their elder brother. A two-for-the-price-of-one offer. They weren't exactly thin themselves, but put beside their sibling they looked like cheese straws. Like Sean, the twins were not lacking in confidence. James is the only person apart from W. G. Grace, as far as I am aware, who has refused to leave the crease upon being dismissed, on the grounds that 'They've come to see me bat, not you bowl.' The 'they' in question were two small boys and a rusty bicycle. (He was, needless to say, physically removed from the wicket.) James did, however, play a lot less cricket than Eiran, for he lived with his Swedish girlfriend. Inexplicably, he generally opted to spend the bulk of his weekends in bed with a Swedish woman, in preference to the raw, pulsing excitement that is village cricket.

Eiran, on the other hand, went through girlfriends like an alcoholic through complimentary airplane miniatures (he went through those pretty fast, too). He even brought them to cricket sometimes. On one occasion at Holkham Hall, the dignified country seat of the earls of Leicester, we were treated to the hideous sight of Eiran's own country seat, bobbing up and down in the long grass. (He was, admittedly, in the midst of a flock of sheep at the time, leading me once again perilously close to the joke that dare not speak its name.) Eiran always carried an acoustic guitar with him, an instrument upon which he was more than adept, so that he could whip it out and impress the ladies. (Stop it. *Now.*) Sean, by contrast, had purchased a small dog for this purpose, which proved even more spectacularly successful. In fact he even procured a girlfriend for Eiran with it. The dog soon became a regular menace at cricket matches. Many's the time an opposition batsman, lured into an error by a cunning slowed down off-cutter, would loop a simple catch up to square leg, only for it to plop harmlessly into the vacant space where Sean had been standing. Invariably, his fat arse would be sticking out of a hedge in the distance, hunting for his wretched springer spaniel.

Personally, I've had a prejudice against dogs at cricket matches since the early days of Captain Scott. It's not just the endless saliva-covered cricket balls thick with toothmarks. Specifically, a team-mate procured two lurcher puppies and named them Harry and Marcus, after his most regular captains. My then girlfriend (what *is* it with girls and small dogs?) begged me to let Harry the lurcher ride with us in the car on the way to a game, snuggled on her lap. I said no. She ignored me. About ten miles up the motorway, the creature woke up in her lap, panicked, and tried to flee, while simultaneously emitting a violent jet of projectile diarrhoea. I couldn't stop: we were in the fast lane of the A40. 'Christ! Point its bum out of the window!' I yelled, whereupon she grabbed its collar and tried to hold on to the wriggling beast. This merely had the effect of turning its squirming, flailing hindquarters into a revolving diarrhoea nozzle, spraying me, her, the inside of the windscreen, everywhere, with a jet of foul-smelling liquid. It was like one of those novelty flower-headed hoses you see in souvenir shops. Only brown. The smell never came out of the upholstery. In the end, I had to sell the car. I even tried to sell her, for the same reason.

The O'Herlihy brothers argued ceaselessly about the best way to stop their dog escaping, as indeed they argued about everything else. The no-ball law, the capital of Bolivia, who'd won the FA Cup in 1911, you name it, no subject was beyond the scope of a good face-to-face slanging match. [Answers for the anally retentive: (a) the front heel should be at least partly behind the popping crease, and the back foot should not touch the side of the return crease; (b) La Paz: (c) Bradford City.] They were, of course, entirely devoted to one another. And they offered qualities (to everyone else but their siblings) that we'd been missing: voluble, good-natured bonhomie, married to boundless optimism. It wasn't that they were any better than the rest of us—yet—although they clearly had the potential to streak far ahead. Sean's batting was riddled with technical flaws, while Eiran and James were too busy showing off, swashbuckling, trying to hit everything out of the ground. I solved the latter problem, incidentally, with a simple stratagem—a spread bet. For every total they amassed below 15, they had to pay me 50p for each run short. Over 20, and I had to start paying up. The first season, I was quids in. Thereafter they put two and two together, got their heads down until they reached 15, then systematically emptied my wallet.

I'd actually tried something similar many years previously with Terence, when we were hanging on for a draw at Steep in Hampshire. The home side had scored 160 odd, we were about 40–9, and there was an hour to go. Marcus (at the other end) I could trust to defend his wicket, but Terence, who was last man, would have to bat for fifty-nine minutes longer than the duration of his average innings for us to make it to safety. Knowing his love of the folding stuff, I held a whip-round, and raised a £25 bribe. Should he make it to the end, he'd get the lot. But if he failed, he'd have to give me a pound. Suddenly Terence became Trevor Bailey. Even when the home side brought back their pacemen, one of whom felled him with a vicious bouncer to the head, he refused to budge. Various fielders tried to carry his prone form to the boundary, whereupon a squawk like a chicken emanated from the unconscious batsman: 'But I'll lose my money!' And up he got, and got on with it, and made it heroically to the end, and didn't buy a round in the pub afterwards. It's important when making bets with one's team-mates, however, not to leave any loopholes. One big-mouthed Lancastrian batsman insisted loudly that he could score a century in twenty minutes. Knowing this to be impossible, I accepted his lucrative wager. But when he was clean bowled for 11, eighteen minutes later, he refused to pay up, on the grounds that he hadn't had the full time allotted to complete the task.

The fourth lawyer to join up, who had nothing to do with the other three, was a man who needed no incentives to do well. His very name was a daily challenge for him to overcome: Paul Daniels. He had been born, of course, long before *the* Paul Daniels had invaded our screens; then, all of a sudden, in his childhood, this impish, grinning apparition babbling on about the lovely Debbie McGee had turned up on TV and ruined his life. It could have been worse, I suppose. He could have been called Dennis Nielsen, or Peter Sutcliffe, or even Paul Pot. Actually, on second thoughts, that probably wouldn't have been worse. *Nothing* would have been worse. Daniels (our version) was a burly, beery, jolly, hyperactive, rugby-loving Welshman and fanatical Blairite, whose legal speciality was the defending of radical causes (and who was probably therefore wildly overpaid). He was also—although we had no inkling of this when we recruited him, on the usual friend-of-a-friend-of-a-friend basis—a quite exceptional batsman. Whenever he played, we won. When he didn't play, we lost.

Centuries flowed from his bat. Sides that ran into him could do nothing but pray. When he finally threw his wicket away at Great Yeldham, several of the opposition fieldsmen literally fell to their knees, hands clasped together, and gave thanks to the heavens. I batted with him against Sir Tim Rice's team, the Heartaches, a well-marshalled side of solid, well-bred, gung-ho league players, who had been content to batter us to the consistency of porridge on a regular basis. Suddenly the boot was on the other foot. All I had to do was stand at the other end and watch, and prod the occasional single to rotate the strike. Daniels simply hit everything that came his way out of the ground. Together we put on well over 200 runs. The layabouts, despite their professed love of violent batting, were utterly, totally horrified. Francis drove home in a huff again. No amount of 'creative' umpiring could get rid of this man. Obviously we didn't win the game, as sufficient creativity was put into the bowling and fielding to ensure a draw, but the Heartaches declined to play us again. They preferred the boot, it seemed, to remain on its original foot at all times. Personally, I found this hilarious. All those years losing fixtures hand over fist because we hadn't been up to scratch, and now, finally, we'd lost one because we'd been *too good.* It was novel to say the least.

The response to all this new blood, for the layabouts, was to co-ordinate their appearances. They were older now, and had been playing for nigh on twenty years; there were marriages and children and arthritic knees (and, in one case, lumbago) to think about, which meant less cricket. They tended to play about six or seven Sunday games a season these days, but started colluding to make sure that they were the same six or seven Sunday games—invariably the plum fixtures in the prettiest villages. The combined age of these teams usually topped 400 (although any self-respecting 400-year-old would have been ashamed at the level of commitment and dedication on display). This, of course, was an utter disaster for our selection procedure. A whole alternative side had to be found, who would be glad to turn up, bat, bowl and field on a regular basis, but who would then happily stand aside and let someone else take their places for the most glamorous games. Unfortunately, such people do not really exist.

Sean O'Herlihy came to the rescue. He'd already proved himself adept at finding last-minute players, mainly by sitting on their heads until they complied (we were the only team in England with a large contingent of pancake-headed fielders). During his evenings moonlighting as a nightclub bouncer, he'd discovered that free skiing holidays were available to anyone large who was prepared to stand outside, rather than in, the après-ski bar at the end of the skiing day. There he had run into a whole glut of South Africans, newly released from their international pariah status, who had cottoned on to the same scam. Some of them were on their way to London. So, come summer, he called a couple of them up and invited them to play. They were keen, vocal, athletic and punky, and they fielded like killer bees (yes, yes, I know, killer bees can't catch cricket balls either, but I wouldn't argue the point with one). They batted with the sturdy resolve usually employed to ride unsaddled wildebeest around the Highveldt. They wanted to win everything, and refused to give in until defeat had punched their teeth out. Whatever they'd been taught at the F. W. de Klerk Correctional Facility of Kaffirbashersdorp West, surrender wasn't in the curriculum. And they were *keen*. Boy, they were keen. One of them promised his girlfriend a 'romantic weekend in Oxford', which turned out to be two games of cricket for us, interspersed with a nocturnal kip in a sleeping bag on the pavilion floor. She didn't mind: she was South African too.

We'd seen colonial keenness before, of course. Cliff, our Australian, had once been unable to play at Selborne in Hampshire, partly because of a broken hand, and partly because his parents had flown halfway round the world to see him. He'd actually arranged to take them on a walking tour of the Oxford colleges they'd heard so much about. In the event, he turned up at Selborne, which is on a minor road near Alton, fifty miles from Oxford, claiming in all wide-eyed innocence that he'd 'got lost' on the way. He then took the field, broken hand and all. There'd even been one game when we'd had *two* new players, *both* Australians, who'd chivvied and encouraged our bowlers throughout the opposition innings, an activity which had gone down about as well with the layabouts as if the pair had defecated in the outfield. Marcus had eventually placed one at deep extra cover and the other at deep midwicket, as far apart as possible, from where they continued to chirrup, producing an interesting stereo effect in the middle. But this had been an isolated incident, and it had been ruthlessly suppressed, Tiananmen Square-style. In the context of the team's twentieth anniversary, the arrival of the South Africans seemed to portend much, much more.

In fact there were only the two South Africans at first, who played just eight games between them all season, and who were—statistically speaking—not much better than the rest of us. But it was their *attitude* that made all the difference. As soon as they joined the team, they transferred their loyalties to it wholesale. They really didn't care about their own performances, as long as the team did well. Like Cie, they were genuinely delighted by their team-mates' success. They'd bust a gut in the field to save a run. They always tried hard. And they were always good-natured and friendly; they never bickered, bitched or griped. In short, they were, in every sense, un-*British*. I thought they were a breath of fresh air.

Marcus called me at the end of the season to tell me that the layabouts were resigning en masse in protest, and that he was starting a new team. We were divorced at last.

5

Kuala Lumpur

The O'Herlihy brothers being half Malaysian, it seemed entirely logical to them that we should all pack our bags yet again and move the whole circus halfway round the world to Malaysia. I wouldn't have to do much—with their family contacts they could arrange all the games, secure cheap flights and hotels, and so forth. Clearly, they felt they'd missed out.

'We've heard the team has just been on two great overseas trips,' they said.

'Well . . . they started well enough,' I ventured guardedly. 'They sort of . . . all went wrong though, in the second week.'

'Then we'll only go for a single week.'

Cunning.

We'd have to find a load of new players, of course. But if anything went wrong on the field, Paul Daniels would pull us through. Or would he? Something very, very strange had begun to happen to the Welsh wizard. Initially there'd been a run of low scores—a glitch, we thought, or a trot of bad form of the kind that can affect anyone. His batting average had tumbled from a healthy 100-plus to a distinctly mediocre 18. But then he kept getting worse, and worse, and worse. He would come back from the crease scratching his head and staring at his bat, which he said 'felt heavy'. Pretty soon, double figures became a distant dream. Someone somewhere in the National Heath

Service should do a survey on sporting form as a precursory indicator of long-term illness, for it became clear before long that Paul was extremely unwell. The cause was eventually diagnosed as the severely debilitating Epstein-Barr syndrome. In due course he had to retreat to his parents' house, and became bedridden. Even when he finally emerged from his sickbed, following months of treatment, his top score for two years was to be 4. Our superman had been laid low by green kryptonite. It was a development that was not entirely without irony.

In his place came Sam, a former Wasps rugby player and chest-beating fast bowler; the extraordinarily monickered Wolfram Finger, surely the only German cricketer in the history of the sport; and Giles, a garrulous *Times* journalist, who claimed to be a spin bowler. Well, to be fair, he claimed to have been—statistically—the number-one spin bowler for his age in the entire country, at thirteen years old. Undoubtedly, though, his crown had slipped during the intervening years. In fact, were he to be seated at his grandmother's bedside, he would have been hard-pressed to call himself the best spin bowler in the room. But, despite a tendency to volubility that verged on the bombastic, Giles invariably won people round in the long run, especially as he was always prepared—after the event—to admit that he had been wrong. Keeping wicket once, as he occasionally did now that Terence was gone, he complained loudly of a rival spin bowler that 'If there's a caught-behind chance off this bowling, I'll eat my cricket kit.' Of course, the batsman neatly snicked the next ball through to Giles, who predictably dropped it. At our annual dinner that year he was presented with a special pudding: part of his own batting pads, dipped in whisky and flambéed, with a scoop of vanilla ice cream on the side. To his immense credit, he wolfed the lot.

Even if our new-look side was not especially strong on talent, it differed from its predecessor in that it was bursting with self-belief, team spirit and the will to try hard. And, of course, having the occasional South African accent in our armoury did no harm either. In one charming Oxfordshire hamlet, our rather innocuous opening bowlers ran through the village top order in double-quick time, because the home batsmen—one after another—backed slowly away towards the square-leg umpire, leaving their wickets unprotected. It was clear that we were witnessing a premeditated pattern of ball-avoidance. After the game, I sought out the opposition's opening batsmen and asked for an explanation.

'Well,' said one, 'when we 'eard them South African accents down the Swan at lunchtime, we knew we was done for. Didn't seem much point after that.'

It occurred to me that this was a peculiarly British attitude. As a nation, we tend to assume that foreign opposition will be better. OK, that's invariably true. But that doesn't mean that foreigners are better *as of right*. It doesn't mean there's no point *trying* to beat them. Look back at the desperate years of English Test cricket. Was Merv Hughes really that good, with his fat neck and his Freddie Mercury moustache? No. But he genuinely believed he was, and woe betide any

English batsman prepared to dispute the fact. Remember Waqar's strut, and Wasim's swagger? Remember Curtly's icy stare? Now compare them to Mike Atherton's attempts to glare aggressively back down the wicket. He looked like a sullen schoolboy whose calculator had been stolen from his satchel by an unknown classmate. Even Alec Stewart's 'defiant' mode resembled the chipper cockney stoker who kept the destroyer going under enemy fire in all those old war films. Solid, reliable, dependable, yes. Intimidating, no. The only player we had who went out of his way to look intimidating was Chris Lewis, who shaved his head for the purpose, and immediately took to his bed for several days with sunstroke. Which made a change from the mystery toe injury he invariably developed when any of the stronger opposition teams pitched up in town. No, the problem with the national side in those days was—at least in part—that we used to turn up expecting, from the start, to defy, to resist, to hang on pluckily despite being second best. Even the all-conquering, Ashes-winning side of 2005 had its sticky moments: during the Trent Bridge Test, with Shane Warne defending the most meagre of totals, you could see a number of the England batsmen staring deep into their own souls, as if unable to believe that victory was really possible.

Duncan Fletcher's biggest achievement has been to instil colonial levels of self-belief into the England team. Famously, the only person who seemed to possess this attitude in the bad old days was Ian Botham, who welcomed Graham Dilley to the crease during the 1981 Headingley Test victory, with only three wickets remaining and

England needing 92 to make Australia bat again, with the memorable phrase 'OK, Dill, let's give it some humpety.' It's this attitude, this refusal to accept defeat, that seems to permeate Australian and South African society and sport; and it's this mental approach, over and above technical ability, that has traditionally made their players better than ours at most levels of the game. For it filters right down to ground level. Another new player in our team was Greg, a little Australian. Except that he was not Australian: he had been born near Portsmouth, and had emigrated to Sydney as a child. As a result, he was more Australian than any real Australian you could hope to meet. He dyed his hair green and gold, said 'g'day' a lot, and swore that there were no poofters in Oz. He was, in fact, a parody Aussie. But when we were 9 down with 60-odd still needed to win, and he was last in, and I told him just to go and have fun as the game was probably a lost cause, he wasn't having any of it. 'Rubbish, mate. I'm gonna get these.' *But your top score is 7 in eighteen months*, I thought. He got them. He made 55 in three overs. Even though he wasn't a real Australian, he'd been educated there, and the possibility of defeat had clearly been rerouted into the dump bin of his brain. Colonial self-confidence is strangely infectious. Gradually it began to seep into the collective consciousness of the Captain Scott XI.

Of course, we still had one very tangible link with old attitudes in the shape of Anuj, our spherical Indian princeling; he continued to stand idly by while balls passed mere feet away in the outfield, to turn down easy singles that had come off someone else's bat, and to protect his batting average when quick runs were needed for a win. He was one of the twelve on the list to tour Malaysia. When he told Sean that he was '100% definitely coming', though, the alarm bells began to ring in my mind. As everyone knows, 110% is the bare minimum percentage applicable in sport (which, like Polish spirit, is permitted to transcend mere mathematics). Sean was inclined to give Anuj the benefit of the doubt. He did grill him fiercely about his intentions, of course, but Anuj never wavered, never once dipped to the fatal 99% mark. Come the Sunday night before Sean had to buy the air tickets, Anuj still had not paid, and had failed to turn up to a rendezvous with the cash. Instead he telephoned, insisted once more, worryingly, that he was 100% definitely coming, and promised that—as he would be at work on the Monday—his mother would bring the cheque to the airline office. As it happened, Sean too being at work, the task of buying the team's tickets had fallen to *his* mother. The Malaysian lady waited in the rain for hours for the Indian lady, but she did not show. Neither was Anuj reachable. So, not knowing what to do, Mrs O'Herlihy bought Anuj's ticket with her own money. It was non-refundable.

At long last, Anuj was located.

'I've changed my mind,' he told Sean. 'I won't be able to come.'

'Then you owe my mother the price of your air ticket,' retorted Sean bluntly.

'Oh no no no no,' insisted Anuj smoothly. 'You see, I never technically instructed her to buy my ticket.'

The equation was simple, Sean informed me. Either Anuj never played for the team again or he didn't. It was not the hardest decision I had ever had to make.

*   *   *

One thing I could rely on, at any rate—as the tour was being fixed up by a sensible member of our own side—was that we wouldn't be matched up with such ludicrously tough opposition as before. I checked with Sean exactly whom we were due to face.

'First up is the Malaysian armed forces.'

'Phew. Sounds tough. And after that?'

'On the Tuesday we've got Malaysia.'

'Malaysia what? Malaysia juniors? The Malaysian Blind Cricket Association?'

'Er, no . . . Malaysia.'

'*Malaysia*?'

'Er, yeah. The country.'

'Jesus Christ, Sean. We're a village team.'

'They're not as strong on a Tuesday. And they've got a really nice pitch.'

Oh God.

*   *   *

The trip got off to an inauspicious start as the O'Herlihy twins passed through Malaysian immigration. We stood in an antiseptic hall being reminded by a soothing, shopping-channel-style voice-over that the penalty for drug possession was death, which might have given the pair pause for thought for a moment or two. James was waved through without incident, but Eiran, following on behind, was stopped by the same immigration official on the grounds that he 'looked suspicious' and that his passport was 'possibly forged'. Naturally, we remonstrated. If his identical twin had not looked suspicious, how could he? If his identical twin's near-identical passport, with its consecutive serial number and its identical place and date of issue, had not looked like a forgery, then how could his? This blizzard of logic served only to confuse the clearly chicken-sized brain of the immigration official, who presumably feared a plot to flood Malaysia with identical long-haired semi-Irish clones. Only the summoning of the man's superior's superior's superior finally cleared up the situation.

Free to explore the delights of Kuala Lumpur, the majority of the eleven made straight for the hotel pool, which was admittedly rather splendidly situated beneath the twin spires of the gigantic Petronas Towers, the world's tallest building. Only Sam and I, along with one of the South Africans, opted to see the city. KL (as it's invariably called) is the capital of a Muslim nation, but it's the most liberal Muslim capital city I've ever seen, possibly because of the vast crowd of irreligious pork-crazy Chinese dwelling there. The women do not wear burkas or headscarves. The young spend their evenings knocking back cocktails in gleaming chrome-and-neon nightclubs, where boys in skintight black polos rub shoulders with heavily made-up girls in strappy tops. The markets are crammed with counterfeited Western designer goods. The Petronas Towers that steeple over this teeming morass of conspicuous consumption may indeed be 'based on an eight-sided star pattern echoing the Arabesque patterns of Islamic art', but they were designed by Americans. They are the minarets of a temple consecrated to the worship of oil money.

Minorities in Malaysia, like the British and the Indians, carry on their cultish activities in suburban enclaves. We made an eight-mile trek into the northern suburbs to see the remarkable Batu Caves, a huge limestone formation set into a cliff-face, and reached by a flight of 272 hand-carved steps. The delicate tracery of nature has been overlaid with the gaudier work of man: the whole complex was turned into an elaborate Hindu temple during the nineteenth century. Brightly coloured images of Lord Subramaniam, an aspect of Shiva, and the fearsome Durga, representing the same deity's feminine side, take their place in the usual Hindu pantheon of bulging-eyed gods and monsters. Christianity, of course, presents a much more visually austere face to the world, but the faded murals of the early Church, and the scraps of faint terracotta plaster that adhere to the base of crumbling columns, would suggest that the West, too, began its spiritual life in a riot of kindergarten colours. Our austerity, perhaps, is cyclical, feeding on a faded image of itself; maybe the Indians remain truer to the original concept of a place of worship as a dazzling, enticing entertainment for impressionable eyes.

Certainly the Batu Caves would be a marvellous place to bring children, being overrun not just by Technicolor gods but also by real hairy little monkeys. A marvellous place to bring children, perhaps, but not huge fast bowlers.

'You never said there would be m-monkeys,'

quailed Sam.

'I never knew there'd be monkeys. why, what difference does it make?'

'I have a m-monkey phobia. I'm terrified of them.'

'Sam, they're ten inches high. They drop their bananas and scarper if you go anywhere near them. You used to play rugby for Wasps. What on earth could they do to you?'

'It d-doesn't matter. P-please, keep them away from me.'

He dodged behind me hurriedly as a distant monkey, scratching its arse on a stone banister, momentarily gave him a baleful glance. Sam was the closest thing in our team to one of the great apes himself. In fact he was so hirsute he was in serious danger of being poached in the outfield. He was six feet two and sixteen stone, and had thought nothing, during his rugby career, of standing in the path of an onrushing Jonah Lomu. Now—like the proverbial elephant who was afraid of mice—he was shaking like a baby at the sight of a ten-inch quadruped. Tragically, we had to beat a retreat from the caves.

We got back to our hotel just before the afternoon downpour. Every day in Kuala Lumpur the skies clouded over after lunch, becoming increasingly brooding and forbidding until by mid-afternoon a hellish black swirl made the heavens a witches' cauldron. Invariably, a pounding rainstorm would follow, of the kind usually associated with TV disaster appeals, or optimistic predictions by Michael Fish. Giles, who had already run up a personal lager bill of £95, was too drunk to move from his sunlounger; Herr Finger, who had unwisely attempted to keep pace with him, was in a similar state—glassy and monosyllabic—a condition that would persist until the end of the week. Only when an official came round and put up a wooden stand announcing that the pool was now closed did Giles budge: he threw it into the deep end, then went for a swim on the pretext of retrieving it.

All of this begged the simple question: if meteorological Armageddon was visited on the city every day at about 3 p.m., how on earth were we supposed to finish a full-length cricket match with a 10 a.m. start? The answer was equally simple: we weren't. The British are as keen on their religious rituals as any Hindu or Muslim. Empire etiquette dictated that cricket matches of eighty-overs duration must begin at 10 a.m., irrespective of the impossibility of eighty overs being bowled. 'Why don't we just have a shorter match?' I suggested, and received the kind of withering stare that would have greeted the idea of whizzing through the Pope's funeral in five minutes, in case of drizzle. What happens in Malaysian cricket—not that we knew this at the outset of our first game—is that there's usually room for half an hour's cricket on the sodden field at the end of the day, at which point the umpires randomly make up a reasonable target for the batting side to aim at. It's a bit like the Duckworth-Lewis system used in Test cricket, except without the logic or maths.

We convened on the usual gorgeous Malaysian morning, sunny, stifling and sticky, at the Armed Forces Ground. I won the toss and was left with the tricky conundrum of what on earth to do. I've been captaining a cricket team, on and off, for a quarter of a century, and I'd say it took me at least the first decade to learn to read an English pitch. It's all about what will happen to the soil during the course of an afternoon: will a damp pitch cut up and crumble, or will it hold steady? Will a dry surface crack apart, or will it stay intact? Will a dead surface liven up, or will the ball bounce ever lower? If a hard, fast surface has a thin, grassy covering, should one opt for the advantage of the ball coming on to the bat, or the advantage of a seaming new ball? For most players, the equation is simple. If they're batsmen, they want to bat. If they're bowlers, they want to bowl, and have five slips like on the telly, even if it's so muddy that no edge could conceivably reach the slips, and none of the team's slips has ever actually held a catch anyway. Captains know different. I'd say that a good third of all the games I've been involved in have been more or less settled by the toss. But here in Malaysia I was at a complete loss: the pitch was fashioned from a powdery red clay, held together by visible clusters of white roots. What this might do over the course of half a day followed by an intergalactic thunderstorm I had no idea.

I was immediately put in mind of a trip I'd once made to watch a strongly fancied England side play two back-to-back one-day internationals against the West Indies in St Vincent. Adam Hollioake, who was skippering, had presumably been faced with a similar conundrum. He had opted to bat—a decision which had evoked chortles all round from the locals in the stands.

'Ho ho ho—that man's made a very big mistake.

The tide is in—any side bat at St Vincent when the tide is in, they gonna lose! Your boys have had it, man!'

The St Vincent ground was indeed a low-lying coastal stadium, the tide was in, and sure enough England were easily rolled over. That night, St Vincent being a small place, the England fans found themselves in the same bar as the England players. Should I go over and say something? I wondered. The England team were being incredibly charming and patient with their supporters, but surely the last thing Adam Hollioake wanted on a night out was to be bearded by some armchair captain. Finally, a few beers made the persuasive case that it was my patriotic duty to say something to him. I went over and introduced myself.

'Look, I really don't like to bother you like this, it's just that, well, I was sitting in the middle of a crowd of locals today, and they said that when the tide's in—'

'—the side batting always loses,' he smiled, finishing my sentence for me. 'Don't worry, I know. You're the tenth person tonight who's come up and told me all about it.'

The next morning, with the tide in as per the previous day, Hollioake won the toss again. He elected to bat again. England were comprehensively destroyed again. Like I said, it takes a decade or so.

My Malaysian conundrum, of course, involved other factors besides the unusual-looking pitch. The rain, I thought, held the key. If we batted second, then (a) the wicket would still hold firm, as there were rain-covers, (b) we'd have a smaller target to go at, hell for leather, a lottery which would presumably equalize the teams somewhat, (c) we would field in the cool of the morning, and (d) we wouldn't have to stand around in the swamp later, and get our trousers all muddy. Yeeuch.

I believe I even used the phrase 'the cool of the morning' to my team-mates. In reality it was like playing cricket in hot strawberry jam. The sweat ran from us in rivulets. After the game we worked out, on the hotel's bathroom scales, that we had each lost between five and ten pounds inside a few hours (Dr Atkins, eat your heart out). Our opening bowlers were magnificent—after five overs each, the Malaysian military had mustered just thirteen runs for the loss of two wickets—but then they both literally sank to their knees, unable to go on. Even Sam, the nearest thing we had to a professional sportsman, was utterly incapable of completing his ten overs. If only I'd thought to bring a small monkey with me, to threaten him with. But the rest of us plugged away, and we fielded like demons. Like the teams we'd faced in South Africa, the opposition had a paid ringer in their ranks, a Pakistani pro called Nadeem. He put us to the sword somewhat with an elegant 46, but all in all we were very pleased to restrict our hosts to 110 off their forty overs.

Nadeem did the damage at the top of our order too, beating me and a couple of others all ends up; but two of the O'Herlihys stabilized matters, and we had scored 52 for 3 off nineteen overs when the rain came.

The waters receded at a quarter to six, leaving time—by the umpires' calculation—for eleven more overs. Thirty-three runs, they arbitrarily decided, would make a competitive target. Three an over, and we had seven wickets still to fall. Surely we were in with a real chance. I had, however, reckoned without one or two important factors. The tarpaulin covers had proved utterly worthless against the beating tropical rain, and the resulting water leaks had turned the red clay of the wicket into a slippy, slithery mess. It had become an old-fashioned 'sticky'. Furthermore, the umpires had not thought to reduce the bowlers' allocation commensurate with the overall reduction of overs, so the dangerous Nadeem would be allowed to bowl six of the eleven overs remaining. He was to prove as good an off-spinner as he had been a seamer, his fizzing deliveries biting into the adhesive red clay. The outfield, of course, was drenched, so runs would be hard to come by. Paralysis set in. The two O'Herlihys were quickly removed, together with the rest of the middle order, for a combined total of one run. After seven of our eleven overs, we had scored just seven runs. Giles and Wolfram, both nursing king-sized hangovers, came to the crease with four overs to go, still needing to score 26.

A sizeable crowd was gathering now, made up in the main of Malaysian army personnel, sensing a tight finish. Having an audience present can change the dynamic of a game: concentration becomes harder; self-consciousness becomes an enemy. I should say at this point that I've hated playing in front of crowds, however small, ever since Griff Rhys Jones inveigled me to play in a charity cricket match in Suffolk. He'd called me out of the blue, saying that he'd fixed up a celebrity side for the following day, that one of the celebrities had dropped out, that he couldn't find another, and that—as nine of his team had never played cricket before, and he remembered from Cape Town that I had—would I mind making up the numbers? Foolishly, I'd said yes. I still toss and turn in the night, bathed in sweat, as that game rewinds itself in my dreams.

It had started well enough: it was a gorgeous day, sizzling hot, the sun a burnished disc in a cornflower-blue sky. We'd assembled for a lavish lunch, laid out on trestle tables in the half of Suffolk that Griff owns, before making our way to the ground—somewhat bizarrely—on a flatbed trolley pulled by a tractor with Griff at the wheel. There were Clive Anderson, Rory McGrath, Hugh Laurie, Samantha Janus, six other celebrities, and, rather irrelevantly, me. Hugh Laurie was the only one among them to have played before. Astonishingly, when we got to the ground, we discovered that a crowd of six thousand people had assembled. An even more horrible discovery, though, was that Griff and his fellow captain had got their wires crossed. The other team consisted not of eleven cricketing celebrities, but of *eleven celebrity cricketers*. They were all county players.

Griff won the toss and asked me what to do. The wicket was a peach, a real shirtfront, with nothing in it for the bowler.

'Griff, you've got to bat,' I said, 'and you've got to stage-manage the game. Tell them to feed us a hundred runs, then get them slowly. If they bat first and take it seriously, there'll be a massacre like you've never seen.'

'OK,' said Griff, 'we'll bat.'

'Oh,' said the opposition captain disappointedly. 'I was really hoping you'd bowl, in this heat.'

'OK,' said Griff brightly, 'we'll bowl.'

I raised my eyes to heaven.

After a short interval, the batsmen made their way to the crease and took guard. Griff tossed me the ball.

'Here, you can open the bowling.'

'Me? But I haven't warmed up or anything.'

'Tell you what, why don't you captain as well? I'm not really sure if I'm doing this right.'

I paced out my run-up and prepared to bowl, to Ray East of Essex. But there was something wrong—something missing. I couldn't put my finger on it at first, but then, as I began my run-up, I realized what it was. No wicketkeeper.

I stopped. The crowd began to slow handclap. The nearest fielder, a bearded musician I had failed to recognize, was twenty yards away.

'Do you want to keep wicket?' I called desperately.

'What?' he shouted.

'Do you want to keep wicket?' I screamed, fighting to make myself heard over the noise of the restless crowd.

'Sorry. Can't hear you,' he shrugged.

I ran over and commanded the poor fellow to go back to the pavilion, double quick, and change into wicketkeeping gear. Finally, with the crowd in a state of near-rebellion, the match was able to get under way. Ray East watched my first ball pass harmlessly. I breathed a sigh of relief. But that was all the respite I was going to get. He'd just been having a look, checking that I was indeed rubbish. After that he slapped each ball to distant corners of the ground, lazily but clinically. I was, as the expression goes, mullered.

The county players took the game very seriously indeed. There is something rather dispiriting about watching first-class cricketers joyfully carting Samantha Janus out of the ground for a succession of mighty sixes. No doubt the old Captain Scott XI would have loved every second of it, but I can't say that any of us did. Thank God, then, for Hugh Laurie, who turned out to be a brilliant cricketer (he's a good all-round sportsman, in fact, who once featured in the University Boat Race). He took a handful of wickets and scored the only runs when it was our turn to bat, saving a tiny little bit of face on our behalf—perhaps a nostril-hair's worth. As to my own batting failure, I was determined to have a go, at the very least. Facing Don Topley, also of Essex, I surprised myself by essaying a perfect off drive, which screamed off the bat, about four inches off the ground and a yard or two to the bowler's left. Wow, what a shot, I thought. Topley watched it go by, then, at the last minute, leaned across almost absent-mindedly and plucked it from the air with all the grace of a professional athlete, as if picking a ripe apple from a tree. We lost by I-can't-remember-how-many hundred runs. It was no sort of spectacle. By the end, the crowd of six thousand had thinned to about sixty. People like to watch real contests.

Back at the Malaysian Armed Forces Ground in Kuala Lumpur, Giles and Wolfram were—fortunately—turning things into a real contest. Still too drunk to be aware of the odds stacked against us, they had taken the fight to the opposition, and were whacking the ball to all corners. The crowd were cheering every hit, and every miss, with that indiscriminate fervour peculiar to Asian cricket fans. We began the last over needing nine runs to bring the scores level, which—as we'd lost fewer wickets—would give us the win.

The first ball was a wide, acknowledged by the scorer but largely missed by the crowd and most of the players in the general pandemonium. 'Five balls to go!' shouted the spectators erroneously. The next four balls yielded a two and three singles, the crowd continuing its inaccurate countdown with every ball. Three were still needed from two balls, but, thanks to the spectators' collective inaccuracy, the fielders and Giles all thought it was the last ball of the match. He smashed it to long on and the pair completed an easy two; then he came back for a crazy third, believing it our only chance of victory, while Wolfram, knowing there to be another ball left, stayed put. The pair were now at the same end. The Malaysians whizzed the ball to the other end, but the bowler, in a panic, attempted needlessly to hurl the stumps down and missed. Giles screamed at Wolfram to run. The German, obeying the order unthinkingly with the biological instinct of centuries, set off at speed. His despairing dive reached the crease a split second after the ball broke the stumps. He was out.

Technically speaking, we needed one to win off the last ball, but the whooping, celebrating home side were wheeling off the field in triumph, into the arms of their supporters. They had beaten the mighty English village side. The next man in, padded up amid a heaving crowd of celebrating Malaysians, made futile attempts to propel the fielders back on. Giles was already walking off, thinking we'd lost. Wolfram was limping off in his wake, trying to catch him up to ask him why he was walking off. Whether the language barrier was a genuine obstacle or a convenient excuse (I mean the Anglo-Malaysian language barrier, not the Anglo-German one), it took half an hour to sort out the confusion. Eventually an honourable draw was declared and an awards ceremony was held, at which the Malaysians unexpectedly presented us with a beautiful engraved shield commemorating the game. We had brought nothing to give them. Ruefully, Sean produced his Captain Scott cap and jumper, both brand new, from his kit.

'Er . . . we brought you this,' he lied.

By the end of the week we had enough shields to open a market stall and almost no kit left.

*   *   *

Utterly shattered, we had to pick ourselves up the next day to play Malaysia. The *country*. It was, however, as Sean had mentioned, a Tuesday. The opposition players were all amateurs, which meant that all the best ones would be at work. And, as this was the national side, there'd be no Indian or Pakistani ringers. Our self-belief had grown and grown: we genuinely thought we were in with a chance. The venue for the game, the prosaically titled Rubber Research Institute at Sungei Buloh, was magnificent, a Commonwealth Games ground with a mosque alongside. This, incidentally, was to be the only time on the entire trip that I had any real sense of Malaysia as a devout Islamic nation: it was an unusual experience, playing cricket while a muezzin wailed his call to prayer across the ground every hour or so.

The first obstacle of the day, though, was to get the O'Herlihy brothers out of bed. At the appointed start time they were still lying in blubbery piles in their darkened hotel room, farting and belching like elephant seals amid a pile of hamburger wrappers. Eiran and Giles had spent the night dueting in a karaoke brothel. Don't ask. I will simply confirm that, yes, such places exist in Islamic Malaysia. By the time we got to the ground it was half past eleven, but obviously—amid all my profuse apologies—the idea of shortening the match was out of the question. Once again, and not without a certain satisfaction this time, I chose to field in 'the cool of the morning'. Again the sweat ran off us in streams, but again we bowled and fielded like dervishes, flinging ourselves full length to stop each and every ball. (As per my previous objection to the panther-fielder analogy, there is absolutely no reason that the Islamic dancing-warrior order of dervishes, who find their spiritual home at Konya, in the central Anatolian plateau, would be any good at stopping a cricket ball. But you get the general idea.) By the time we adjourned for a fierce curry lunch, the Malaysian eleven had been restricted to a pallid 106.

Being miserably out of form, I departed early yet again for a hopeless duck, but my colleagues were made of sterner stuff. We had reached 37–1 off ten overs when the thunderstorm came and huge forks of Frankenstein lightning jagged across the sky, forcing us to make a run for the pavilion. This time, though, the storm did not spend itself completely, and the rain did not cease. Unusually, the tempest retreated to a distance, where it continued to rumble threateningly. Over our heads, meanwhile, it was reduced to a mere drizzle—sufficient, decided the umpires, for the home side to take the field once more. The reluctant Malaysians were dragooned out into the quagmire left by the retreating gale. The new target, the umpires decided, would be 71 off twenty-five overs. In other words, a further 34 from fifteen overs. This was incredibly, unaccountably generous, and eminently gettable, if only the rain would hold off.

We lost two further wickets without adding to the score; but the Commonwealth Games covers had done their job better than their military counterparts, the wicket was dry, and the outfield was cropped shorter than it had been the previous day. And, we were very, very determined. Giles and Eiran came to the crease and, karaoke brothels notwithstanding, made short work of the total. The winning runs came up with seven overs to spare. As the umpires signalled the victory, the thunder and lightning, which had been brooding over in a corner, idly barbecueing the odd tree stump for fun, rolled back extravagantly across the ground, drenching all and sundry. We fell to our knees in the rain. We had beaten an entire country. All right, a country with no professional cricketers in its team. On a Tuesday. But we had beaten an *entire country*. It seemed a very, very long way from that thumping defeat back at Bladon in Oxfordshire, in our inaugural match, more than two decades previously.

The thunderstorm continued to rage apocalyptically for the rest of the night.

*　　*　　*

After that, we were utterly spent. We had two more games scheduled for the final weekend, but we knew we had no prospect of winning them, nor did we care. We felt like kings. We had four days off to celebrate, so we went to the beach at Langkawi island to eat seafood and get drunk. The afternoon thunderstorms followed us there, but usually overflew the beach in order to pound targets further inland. Unwisely, most of the team went off on motorcycles one afternoon to play golf. They came back several hours later, grazed and bedraggled: a mammoth downpour had flooded them out, washing away their motorcycles, carrying off golf balls, clubs, carts and unwary caddies on a rushing tide of brown water. It didn't matter: nothing could dampen our mood. The only thing missing, Eiran declared, was women. Not that there weren't any women on the beach, but for such a Romeo he seemed surprisingly shy about going over and talking to them, perhaps because he was so young.

'There's a woman. I'll go and talk to her,' I said.

I did. She was Welsh. Eiran spent the night loudly shagging her in the hotel jacuzzi. This made me feel uncomfortably like his pimp, and I wondered whether I should invest in a purple leather coat and broad-brimmed hat.

For me, the highlight of Langkawi was the Pulau Payar marine park, a remarkable little island set aside for scuba-diving and snorkelling. A floating platform sits offshore, replete with restaurant and bar, around which tropical fish of every description swim, almost literally, in thick clouds. Slip over the side with a face mask and you can barely see the sea for the fish, their inquisitive stripy noses bumping into the plastic an inch from your eyes. Some helpful soul, quite clearly, had been feeding the little buggers. Eco-conservation this wasn't. But as someone who's spent several hours trudging through a Costa Rican rainforest without seeing a single parrot, not to mention passing the best part of two days in a viewing platform high above the Indian jungle for the meagre return of a single pig and an irritated scorpion that leaped out and tried to sting me when I opened the window, I felt that nature owed me one. It's all very well for these conservationists who get to spend three months in a camouflaged hide, or six months on a yacht with an underwater camera. Slip the wildlife a few breadcrumbs, I say.

Just off the beach at Pulau Payar was an even more amazing sight: a vast flock of tame baby sharks, openly being fed this time, by hand, by tourists with fish supplied from a bucket by an attendant. I stood in the shallows, shoeless and sockless, as yard-long sharks shot around and in between my ankles at lightning speed. Offer them a piece of fish from the beach, a few feet away from the water's edge, and they'd leap out on to the sand, grabbing it deftly with their savage little jaws, before thrashing inelegantly back into the sea. Admittedly, taking the conservationist view here, I could see that this might go on to present problems when the beasts were fully grown. No one would want to be sat with their family on the sands at West Wittering, just about to tuck into a prawn sandwich, only to see a thirty-foot Great White hurl itself out of the Channel, deftly snatch the sandwich with its multiple rows of teeth, perhaps half-inching a packet of Walker's cheese 'n' onion for good measure, then squirm back down the beach and disappear into shallows thronged with bank-holiday bathers. Point taken, David Attenborough. But, with the little fellows only a yard long, I have to say it was the most tremendous fun. Around me, Muslim Malay women stood squealing with a mixture of fear and delight, teetering in their tiny string micro-bikinis. They had, of course, all politely refused alcohol at lunch.

* * *

By the time we staggered back to KL, we knew we had one more evening's worth of bragging rights before the upcoming reality check. Sean's self-confidence was in overdrive. Waxing lyrical about the quantity and quality of the Malaysian food on offer at a recent family function, he loudly claimed to have eaten 300 satay sticks at a single sitting. 'That's nonsense,' I said. 'Nobody could possibly eat 300 kebabs in one go.' 'Oh no?' he said. 'Put your money where your mouth is. Just watch me go.' 'OK,' I said—'a hundred quid says you can't do it.' 'I'm having some of that,' said Giles, adding another hundred quid. By the time we reached the satay restaurant the side-bets had become labyrinthine.

Now, Sean is big. very big. And very, very determined. But *three hundred* kebabs? I just couldn't see it. I mean, I ate five of the things, and I was utterly stuffed, and I'm twelve stone ten.

Eiran had offered to keep his brother company, as had one of the South Africans. They fell away after sixty and seventy satay sticks respectively. But Sean kept going. He just kept chomping. We'd started at 8 p.m. At eleven he passed the 100 mark. By this time he had been looking green around the gills for a little while: indeed, he had made the transition to a sort of cerise colour. At 120 kebabs he disappeared to the lavatory, and didn't come back for half an hour. Had he been sick? We didn't dare ask. One thing was for sure: he was going to go on all night if necessary, and he was going to make himself extremely ill indeed. Giles and I decided we all needed a way out. An easy one presented itself: at his current rate, Sean wouldn't reach the 300 mark until somewhere around breakfast time. Given that he had slowed considerably after an initial burst, he would probably even miss the next day's match. Certainly the restaurant would be wanting to close, despite the steady income stream that was coming its way. That was our exit strategy: it was unfair, we decided, to expect the waiters to stay up all night. All bets were off, null and void. Face had been saved all round, which after all is the essence of Asian compromise.

Little of note happened in our remaining two games, except that we were blown away as expected, first by a team of KL's expatriate Indians, and then by the expat Australians. We were made to bat first both times, so the meteorological boot was on the other foot. My own wretched run continued until the final match, when I managed to score a few runs, principally because I was the only one of us remaining who was sober enough to do so. This pleased me, as the Australians sledged and swore a lot, in their usual charming Antipodean manner. Without doubt, though, the most interesting aspect of the two games was the venue: the Royal Selangor Turf Club, another slice of Empire. We were playing in the middle of the racetrack, and towering above us a packed grandstand heaved with shouting, excited Malaysian race fans. Bizarrely, however, the track itself was devoid of racehorses. It was completely empty. The only sporting activity taking place below them was the not even peripherally interesting antics of twenty-two sweat-soaked foreign cricketers. The whole thing put me in mind of an episode of *The Avengers.* I could even picture the pre-credits sequence: a panting middle-aged civil servant running for his life down a deserted racetrack, before expiring with exhaustion, to the cheers of the crowd. Into the close-up of his corpse would come the shinily shod feet of two evil jockeys. The caption: 'Dead Cert'. The answer to this mystery lay once more in Malaysia's uncomfortable religious position, teetering schizophrenically atop the spiritual/secular fence. Betting should, strictly speaking, be illegal in a Muslim country. But in Malaysia it is allowed to take place at racecourses. The punters in the stands were betting on that day's Singapore races, and each of them had a radio pressed to his ear; but they had to take a seat in the stands of the Royal Selangor Turf Club for their bet to become legal. It made for the oddest game of cricket, with thousands of spectators breaking into wild cheering at entirely random moments.

The cricket at an end, a few of us fitted in a

magical trip up the Selangor river by night, the banks glittering with fireflies, and, before that, a long haul by switchback road up to Fraser's Hill, one of two remaining British Empire hill stations (the other being the even more impressive Cameron Highlands further south). The premise behind their construction had clearly been a simple one: go ever higher above the prickly heat and lashing rainstorms of the primordial jungle until the climate approximately resembles that of Surrey. Then build an exact replica of Surrey, with half-timbered houses, neat lawns and golf courses aplenty. Personally, I find almost any colonial architecture fascinating. Conquerors always put up the most impressive buildings in order to show off, from the mighty mosques and minarets of India or Andalusia to the fortress cathedrals and regimented streets of Latin America. But the British legacy has often been quaintly incongruous: not the usual statement of power and glory, but a sentimental recreation of a mythic old England that wavers somewhere between the touching and the mawkish. The results are inevitably as surreal as race day at the Royal Selangor Turf Club. We played crazy golf and ate clotted-cream teas thousands of feet above the jungle, reminded at intervals that this was *faux*-Surrey by huge, hideous, six-legged creatures that had strayed up from a lower altitude, suddenly plopping on to the Irish-linen tablecloth and taking a nibble of strawberry. Sadly, none of the British players came with me to see this bizarre tableau, only German and South African companions. Delightful though my new team-mates were, they almost invariably preferred the inside of a sports bar showing old Premiership football games to the wonders of the country they had come to visit.

Such limitations notwithstanding, it had been a tremendous tour. All any of us could talk about was where we were going to go next. Australia? The West Indies? I myself had a sneaking interest in Argentina. But who was going to organize this next jamboree? 'You are,' they all told me. Oh no. I had vowed never to organize another tour as long as I lived. 'Go on,' they said. 'Just one more. One more won't hurt.' Of course, organizing a cricket tour, like climbing a mountain, is misery when you're doing it, satisfying when you've reached the summit, and misleadingly easy in the memory thereafter. I climbed a 17,000-foot mountain in Mexico once. I vomited with altitude sickness halfway up, and could barely breathe or move on the upper snowfields. It was horrible. But whatever fortitude I'd had to display on those slopes was dwarfed by the mental strength needed to remind myself since that—come what may—I must never, ever do anything of the sort again. Repeatedly, I have to take a cudgel to my memory and beat it like a snake. Take that, you little sod. I'm not giving in to your blandishments.

I gave in, of course. Just one more tour. But then I had an idea that seemed at once brilliant and unbelievably stupid. We would travel to all of those places at once. Australia, the West Indies, Argentina, the lot. We would go right round the world. A game of cricket on every single continent. Then I could finally retire from travelling the world with a bat. It would cost a fortune, of course. But I could rely on each and every one of my team-mates, I knew, to be absolutely 99% certain of coming.

6

The Whole World

The plan, which sounds simple enough on paper, was to visit Barbados (counting, geographically at least, as North America), Buenos Aires (South America), Sydney—to see an Ashes Test—and Perth (Australasia), Singapore (Asia) and Cape Town again (South Africa). We would travel 39,820 miles, be in the air for more than 100 hours, and earn enough air miles to travel most of the way from Heathrow to Exeter. Most of our prospective locations had been selected for the likelihood of sunny weather in January: the trip could not be done in less than three weeks, which was a lot of holiday for anyone to set aside for a cricket tour (well, anyone with a life), so the idea was to leave on Boxing Day, thereby hiding a week in the general Christmas/New Year seasonal laziness that the British pull off so well. Of the two remaining continents, Europe, we felt, had been covered by innumerable wet Sunday afternoons at Charlton-on-Otmoor, but to be on the safe side we thought we'd find a park near Heathrow on our return and—if it wasn't pouring down—have a ten-over thrash. As for Antarctica, well, that wasn't going to be included in the itinerary, but I had recently returned from having my innings there disrupted by hooligan penguins. I did a bit of quick thinking. It occurred to me that I was about to become, in all probability, the first man in world history to play cricket on all seven continents. What a supremely preposterous achievement, I thought. How thrillingly pointless. It would make all those men in *The Guinness Book of Records* who lie for hours in baths of baked beans seem positively serious-minded.

So far, so simple. The tricky bits would be (a) finding twelve people prepared to cough up what would surely be a colossal amount of money, (b) finding a minimum of five teams who would *guarantee* to play us on a given day, whatever the weather—for we could hardly afford a cancellation—and (c) finding an airline prepared to ferry us around the bottom half of the world. There are plenty of discounted round-the-world tickets, of course, but they tend to follow the ley lines of unadventurous WASP-gap year students—London, New York, LA, Auckland, Sydney, Delhi (ooh—careful—one or two people in turbans there), London. Our route, we soon discovered, simply did not exist as a pre-discounted fare. We would have to pay full whack. And there was even worse news: the only airlines that flew from South America to Australia—Qantas and Lan-Chile—were part of the One World group, which meant we would have to book our journey through the World's Worst Airline—British Airways. As anyone who's ever had the misfortune to fall foul of this wretchedly incompetent organization will know, this promised to be a surefire disaster.

To be fair, perhaps they're not *the* worst airline in the world. That honour surely goes to Yemen Airlines, with whom I once had the privilege of flying on two internal flights. The first time, I crawled out of bed at 3 a.m. in order to reach the airport by the appointed check-in time of 5 a.m., only for the plane to sit on the tarmac until early afternoon. *The following day*. After thirty-three hours in the departure lounge, the flight finally being announced, it became clear that there were at least twice as many passengers with tickets as there were seats. The issue of who got on and who didn't was settled by a mass brawl. I must confess I'm not much good in such situations, but there were five bearded German cyclists ahead of me who were booked on a cycling tour of the Arabian Desert (it's the kind of thing bearded Germans get up to), and who were determined, in characteristically Teutonic fashion, to assert their rights. I tucked in behind, and said 'Jawohl' when a bruised and battered Yemeni airline official asked if I was part of their group. Once on the plane, I discovered that my seat could not or would not remain upright, meaning that I had to spend the entire flight in a horizontal position, with my head nestled in the lap of the woman behind, an elderly Yemeni lady in a chador, whose letterbox eyes burned into mine for several hours. When we finally arrived at our destination in the east of the country, the German cyclists discovered that Yemen Airlines had put all their bicycles on a plane to Saudi Arabia. Which told them. So much for inherent Teutonic superiority. All in all, you had to hand it to the Yemenis—to mess up so many things on one flight was some accomplishment. So, which company is worse, Yemen Airlines or British Airways? It's a close call, but I'd have to say, in all fairness, that the

Yemenis shade it. Just.

British Airways have, in the past, given me food poisoning. They have lost my luggage twice. The first time, in Istanbul, I had made the mistake of travelling with a vintage leather suitcase, in a misguided attempt to play the old imperial traveller, an affectation which BA ruthlessly punished. An official finally called me at home in London and told me they had located the case, and would drop it off that evening. I cancelled my plans and sat in all night, calling them occasionally, getting only the 'any minute now' minicab mantra in reply. By midnight I lost my middle-class reserve and actually demanded to know where it was.

'Er . . . it's in Istanbul,' said the voice on the end of the phone.

'Then why did you say it was in London and about to be dropped off at my house?'

'Well . . . we, er . . . we thought it sounded better than saying it was in Istanbul.'

Genius.

When the case finally showed up, it had literally been ripped into two parts, no mean feat of strength, even if the leather was over sixty years old. I imagined an old-fashioned bald strongman with twirling moustaches down in the BA luggage department at Heathrow, systematically ripping cases in half as they came off the carousel. The two pieces arrived (with no word of apology) in a large polythene bag, together with about half the contents, each item of which had been assiduously trampled with large, black, muddy footprints, like the ones in cartoons.

'Sign 'ere, mate.'

'But what . . . ? How . . . ?'

'Nuffink to do with me, mate.'

The second time British Airways lost my luggage, they were not nearly so efficient or polite. They simply refused to answer the telephone, or any letter, fax or email. Eventually I had to take them to court to get compensation.

And then there was my planned week's holiday in Cuba. Despite our checking in well ahead of time, BA told us (and the twenty or so people behind us) that the plane was seriously overbooked, so they'd be putting us on the next flight instead, which left in a week's time. By a not-so-extraordinary coincidence, that was the very plane we were due to return on. Are you seriously suggesting, I asked the woman behind the counter, that we fly all the way to Cuba, clear immigration, then get straight back on the same plane and fly home?

'It's an option,' she said, with a gleaming training-course smile.

An agonizing wait followed, to see if two late first-class passengers would turn up. They didn't.

'There,' enthused the check-in girl. 'See? You *can* go. And you'll be travelling first class! So everything's fine, isn't it?'

The twenty people behind us, still hoping in vain for a miracle, fumed. We made our way to the gate. There, the woman at the desk took our first-class boarding cards, ripped them up before our eyes, and issued us with second-class ones.

'Excuse me,' I said in my most ineffectually polite tones, 'but the lady at the counter said we'd be travelling first class.'

'*What,*' she sneered, 'does it say on your tickets?

"First class"? No. It says, "Second class". You *can* read, can't you? So, you're travelling second class. OK?'

Feeling like lepers, we boarded the plane. It was cold. I took a jumper from my bag.

'That jumper has to go in the overhead locker,' said the stewardess. 'You can't have anything in your lap.'

'It's all right, I'm about to put it on,' I explained.

'No, it has to go in the overhead locker.'

'No, I'm going to wear it.'

'It has to go in the overhead locker!'

'I'm going to wear it!'

She grabbed one end and pulled. I held on to the other end. We stood there, having a knitwear tug-of-war in the aisle of a British Airways jet. I heard the sound of ripping seams. My temper came apart in similar fashion.

'Let go of my FUCKING JUMPER,' I screamed, 'because I'm going to FUCKING WEAR IT!'

The whole plane stopped dead, and stared at us.

'Keep your hair on,' she spat, glared at me, turned on her heel, and stalked away. Suffice to say that in-flight service was hardly at its most effective for the rest of the journey.

* * *

It was not without trepidation, therefore, that I made my initial approach to British Airways. I'd tried travel agents and bucket shops, of course, but no, none of them could handle it. It had to be the group-bookings section of BA. They did not disappoint.

'I'd like to make a group booking for twelve people to go round the world, please.'

'Oh, I can't do a booking for twelve people.'

'Why not?'

'Once a group booking gets into double figures, our computer gets confused. I can only do bookings for nine or less.'

'So if I'd asked for two bookings of six people each, that would've been OK?'

'Yes.'

'OK, I'd like to make two bookings of six people each, to go round the world, please.'

'Oh, I can't do that.'

'Why not?'

'Because I know that you're not two parties of six. You're one party of twelve.'

'Yes, but just for the purposes of this booking can't we be two parties of six?'

'That would be unethical.'

'Would it help if I rang back and spoke to someone else?'

'No.'

'Would it help if I made one booking of six, and someone else called up to make the other booking?'

'Certainly not. What are you suggesting? Nobody in this office will have anything to do with that sort of behaviour. We *know* you're a party of twelve. You can't pull the wool over our eyes.'

So that was a no then.

In desperation, I called the PR section, who put me on to a department called Special Accounts. They seemed singularly unwilling to answer the phone, but eventually I made it through to a woman called Sabahat, who—at last—agreed to book twelve round-the-world tickets at a price of £2,035.45 each. We were not actually due to leave for fourteen months, but, with Christmas and New Year air traffic so congested, I thought I'd better get in early. At this stage, explained Sabahat, she couldn't actually make the bookings—they could only be actioned twelve months ahead—but as soon as each flight was opened she'd book us in, then call me back when all was done.

She never called.

At last, when more than enough time had elapsed, I telephoned her direct line. Thirty times. At no point did she pick up the phone or return any messages. So I tried the main number. Twenty times. Finally, someone answered—a confident, wide-boy estate-agent-type called Sedleigh.

'Can I speak to Sabahat, please?'

'She's left.'

'She's *left*?'

'Yeah, man. Gone.'

'She was doing a booking for me. So she must have left the paperwork behind.'

'Nah. All her paperwork's been shredded.'

'*Shredded*?'

'Yeah, when someone leaves, we chuck out all their paperwork.'

British Airways, it seems, had no record of our existence. 'No worries, man,' said Sedleigh. 'Leave it with me—I'll fix the whole thing up. Call you back in a week.'

He didn't, of course; nor did he answer his phone, or return any messages. After I'd tried the main number innumerable times, one of my calls was finally answered by Sheila, an Indian-sounding woman.

'Is Sedleigh there, please?'

'He's left.'

'He's *left*? Look . . . he was doing a booking for me. Did he leave any paperwork behind?'

'No. I'm afraid that when someone leaves, their paperwork is—'

'—shredded. Yes, I know.'

British Airways *still* had no record of our existence. Fourteen months had become eight. I insisted that Sheila stay on the phone, all afternoon if necessary, while she made the booking there and then. Why, I wanted to know, did nobody in her office ever answer the phone?

'We're an extremely busy department.'

Pace the Monty Python cheese shop, they certainly weren't busy booking any flights.

Finally Sheila broke the bad news. Many of the flights we wanted no longer had twelve free seats. The same went for any alternative flights I could suggest. We were too late. The trip was a non-starter. It was all off.

* * *

This news knocked us all for six. A ton of planning had already gone into the playing side. I'd booked a hotel-and-match package in Barbados through a company run by the former Leicestershire bat Barry Dudleston. I'd been in touch with the incredibly friendly and helpful people from the Argentinian Cricket Association, who'd fixed up a game for us at no less a place than the Hurlingham Club in Buenos Aires. Sean was brokering a match at the equally famous Singapore Cricket Club via his Malaysian contacts, while Greg, our fake

Aussie, was arranging for us to meet his old club in Perth. And we were going back to Rygersdal, in Cape Town, for another picturesque fixture beneath Table Mountain. Hotels and vehicles had been booked all around the world. It had been a mammoth task, and all of it had now crumbled to nothing.

It was a travel-agent friend of a friend who provided a chink of light. He just couldn't believe that quite so many flights were booked up so far ahead.

'It could be', he offered, 'that British Airways are just being useless.'

Now you're talking my language, I thought.

'It's possible that only a small number of seats on such distant flights are accessible from BA's London computers, especially as you're talking about seats on other airlines. There may be many more free seats that just aren't coming up—in which case, all they'd have to do would be to request them through the local agent. I mean, anyone who knows anything about the airline industry would know that. But we are talking British Airways here.'

Finally I got through to Sheila again. The travel agent had been right.

The tour was back on.

*   *   *

All that remained was to find a further eleven suckers. I had a flatmate now, an Old Etonian friend named Tom. A sensitive soul (or a caddish rake, depending on your point of view), he and his wife were on a 'temporary break', despite which

Tom had somehow acquired a girlfriend. He was currently using my place as a bolt-hole, a metaphorical garret in which to go through agonies of indecision as to how he was going to win his wife back. He was definitely coming on the world tour. At least he was if he wanted to continue his agonizing, rent-free, *chez moi*.

The history of the Captain Scott XI is littered with inadvertently entertaining Old Etonians. It's not that they've been stupid—far from it—it's just that in almost every case a piece of the jigsaw seems to have mysteriously gone missing. One splendid chap, for instance, who played in the era of Ian Hislop, was reputed to be the part-inspiration for Hislop and Nick Newman's creation, the Harry Enfield character Tim Nice-But-Dim. When a fellow player, a working-class Lancastrian, told him of a mate down from Blackburn who was having trouble finding an affordable room for rent in Stockwell, the Old Etonian looked puzzled and replied, 'So . . . why doesn't he just buy a flat in Kensington?'

The same man called me once, to ask the name of the pub we were due to meet in at Great Yeldham.

'Have you got your fixture list?' I enquired.

'Yah. Right in front of me.'

'Is it open? Can you see the entry for Great Yeldham?'

'Yah. It's open on that page.'

'What pub does it say?'

'The White Hart.'

'Well, the name of the pub we're due to meet in at Great Yeldham is: The White Hart.'

'The White Hart. Right. Yah. Great. Excellent.'

He went into the city and became a multimillionaire.

But even he was trumped by a delightful Old Etonian named Dobbs, who turned out for Captain Scott during our student years. Tall and elegant, Dobbs was from Northern Ireland—not that you'd know it from his cut-glass accent. I needed his address so that I could send him a fixture list during the Easter holidays, but he was reluctant to reveal it for 'reasons of national security'.

'Sorry, old boy. Can't give it out. You see, my father's the Lord Lieutenant of Ireland, and it's absolutely vital that our address is kept secret from the IRA.'

'But *I'm* hardly going to give it to the IRA, am I?' I pointed out. 'I don't have their address either. I'm just going to send you a cricket fixture list, in the post.'

'Hmm . . . Well . . . OK. If you absolutely promise faithfully not to reveal it to *anyone* else, under any circumstances.'

'I promise faithfully. As soon as I've used it, I'll throw it away.'

'OK, here goes. My father's address is: Lord Dobbs, Castle Dobbs, County Antrim.'

A delicious image immediately swam into my mind, of the local branch of the Provos clustered around a pint in the Castle Dobbs village pub, trying to work out where Lord Dobbs lived in order to assassinate him.

'Fergal. Any leads yet on where Lord Dobbs lives?'

'Nothing. The Brits have kept this one under their hats all right.'

'Damn.'

'We could ask up at the castle—they might know.'

'Don't be ridiculous. They're not going to tell us, are they? We'll never find out.'

Sadly, my flatmate Tom was an altogether different kettle of smoked salmon, and not prone to such twitticisms. He was more the Hugh Grant type: a floppy-haired actor by trade, but marginally less professionally successful than his august predecessor. His most important role to date had been playing a policeman in a scene that had been cut from *Patriot Games*. On the field, Tom was not the sort to take the bowling by the scruff of the neck, or roar in off fifty paces and make the ball rear: rather, he was the slender, elegant type, his playing style refined and dignified, distinguished as it was by a simple clarity and harmony of proportion. Or, to put it in less flattering terms, he was an utter weed. His biggest TV role had been playing a baddie in *Dalziel and Pascoe*, an episode which had climaxed in Tom having a punch-up with either Dalziel or Pascoe, I forget which. The lack of suspense would have killed me, if I hadn't died laughing first. Tom v. Dalziel and/or Pascoe? why, Miss Marple could have beaten him to a pulp. I should add that Tom was, unlike myself, fantastically neat. He was the kind of man who puts his socks in alphabetical order. When we finally went around the world, one of his suitcases was reserved for his favourite pillow from my spare bedroom, lest one of those beastly hotel pillows disturb his nocturnal equilibrium. It was hardly surprising that some of our team-mates had already begun calling us 'Felix' and 'Oscar'.

Another of our first-time tourists also made his living from the creative arts: Matthew was a highly successful modern artist, although for most of us this translated into a vague excitement that one of his paintings had been used on the cover of *Carry On Up The Charts* by the Beautiful South. Matthew had a special reason for coming on the trip: his father had abandoned his family when Matthew had been just two, and had vanished to Sydney. All he knew was that his dad probably still lived somewhere in the city. This would be his first visit to Australia, and he hoped that somehow, when he got there, he might be able to locate his missing parent. Matthew had since become the father of two boys himself, the younger of whom, Cosmo, was without question the finest young cricketer in the world aged six. From age four he had been able to play a better forward-defensive shot than me; but his, for some reason, screamed to the boundary for four instead of plopping inoffensively on to the turf.

As previously mentioned, the Captain Scott XI's encounters with opposing small boys had never been especially blessed; but we had enjoyed equal ill luck when fielding small boys on our own side. On one occasion, when we had been two players short at the village of Hambleden in Bucks, I had reluctantly agreed to field two nine-year-olds: the son of one of our players, and his best friend from school, who just happened to be the son of Maureen Lipman. All proceeded smoothly until a very large West Indian came into bat for the opposition, twirling a 3 lb bat. Nervously, I moved Lipman Jr further back to long on. The rampant Caribbean's first ball being a gentle half-volley, he wound up big-style, before launching into one of the most violent aerial on drives ever witnessed in the history of the game. All heads immediately craned to see where the ball had gone. A soft 'plop' from the wicketkeeper's gloves informed us that the batsman had in fact missed it completely. But *something* had gone flying. Ah, yes, that was it. The West Indian behemoth, somewhat mystified, was standing in his crease staring at his gloves, which still held the rubber from his bat handle. The bat itself, meanwhile, was airborne like a cruise missile, on a trajectory that seemed certain to bring it down on the tiny, paralysed form of Ms Lipman's kid. All of us, in fact, were paralysed. No one could bring himself to move or speak, including the potential victim himself. All we could do was track the course of impending, unavoidable doom like the war-room controllers in *Dr Strangelove*, and riffle mentally through the next day's tabloid headlines. The bat's flight cannot have lasted more than a few seconds, but it felt like an hour. As it happened, the offending implement embedded itself in the earth like a javelin, a foot behind the child's head. Had I moved him back a further twelve inches for his own safety, the bat would have embedded itself in his brain. The subsequent sound of twenty men and two children exhaling was audible across all seven Home Counties.

Cosmo, one suspects, would have simply caught the bat and fizzed it horizontally in to the stumps, fatally impaling the wicketkeeper. If Damien in *Omen III* was possessed by Lucifer and all his demons, then this extraordinary blue-eyed child was possessed by the ghosts of Wally Hammond and Colin Dredge. But he wasn't merely adept at cricket: he lived, breathed, ate and slept the game. He memorized old copies of *Wisden*, and at the age of six knew the batting averages of innumerable pipe-smoking, Brylcreemed pre-war batsmen to several decimal places. He wasn't interested in *Postman Pat* or *Pingu*, only VHS tapes of ancient Test matches and one-day internationals. Visiting his parents for dinner one evening, I was grabbed by Cosmo and ordered to follow him upstairs, just a few minutes before dinner was due. 'I've got something *really* important to show you,' he insisted. There he switched on the television and popped a tape into the slot. A fuzzy cricket match began, identified by the Neolithic cave-painting graphics as an ODI between England and Australia from 1983. I waited. The first few balls passed without incident. Eventually, I said, 'Cosmo, what is it exactly we're here to see?'

'This game,' he replied. 'It's brilliant.'

'What, the *whole game*?'

'It's only eight hours.'

Unfortunately for Matthew and Cosmo, Matthew's wife, an art dealer by trade, found the whole business of cricket rather frightful. Any encouragement of Cosmo's excellence at the sport would, she felt, only serve to exclude their other son. Above all, she had a peculiar aversion to her six-year-old starting to watch eight-hour cricket tapes immediately before bedtime. Cosmo was man enough to put up with restrictions on his diet of archive cricket—the VHS would wait, after all—but the live stuff was a different matter. In particular, the Ashes series from Australia that immediately preceded our world tour had an awkward tendency to start transmitting at 3 a.m., or thereabouts. More than once, Cosmo's mother woke in the middle of the night to hear the patter of tiny footsteps and the sounds of muffled match commentary from the TV (it was usually Tony Greig that gave the boy away). Eventually she issued an edict: he was not, under any circumstances, to begin watching the Test match on TV until 6 a.m. at the earliest. The following morning she was once again wakened by the distant orgasmic shrieks of T. Greig & Co. She checked her bedside clock: 6 a.m. Satisfied that Cosmo had been a good boy, she went back to sleep. Indeed, it was only an hour or so later, at seven, when she got up and made breakfast, that she discovered it was not seven but four o'clock in the morning. Cosmo had crept about in his socks while she slept, altering every clock in the house, including the digital alarm by his parents' bed.

The lady's disapproval of her son's cricket obsession extended, one gathered, to her husband as well. Personally, I was amazed that Matthew was being allowed to travel at all. At the end of every season we award an engraved rolling pin to the player who is deemed to be the most severely under the thumb: that year Matthew had come a narrow second to his own son. But he insisted he was coming, and as a successful artist he could at least afford the airfare. Altogether, the addition of Matthew made for nine confirmed tourists: Matthew and I, Old Etonian Tom, Giles, Greg the fake Aussie, Paul Daniels (now crawled off his sickbed), an old college friend of Paul's whom nobody knew, and Sean and James O'Herlihy.

Sadly, Cie would not be among the party, even in the unlikely event of his being able to afford it. He had decided to become a black-cab driver, for it was that rare profession, a job he could fit in around cricket matches, and his all-important taxi-driving exams had been scheduled for the middle of the tour. We promised to call him regularly from wherever we might be on the face of the globe, and keep him posted.

'Hey, man, I know you're going to win every game,' he assured us.

We were doomed.

There was a further question mark, as the sporting journalists like to say, over the involvement of Eiran O'Herlihy. He'd found work the previous winter as a junior solicitor in Manchester, and had immediately been allocated, as grunt solicitors invariably are there, to one of the nastiest murderers ever to come out of Moss Side. Introduced to his new client for the first time, he'd been ushered into the man's jail cell with a pad and a pencil, and the door had been locked shut behind him. Immediately, the murderer (who was exceedingly large) had grabbed both Eiran and his pencil, and had jabbed the lead point half an inch through the underside of Eiran's jaw. If he was not given a helicopter to ferry him to a destination of his choice, he'd informed the warders, he would drive the rest of the pencil right up into Eiran's brain. After all, what was one more murder, added to his already considerable charge sheet?

It had taken eight hours for the man to be talked out of this ingenious plan—all in all, quite a long time to spend with a pencil sticking into your throat. Eiran had been given six months' sick leave to get over the stress, but the six months had elapsed and he was in no hurry to return. He continued to be haunted by nightmares of large men brandishing even larger pencils. What he really needed was a little light legal work no more controversial than, say, a wheelie-bin dispute in Thames Ditton (although some of those can get pretty heated). He was, as a result, unemployed and short of cash.

It had occurred to me right from the start that this trip, extravagant as it was, would probably never take place unless I raided my life savings—in fact I'd been putting money by for just such an eventuality. I had £10,000 saved, of which £3,000 was reserved for my own ticket and expenses. I decided to give away £5,000 of what remained, to enable two or three of our more penniless but deserving players to come on the trip. A grand, then, went to Eiran. The rest was divided equally between the two South Africans who'd stuck with us through thick and thin—Riaan and Aidan.

Riaan and Aidan could not have been more different. The name Riaan was short for 'Adriaan', the Afrikaner version of 'Adrian', which I found surprising in view of its restrained use of only three *a*s. why not Adriaaan? Or even Adriaaaaaan? Certainly Riaaaaaan is what we called him. Riaan was what cockneys would term a 'diamond geezer'. A tall, blond, silent, God-fearing farmboy from the Transvaal, he was unwaveringly steadfast, friendly and loyal: in short, exactly the sort of chap you'd want in the vicinity if you were hanging by your fingernails above the Victoria Falls, or something like that. In all the time he spent with us, I never once heard him say a bad thing about anybody or anything. He wanted to stay in Britain, of course, and had a lot to offer: he was a banker by trade, being a bright, bilingual economics graduate. But our Home Office, in their infinite wisdom, not only limit South Africans to two years on these shores, but mysteriously insist that only one of those years may be spent in any sort of remunerative or important job; so, after twelve months, he'd had to leave the bank and trawl bars and construction sites in search of casual labour. His mistake, of course, was that at no point had he planned a biological or nerve-gas attack on the London Underground, or any of the usual criteria for being allowed to stay here. Sadly, his devout Christian beliefs militated against such behaviour. Taking pity, I employed him as my secretary (not the best paid of jobs, unfortunately). On the plus side, I got a very good secretary out of the deal. On the down side, my office was swamped by bewildered and disappointed middle-aged male executives, who'd popped up to check out my new six-foot blonde secretary.

Riaan's steadfastness translated to the field of play. He and Aidan were our opening bowlers. Riaan was like a metronome, always putting the ball on the spot, never letting a setback get him down, never letting his head drop. Aidan (why 'Aidan'? why not 'Aidaan'?) was the opposite: brilliant, mercurial, unplayable when he was on top, but fatally liable to lose his rag or sulk when things went wrong or fielders dropped catches. I've seen him devastatingly reduce the star-studded upper order of Earl Spencer's XI to 1–4, a line-up which included a former county opener and a retired Test captain (both of whom were so cross they got in their cars and drove away there and then). I've also seen him get slapped around the field by fat estate agents tanked up on lager, then work himself into a rage and berate the nearest fielder for not doing enough to prevent that last towering six. Sporting a marine haircut, Aidan was barrel-chested and garrulous. Good-humoured off the pitch, nothing could induce him to stop talking on it. He also liked to stare at batsmen, which made us giggle. Whichever of these attributes it was that offended their prejudices I don't know, but opposition umpires resented Aidan on sight. In the season before our tour he bowled 160 overs and clean-bowled 42 people. He was awarded just one lbw. The more he appealed, the more they glared at him with barely disguised *Daily Mail* suburban disapproval. He had as much chance of getting an lbw as Abu Musab al-Zarqawi in a kibbutz game. Riaan, on the other hand, with his neat hair, his yes sirs, no sirs and thank you sirs, got a whole stack of decisions. It was a lesson that Aidan, disreputably shaven-headed, snorting like a bull, and doing a passable imitation of the poster for *Platoon*, never really took on board. Still, he was happy enough to be handed the tour airfare on a plate, for, by an amazing coincidence, he was due to marry his childhood sweetheart in his home town of East London (the one in South Africa) just after the end of the tour, and had been wondering how on earth he was going to get there. Hey, I was glad to be of service.

Aidan always enjoyed bowling at English batsmen when there was a fellow South African behind the stumps, so that he could inform the keeper in Afrikaans exactly what he was planning to do next. We eight or nine Englishmen in the side, feeling as excluded as the batsman in all of this, did some research into the language, searching for suitable phrases that we too could chip in at opportune moments. Thus it was, when Aidan ran in to bowl on Evenley village green in Northamptonshire, that he was stopped in his tracks by a shout of 'Jou ma buk vir renoster!' and collapsed laughing before he reached the crease. Apparently 'Your mother bends to take it from a rhino' is about the rudest thing you can say on the Highveldt. It quickly became our tour motto, and we had special caps made with the phrase embroidered into the front panel, an idea that was to make us very popular indeed in Cape Town.

Armed with some sponsorship cash provided by the nice people from a wonderful London pub called the Larrik (advertisement), we also went out and bought helmets, arm guards, chest guards, and all the other paraphernalia of real cricket: bitter experience had taught us that no amount of brandishing the 'village-cricket' tag would make any difference when we arrived overseas. In the Caribbean and in Australia especially, we could expect the ball to be aimed at our heads, probably by seasoned pros desperate to get one over on whitey/the Poms. It was going to be tough. My final purchase was two boxes of new balls, because after all, if someone in a distant land wishes to stove your head in, it's only gentlemanly to supply the ammunition for him to do it with. I had to buy new ones because, after playing cricket for nigh on a quarter of a century, the Captain Scott XI had precisely two elderly, split-seamed cricket balls in the team kitbag. This set my brain whirring, after a mathematical fashion. In all that time we'd played some 600 games, and had supplied some 600 new cricket balls. Where were the other 598? I don't think it's any different for other teams: does anyone have more than a handful of wizened, battered spheres in their bag? In fact some 30,000 games of cricket take place in Britain every summer weekend, which means that some 40,000 new balls are bought and used. Across the entire summer, allowing for rain cancellations, that's about 750,000 balls. Now, let's go back a quarter of a century: over a twenty-five-year period, that's nearly 20 million cricket balls that have been used and, for the most part, have subsequently gone missing. At 5½ oz each, that means someone, somewhere, has stockpiled over 3,000 *tons* of used cricket balls. Who has done this? Is Saddam Hussein planning to launch a comeback, by dropping them all at once on Tel Aviv? Is Ernst Stavro Blofeld building an undersea volcano made entirely of used cricket balls? At the very least, the police should begin searching now for someone with an extremely large lock-up garage.

* * *

By autumn, all was firmly in place. The time had come for everything to go horribly, messily wrong. As luck would have it, I called Sheila at British Airways for an update, and by a million-to-one chance she answered the phone.

'Oh, everything's going really well,' she said. 'All your flights are fine, except the one.'

'What do you mean, "except the one"?'

‘Well, Qantas have cancelled your flight from Buenos Aires to Sydney.’

‘So I suppose we’ve been switched to another one?’

‘No, they’ve cancelled *all* flights from Buenos Aires to Sydney—that service doesn’t exist any more.’

‘So who else is flying across the Pacific from South America to Australasia?’

‘Nobody.’

‘So let me get this straight—you’re saying that our round-the-world trip is going just fine, and everything’s rosy in the garden, except for the small matter of us having to swim seven thousand miles?’

‘Yes indeed, that is the situation.’

I begged, pleaded and cajoled with Sheila. Despite her insistence that there were no commercial airlines in the entire South Pacific, it just didn’t make sense. Somebody, somewhere, must connect the two continents. Finally we struck gold: her computer threw up a Lan-Chile flight leaving Santiago in Chile at 2320 on 4 January, arriving in Auckland, New Zealand, at 0425 on 6 January. Hey, who needs 5 January in their lives anyway? The next plane out of Auckland to Sydney with free seats on it didn’t leave until the end of the day. It meant we’d miss the Ashes Test. It meant we’d have to cancel a match in Sydney arranged tentatively for the following day, because with such monstrous jetlag we’d need at least one rest day before playing. It meant we’d have to leave Argentina early, in order to get to Chile. But at least we’d be able to get across the Pacific without getting our feet wet. I cancelled our twelve Test match tickets, then phoned our prospective opposition captain in Sydney to tell him why we were pulling the plug.

'What do you mean, "no Qantas flights from Buenos Aires to Sydney"?' he said incredulously. 'There's full-page adverts in all the papers here for that very service! Qantas have got a promotional campaign on right now—"Fly to Buenos Aires"! What, are they saying you're not allowed to fly back the other way?'

It took me several days to raise Sheila again. We had a full-scale row. She put her foot down.

'And I'm telling you there are no flights from South America to Sydney!'

'Then why are there massive adverts in all the Sydney papers? Have all the editors been out on the piss together, and thought it would be a good laugh?'

'Listen—nobody flies from South America to Sydney. Not Qantas. Not Lan-Chile. Nobody. You either fly from Santiago to Auckland or you don't fly at all.'

So that was that, then. We were missing the Test match.

* * *

Matthew called me a day or two later to say that he was pulling out of the trip. The Inland Revenue had launched a snap investigation into his finances, and were demanding he pay tax on all the paintings he'd sold, regardless of whether or not the (usually American) purchasers had paid *him* anything. So, for instance, if he'd sold one of his daubs for £10k, but the buyer was sitting out in

Bonefuck, Wyoming, the painting taking pride of place over his mantelpiece, having not the slightest intention of stumping up in the near future, then Matthew owed the taxman £4k anyway. And if the buyer had actually done a runner—not an uncommon event in the art world, apparently—that was Matthew's lookout. All in all, the Inland Revenue wanted more than £100,000 from him. It meant he'd be flat broke until further notice. As reluctantly as the words came out of my mouth, I knew what I had to do.

'All right, Matthew. I'll lend you two thousand pounds.'

I waved goodbye to the rest of my savings.

After that, things went from bad to worse.

Riaan's two-year visa ran out three weeks before Christmas, and he had to stop working for me. We were all hoping that the Home Office would let him stay on as a tourist until the tour began—I wrote numerous deferential letters to dreary, pin-headed civil servants on the subject—but the answer was always the same: no dice. Riaan would have to fly home to South Africa, then fly back again three weeks later. It would cost another £700. All his savings from the secretarial job promptly went up in smoke.

Then Giles called, to pull out of the tour as well. The vacuum-cleaner designer James Dyson had, it transpired, offered him £100,000 to spend the next six months on a vanity project, penning a Dyson biography; part of the deal was that he follow Dyson on a promotional tour of American Midwestern shopping malls throughout January. To be fair, I could see Giles's point entirely: £100,000 is a fair old sum to receive for the chance to surrender one's dignity and journalistic principles, if that isn't a contradiction in terms. If Giles wanted to make himself fabulously rich by becoming the toadying lickspittle of a vacuum-cleaner manufacturer, and by heaping honeyed, obsequious, grovelling adjectives on to the great man's head like some latter-day Uriah Heep, then who was I to criticize? Why, the thought could not have been further from my brain. Giles, an oily, cringing, hand-wringing brown-noser? Perish the thought. We were down to eleven.

I wrote everyone a fierce letter. If anyone else pulled out, I said, then I was calling the whole thing off. I wasn't sneaking round the world with ten players; it was embarrassing enough turning up at Horton-cum-Studley with ten people, never mind Singapore. There, I thought. Tough talking—that'll do the trick. But it had the opposite effect, in a way I could never have imagined. Greg, who still hadn't paid me his fare, called when he got the letter.

'G'day mate . . . Listen, back in the summer you said you had five grand to give away to people coming on the tour.'

'I allocated five grand of my own money to help out players who couldn't afford to pay for themselves, yes.'

'And who got it? Aidan, Riaan and Eiran, wasn't it?'

'Aidan and Riaan had their fare paid in full. Eiran got half of his.'

'Eiran's a solicitor, mate. He must have tons of money.'

'He's a solicitor who hasn't worked for a year.'

'Yeah, but his brothers have. Why aren't they

paying his fare?'

'Maybe they can't afford to. Why, what are you getting at?'

'The thing is, mate, I'm absolutely skint. Haven't got a brass razoo. I need that money.'

'Greg, you're a *banker*. You earn more than any solicitor.'

'Call me "Oz", mate, I prefer it.'

'Greg. You're loaded. You don't need charity.'

'Ah but, y'see, I've already been back down under twice in the past six months. To visit my folks. That's not cheap.'

'Yes, but you knew before you made those trips that you'd have to stump up for the world tour.'

Greg's voice hardened.

'What I'm saying is, mate, if you don't give me a grand as well, I'm not coming. And then you'll have to call off the tour. So you *have* to pay me.'

So that was it. Blackmail.

I convened the O'Herlihy brothers for a council of war. There was absolutely nothing we could do: the little shit had us over a barrel. Sean and James didn't have the money to pay for Eiran's ticket either, but they explained the situation to their parents, who kindly dipped into their own savings and came up with the bulk of the cash. With a heavy heart, I transferred Eiran's thousand pounds across to Greg, when what the little turd really deserved was a fist in the teeth. And I'd thought we had such a great bunch of players. A real team—eleven for one, one for eleven and all that (well, one for ten-and-a-half, anyway). The discovery of a wriggling little worm at the heart of our beautiful big apple threatened to put the most massive damper on the whole enterprise.

I tried to leaven Eiran's financial plight by employing him as my secretary too, for the three weeks following Riaan's departure. In retrospect, this may not have been such a wise move. Eiran was not, shall we say, the most conscientious of workers. I have an extremely vivid memory of walking into my office to find him stretched horizontally on the sofa, beer in hand, simultaneously reading Mike Atherton's autobiography and watching the Ashes on TV. The phone was ringing unanswered.

'So, were you thinking of, maybe, answering that at some point?'

'Hey, chill, the answer machine'll get it. Er, there was a guy looking for you. I told him I had no idea where you were. I forget his name. Oh yeah . . . Peter, that was it.'

That'd be the managing director, then.

I have to confess, though, that the pair of us did bunk off early one afternoon. We took the new helmets over to Lord's for an indoor net with a bowling machine, which was set on 'fast bouncer'. For a whole hour, the contraption (which resembled an H. G. Wells alien from *The War of the Worlds*) did a passable imitation of the bowling action of a big, scary Caribbean quick. Eiran, by this time, had become our best batsman. He was incredibly quick on his feet, almost balletically so, and could get to the pitch of any ball; I'd seen him flay the very best opposition bowling to all corners, with a trademark array of wristy but powerful drives. The short stuff, however—perhaps because it was so rare in the English mud—was not his strong point, and he struggled against the machine. I, on the other hand, got the hang of the thing more quickly, and started to pull 70 m.p.h. deliveries freely from a point mere inches before my nose. Smugly, I began to feel quietly pleased with myself; and smugness, as we all know, is usually fatal.

Paul Daniels came down to see us at the net.

'Er . . . I've got a problem with the tour.'

'Paul, if you're going to tell me you're dropping out, I'm going to ram your head down the lavatory.'

Especially as I've just agreed to give Greg a thousand bloody quid.

'No, no, don't be silly, of course I'm not dropping out of the tour. God no.'

'So what's the problem?'

'I've broken my finger.'

'*What*?'

'Playing rugby.'

With an idiot grin he held up his right hand. His middle digit, encased in a hard plastic shell, stuck out at a bizarre angle to the others in a permanent rude gesture.

'I've got to keep this on for a month.'

'But you won't be able to bat. Or field. Or bowl. Not that you can bowl anyway.'

'Of course I will. I can bat and field with the other four fingers! Just you watch!' he said. Smugly.

*　　*　　*

It was my new secretary, driven to answer the phones at sharpened pencil point, who took the latest call from Sheila. With a fortnight to go, all eleven fares had finally been collected and dispatched to BA. There was only one problem. BA had decided that this would be an opportune moment to put the fares up. I am ashamed to say that I snapped, going berserk with rage Tasmanian Devil-style, and said a lot of things to Sheila that I probably shouldn't have. I threatened her with everything from exposure on TV consumer documentaries to immolation inside a wicker man. Before long, the aggrieved PR lady who'd put me on to Special Accounts in the first place was calling to lambast me for my lack of manners.

'But you don't know what she's *like*,' I wailed. 'You don't know what *any* of them are like. They're all so completely . . . *useless*.'

I was given a dressing down, headmistress-fashion. On this occasion, she told me, the fare rise would be waived; but British Airways were doing us an enormous favour by agreeing to take more than nine people round the world, and if I valued their continued co-operation then I should mind my attitude. All right?

All right.

Like a punch-drunk boxer, I waited for the next setback. It wasn't long coming. Riaan phoned from SA to say he'd got there OK, and was now on his way back. He was all ready to go, kit packed, Australian visa in his passport . . .

Hold on. Australian visa?

'Yes, all South Africans require a visa to visit Australia. I got mine back in July.'

I called Aidan there and then.

'Aidan, have you got an Australian visa in your passport?'

'Er . . . no. why?'

It was 19 December. The Australian High

Commission shut for Christmas on the 21st.

Aidan was ordered down to the Strand in his best suit and tie, while I desperately raked my imagination for anything that might possibly constitute a 'contact'. Finally I located an old friend in BBC Current Affairs who'd had dealings with a senior consular official in the visa section, a pleasant lady called Helen. I outlined the difficulty over the phone. 'No problem,' she said. 'We can rush it through in twenty-four hours, if Aidan explains the situation.' Heaving huge sighs of relief I relaxed, only for my optimism to be shattered an hour or two later when Aidan reported back.

'They've turned me down for a visa.'

'What? But they said they could rush it through in twenty-four hours!'

'It's not the timing. They've turned me down flat. They said I can never, ever enter Australia. Not that I want to, the way I've just been treated.'

'But *why*?'

The answer given, apparently, was 'passport irregularities'. When Aidan had first come to Europe, he'd flown to Ireland to visit his fiancée's family. From there he'd taken the car ferry to Fishguard, where all the ferry passengers had—with the rigour so common to the defence of Britain's borders—been waved through a deserted checkpoint. He had no UK entry stamp.

'But that wasn't his *fault*,' I told Helen, anguish inflecting every syllable. 'UK immigration know he's here.'

'Well, to be honest, it's not really about passport irregularities, or anything like that. Each consular official takes an individual decision, based on the appearance of the applicant, as to whether or not he or she is a suitable person to be granted a visa to enter Australia.'

'He *was* wearing a suit, wasn't he?'

'A leather jacket, apparently.'

Oh, Aidan! So it had been the old shaven-headed, bull-necked, umpiring thing again. Riaan, who looked as if he was about to wheel Whistler's mother off for her afternoon constitutional, had got a visa, no trouble. Aidan, who despite being utterly inoffensive looked as if he was about to kick off a fight with a bunch of Millwall fans, had run into 'passport irregularities'. I told him to get back down there the following day, in a suit and tie this time, and for good measure I asked Tom to go with him. Tom explained the situation carefully to a different consular official, who agreed that there appeared to be no irregularities whatsoever. All seemed to be in order. Aidan paid another £40 fee. The official came back. visa rejected—again.

'But why?' asked Tom.

'Because, once a decision has been taken by a consular official, it's irreversible,' said the official.

'But you knew that when you took the second £40,' said Tom.

'Yes,' said the official.

Humiliatingly, I had to call Sheila—yes, the very selfsame Sheila from BA whom I'd roundly abused just a day or two previously—and ask for Aidan to be re-routed *around* Australia. It was to be a massive, 15,400-mile detour, from Auckland to Los Angeles to Hong Kong to Singapore, before he could be reunited with us on the Asian side. At last it was done. I called Aidan with the (relatively) good news.

'Oh, I can't do that,' he said.

'What do you mean you "can't do that"? I've just spent the afternoon fixing it all up for you!'

'I mean, I can't do that because the Australians never gave me my passport back.'

Gnnnnnnnnnh.

Aidan was despatched straight back to the Strand for a third time, but it was no use. The man who'd dealt with him had gone home for Christmas. No one else was prepared to go through the relevant paperwork. The passport would be returned only when 'routine enquiries' were completed, sometime in January. Mindless bureaucracy, it seemed, was not just a British disease. Apart from anything else, I'd just laid out a non-returnable £2,000 on his airfare. I was beginning to remember why I'd vowed never to organize another bloody cricket tour in my entire sodding life.

I called Helen at the Australian High Commission again, later that night.

'Helen, what are you doing over Christmas?'

'Just relaxing at home with my family in Surrey . . . why?'

'How do you fancy popping up to London? Maybe . . . sort of . . . you know . . . dropping into the office?'

Helen, bless her, went into the Australian High Commission over Christmas and retrieved Aidan's passport. I got it back on Christmas Eve, just before the call from Matthew telling me that this time, without question, he was *definitely* pulling out of the trip.

'It's my wife. She says if I get on that plane she'll divorce me. She says I have no right to go away for three whole weeks on my own. She says I have to decide between the cricket tour and my marriage.'

I spent an hour or so on the phone to Matthew's wife, explaining patiently that it was no longer just about the pair of them. Matthew was now one of the foundation stones of a substantial, elaborate and rather flimsy structure. If he didn't show, I counselled sagely, it would ruin the trip for ten other people (well, for nine other people and a small Antipodean troll). And, of course, she—not me—would be kissing goodbye to two grand. My little homily did the trick. She relented. Matthew was given permission to board the plane.

On an icy Boxing Day morning, we convened at Heathrow at six, in order to catch the 0940 to Bridgetown Barbados via Miami. After my Cuba experience, we were taking no chances with overbookings. As it turned out we were right to arrive early, for BA had only two counter staff on duty, and we had to queue for two and a half hours to check in. Tom (who'd handed out some very neat printed itineraries and a very orderly laminated kit rota) stayed at the back with me, helping to shepherd the other nine forward to receive their boarding cards and US visa-waiver forms from the check-in staff, just in case any of them managed to get lost, find themselves accidentally put on a flight to Saudi Arabia, or fall down one of the cracks in the lino. At last it was our turn. The man behind the desk scanned the screen for what seemed a worryingly long time, before delivering his thunderbolt.

'I'm sorry, Mr Thompson. You're not booked on this flight. In fact neither of you are.'

'What are you talking about? Look—we've got tickets! What are these, if we're not booked on the flight?'

'I don't know where you got those, sir, but neither of you are booked on this flight.'

'We're a *group*. A group booking of *eleven*. How can nine people be on the plane and two not?'

He smiled knowingly.

'I really don't think you can be, sir. You see, we only do group bookings of up to nine. Anything above that confuses our computers. So, you've made a mistake. The other nine are fine. But I'm afraid you two are definitely not travelling.'

7

Barbados

There are some people in this world so rich—so enormously, thankfully, stupidly rich—that they can afford to book holidays in the Caribbean, in places as diverse as Cuba and Barbados, flying first class, and then, when the fancy takes them, not bother to show up at the airport. Either that or said people had simply been run over by a taxi on the way to Heathrow. Whatever the reason, after another agonizing wait it was confirmed that, yes, two first-class passengers had failed to show, and, yes, Tom and I would be allowed to board the plane. Hurrah for the super-rich! Could we actually have their first-class seats? Could we hell. But we could fly to Miami, even if we had to sit fifty rows away from our friends.

Fifty rows on a British Airways jumbo is only, in fact, about twenty-five feet. Easyjet excepted, I have never been on a plane with less legroom. My knees (I'm six foot tall) were wedged like pit props into the back of the seat in front of me, which, as ill luck would have it, contained one of the fattest human beings ever to have graced the known universe: a vast American woman in dungarees, weighing in at twenty stone-plus and resembling a huge inside-out pork sausage. Alongside sat her husband, a mournful cormorant of a man, who said nothing throughout the entire flight. With the plane airborne and the seat-belt signs off, she touched the 'recline' button on her chair arm. With the full weight of the *Graf Zeppelin* behind it, her seat shot backwards to its full extent, causing me to yowl in agony as both my femurs were neatly snapped in two.

'Do you *mind*?' she said. 'I am *trying* to sleep!'

'Sorry,' I mumbled. Sleep?? It was ten o'clock in the morning.

By now the woman's head had settled immediately beneath my chin, in a bizarre reversal of my Yemen Airlines experience. Her buckling seat fought manfully against the impossible strain. I dared not move. I could not move. Unfortunately I became gripped with an overwhelming desire to sneeze. By squirming in my seat, I managed to twist my body slightly, just sufficient to reach into my pocket and extract a handkerchief.

'Do you *mind*?' she said again, fixing me with a basilisk glare.

After what I felt was a diplomatic pause, I lifted the hankie and essayed the tiniest little sniff.

'Do you *MIND*?' she said, twisting round, her face a mask of rage.

There was nothing for it. I wriggled vertically

out of my seat, as she went through her whole repertoire of theatrical grumbles. I would have to spend the rest of the ten-hour journey standing in the aisle. Sean came over to keep me company, and we got into what—looking back—was a quite staggeringly boring conversation about loft conversions. Our half-whisper, however, was insufficiently low for the gorgon's liking.

'It is clear to me', she shouted, 'that the pair of you have issues with women!'

'"Issues with women"?' I replied, rather dazedly. 'I'm sorry . . . I don't understand.'

'Both of you are obviously unreconstructed sexists! I should know! I'm the—' (and here she revealed herself to be a senior academic at a major American university, whose legal budget I could barely begin to measure up to). 'Men have to respect women's wishes, do you hear? You men can't live your whole lives in a bubble!'

The cormorant nodded his acquiescence.

'The only bubble I can see, madam,' I replied gravely, 'is the one in your stomach caused by eating quite so many pies.'

Oscar Wilde it wasn't. It was also, as it turned out, a bad mistake. She stomped off, creating a passable impression of serious air turbulence. Before long, the chief steward came to see us.

'I'm afraid we've had a formal complaint of sexual harassment against the two of you.'

'Sexual *harassment*?' I almost gurgled.

'The, er, lady claims you've been sexually harassing her since the flight began.'

'But that's ridiculous!'

'I'm sure it is. But unless you're prepared to make a formal apology, face to face, then she won't drop the allegation.'

'Why on earth should we care what she alleges?'

'Because if she hasn't dropped the allegation by the time we enter American airspace, then the pilot is legally obliged under US law to notify the American police, who will meet you when you step off the plane, and hold you for questioning.'

'But—but we're on a connecting flight to Bridgetown.'

'You may even be taken into custody for a day or two, until the matter is settled. Sexual harassment is an extremely serious business in the States. It's a situation you'd do well to avoid.'

It was quite unbelievable. I'd always had a very slight worry at the back of my mind, taking ten amateur sportsmen on a three-week trip that involved no less than 106 hours either in the air or in the departure lounge, that someone, at some point, might tank up on miniatures and misbehave. But *me*? Arrested by Miami vice for holding a whispered conversation about loft conversions, the world's most bourgeois subject? America had clearly gone stark, raving mad.

I refused point-blank. It was a matter of principle. I hate bullies, and wasn't going to be bullied into submission. I'd rather have missed out on Barbados. But Sean, who is surprisingly willing to embrace realpolitik when the occasion demands, offered to make the apology himself. In fact he made a thoroughly Levantine statement of curlicued apology, originating somewhere in Kuala Lumpur no doubt, a big Cheshire-cat grin of contempt plastered across his face. I, on the other hand, strode purposefully off the plane the moment we touched down in Miami. Matthew caught up with me.

'What on earth was that all about?'

'Too late,' I breathed. Fatty was on my tail.

'I see *you* didn't have the guts to apologize!' she screamed, puffing up behind. 'Typical man!'

'Typical,' mumbled the cormorant by her side, breaking silence for the first time.

'Look at you both!' She jabbed a finger at Matthew and me. 'You've *both* got a problem with women! You're *both* sexists!'

'Me?' said Matthew, entirely bewildered. 'I'm sorry madam, but I . . .'

'Don't try to deny it! You're a man, aren't you?'

'But I—I . . .'

I put my head down and bulldozed for the exit door, leaving Matthew threshing helplessly in her maw.

I had successfully managed to avoid arrest on American soil. Unfortunately, Riaan and Aidan were not so lucky. On proceeding through immigration and handing over their green visa-waiver forms, they ran into a little problem.

'Where are your blue visa-waiver forms?'

'These are the ones British Airways gave us in London. We all got the same ones.'

'These are green. Green ones are for Brits. You two are South African. You should have blue ones.'

'Well these are the ones British Airways gave us.'

'Don't try to be funny, pal. Tell it to the judge.'

Riaan and Aidan were promptly arrested under anti-terror legislation and taken to a holding cell. The long arm of the World's (Second-) worst Airline had reached as far as the World's Stupidest

Democracy, to create perhaps their finest bureaucratic balls-up yet.

Americans, as we know, have absolute respect for the full majesty of the law and for the rights of prisoners, whatever their nationality. So it must have been an accidental glitch that the 'holding cell' was a windowless plate-glass box placed in direct ninety-degree sunlight, and that neither of the two South Africans were offered anything to drink. After a few hours of this they were sweating like Gary Glitter in a Turkish bath full of fourteen-year-olds. Presently a fat thug with a roll-neck neck, a Texan accent and a shaven head much like Aidan's own came in and plumped himself on the other side of the table.

'Where are your blue visa forms?' he demanded.

'British Airways didn't give us any,' explained Aidan.

'*I* ask the questions round here, mister!' replied the man.

I quote the above verbatim, merely to establish quite how low an IQ it is possible to possess and still secure a job in the so-called War against Terror. Riaan—who, let's face it, with hair like cornstalks and a complexion the colour of strawberry Angel Delight, didn't exactly fit the template of your average al-Qaeda operative—pointed out in his most respectful Transvaal farmboy manner that the flight to Bridgetown was due to leave in about twenty minutes. Fat boy chuckled.

'One thing you can both be sure of, buster, is that you ain't gettin' that flight.'

* * *

But the incompetent officials of the US Department of Homeland Security had reckoned without the extreme incompetence of American Airlines, brother airline to the supremely incompetent British Airways (who presumably are recognized as the 'Big Daddy' of the gang at international incompetence seminars). Some six hours after Aidan and Riaan's arrest, the rest of us hadn't gone anywhere. We were still locked in a departure lounge on the other side of the airport. Our plane lay in pieces on the tarmac, in the manner of Delboy's Robin Reliant. It had completely failed to start. It was two in the morning British time, which meant it was fourteen hours since our last proper meal. British Airways had provided a gnarled mini-sandwich five hours after that, but during the last nine hours we had seen no food or water at all—and we weren't even being interrogated. So we did the only thing that Englishmen could possibly do in conditions of such adversity: we played cricket in the departure lounge, using Eiran's guitar as a bat.

'You'll break that,' Sean told his little brother.

'It's only a tennis ball.'

'You'll break that, and when you do I'm going to say "I told you so." '

'Yeah yeah.'

Paul Daniels' friend Dan, a polite chap with a boisterous streak, who'd worked for a variety of charities, was batting. Somebody bowled him a vicious yorker, which he dug out rather expertly. There was a hideous cracking sound from within the guitar's floppy case. Eiran, like a panicking mother hen, rushed across and extracted the instrument gingerly. A huge split ran from the neck to the bridge. Eiran's trusty acoustic guitar, his mastery of which had proved the spur for so many meaningless sexual encounters down the years, had been destroyed. He was utterly, completely distraught.

'I told you you'd break it,' observed Sean.

Silence.

'And I told you that when you broke it, I'd say "I told you so." '

Silence.

'So . . . I told you so.'

'WILL YOU SHUT THE FUCK UP YOU BIG FAT C**T!'

The whole departure lounge stopped dead. At last we had done something worthy of being censured for, even apprehended for. Frankly, it was about time. But nobody looked up for long. It was approximately twenty hours since we had convened at Heathrow for what should have been a simple hop across the Atlantic, and the same went for most of the other passengers. Eiran's deep feelings on this specific matter had, in a very general sense, caught the public mood.

* * *

We arrived in Barbados in driving rain, deep in the small hours. Aidan and Riaan, panting, had made the plane just as they were about to shut the main door.

There had been nothing to eat on the aircraft.

'You a cricket team?' said the Bajan customs officer, on seeing our kit.

'Yup.'

‘Who you playin’?’

‘A team called North Stars.’

‘Whooooo. You gonna get some licks.’

The arrivals hall was deserted. Our auto-rental company had shut up shop and gone home, as had the only money-changer, so we had to pay a taxi driver with a minivan way over the odds in US dollars to take us through the sheeting deluge to our hotel.

‘So, you a cricket team?’ he said, as he piled our sodden kit behind the rear seats.

‘Yup.’

‘Who you playin’?’

‘North Stars.’

‘Whooooooo! You gonna get some licks!’

On arrival at the Europa Apartments in Sunset Crest, we had to bang on the gates to waken the night porter. There, we discovered, we would need tokens for everything: towels, the telephone, the safe, the air conditioning, you name it—everything except the cutlery (which, interestingly, amounted to a single whisk). Tokens were available from reception. Which was shut. We didn't need tokens for food. There was no food. To be honest, we didn't care any more. We fell on our beds and slept the sleep of the dead. We had made it to Barbados.

* * *

Barbados was once ‘Barbadoes’, rather a lovely old name I think, even if it does sound like the kind of weeping boils that might appear in clusters during an attack of plague. As its line of south-coast towns (Hastings, Worthing, Dover etc.) would suggest, the island was a British possession for an unbroken period of nearly 350 years, and indeed it still feels like one. Back in the seventeenth and eighteenth centuries it was a horror posting for servicemen, a fetid breeding ground for every sort of genuine plague. Today it has metamorphosed into a certain type of Briton's holiday fantasyland, neat, clean and hygienic, with pissy lager on tap and a D-list celebrity on every corner. Barbados is Caribbean-lite. All the islands of the Caribbean are unusual, in that—on account of that sea's eastward opening to the Atlantic—their eastern coasts are the ones beaten by pounding waves, while their western shores are lapped by a gentle backwash; so it is the western beaches that the holidaymakers flock to, and where the D-list celebs appear in clusters. We played a warm-up game of beach cricket on the admittedly idyllic sands before the Sandy Lane resort, for North Stars CC and their apparently big tongues awaited us the next day. Then I strolled into the hotel bar for a cold white wine, my view of the beach considerably impeded by the grinning mugs of Michael Winner and Simon Cowell at the next table. We went off in search of a beer instead, on the main road behind the beach, and could find only a Premiership-football-themed pub with Sporty Spice, this time, sat at the adjoining table. It was like holidaying in the pages of *Heat* magazine.

As giant images of Liverpool v. Arsenal flickered on the multiple screens, Paul Daniels, who was almost hyperactive with excitement that our great enterprise had finally begun, expounded his theory of sports tours.

‘We need two things, see?’ (He tended to get more Welsh as he got more excited, or more drunk, or both.) ‘A kitty and a points system. I need ten quid off each of you for the kitty, and ten for the points system.’

Explain yourself, boyo.

‘The kitty is for a crate of lager to take back to the hotel, so we’ve got beer on tap. The points system is whatever you want it to be. On my last rugby tour, they awarded points for female liasons: one point for a snog, two points for a fondle, three points for a hand shandy, five points for a shag and ten points for a threesome.’

‘What, with each other?’

‘No! With a *girl*. The person with the most points at the end got the kitty. Not that I’m suggesting we do anything as disgraceful as *that*, of course.’

Of course not.

‘I’ve got a girlfriend,’ pointed out James, Riaan and I.

‘I’m getting married,’ said Aidan.

‘I *am* married,’ said Matthew.

‘I’ve got a girlfriend *and* I’m married,’ said Tom.

The upshot of a heated debate was that everyone gave the Welsh twat a tenner for his lager kitty, but only a few of the single players stumped up for a rugby-style exercise in sexual mathematics. Greg, in particular, was just happy to be involved: Sean had pleaded to be allowed to do all sorts of hideously unmentionable things to him the minute we left UK legal jurisdiction, but I was determined that a minimum standard of politeness be maintained. We were a team, at least until we got back to Heathrow, and that was what mattered. It did occur to me, though, that Greg might be keen on a points scheme because he fancied his chances. He was, after all, the right height to commence at least one of the listed activities within seconds of meeting a lady.

Were the points scheme to have come off, we would not have become the first English cricket team to fall prey to the fleshpots of Barbados. The disastrous 1985–6 England cricket tour of the Caribbean fell apart on the field after a series of bedroom scandals, including the celebrated *News of the World* 'scoop' of Ian Botham and the then Miss Barbados actually breaking their bed during a bout of energetic sex. The result was a 5–0 'blackwash' at the hands of the West Indies. I was once lucky enough to work with Eric Idle and John Du Prez on a musical they'd written for radio entitled *Behind the Crease*, about this very episode: Idle had been in the West Indies at the time, there to see the cricket with a phalanx of elderly rock stars, and had witnessed the whole thing at first hand. The truth, as told by him, was even more entertaining than the tabloid version.

What happened, apparently, was this: the England team were determined from the start to party hard, a resolve strengthened when a defiant Mike Gatting—who'd been doing his best to rouse them to a peak of patriotic cricketing fervour with a series of tub-thumping speeches—was carried off to hospital with a squashed nose, courtesy of a Malcolm Marshall bouncer. Gatting's fate, it seemed to the rest of them, was a vivid reminder of the dangers of taking this Test cricket lark too seriously. So, when Elton John held a bash in their honour, the England team turned up gleefully demanding to know where the booze, drugs and women were. But, to their enormous disappointment, the crestfallen cream of English cricket discovered that only the mildest alcoholic substances were available, and no narcotics whatsoever: the middle-aged rocks stars, it had to be gently explained to them, were long past that stage. In fact they enjoyed nothing more than a nice glass of tonic water and a fireside chat about how to spot Abdul Qadir's googly.

Testosterone by now raging unchecked round their systems, some of the cricketers were easy meat for the rat-like armies of tabloid hacks who were swarming round the island. The *News of the Screws* paid Vicki Hodge, the Caribbean kiss 'n' tell queen (who had already ensnared Prince Andrew), for any salacious details that might arise should she, erm, inadvertently seduce Ian Botham. But her boyfriend, a West Indian cricket fan, tipped off the England all-rounder, who greeted Ms Hodge's friendly approaches with a volley of choice epithets. It was not a clever move: the spurned Hodge merely subcontracted the job to her close friend Lindy Field, the aforesaid Miss Barbados. This time, Botham fell for the bait. The siren had a microphone in her knickers and, what's more, her bed legs had been pre-sawn through by *News of the World* journalists. The slightest touch would have sent the bed crashing to the floor. Botham's fate was sealed: the rest was splashed all over the Sunday papers, as was Botham's blood when his wife, Kathy, arrived on the next flight out. And I won't even mention what David Gower was up to, except to reassure you that he's now married to the lady in question.

Idle, Du Prez and I had successfully pitched the musical to BBC Radio 2 FM, but, after it had been arranged, scored, rehearsed and recorded in front of a live audience, it was suddenly banned by the powers that be. The then controller, a ludicrous battleship of a woman called Frances Line, thought the whole thing too legally scandalous to broadcast, even though the story had already been plastered across the newspapers in six-inch headlines. In particular, she rejected outright the notion that an England wicketkeeper might hide in a lady's wardrobe, rather in the manner of Queen Victoria dismissing the existence of lesbianism. Actually, she may have had a point there: the only reason Jack Russell would have hidden in a wardrobe would have been to eat baked beans direct from the tin without having to share them. This, incidentally, was the same woman on whose behalf we received a fascinating edict banning producers in our department from playing music recorded after 31 December 1973 on the station. So 'All Along the Watchtower' or 'Paranoid' were fine for Radio 2, but not 'Whispering Grass' or 'The Wombling Song'. In fact those would be my sentiments exactly, but I'm not sure that's what she meant.

Frankly, almost any music would have been better than a CD of *The Best of Eddy Grant*, which superannuated nonsense Paul Daniels wasted part of our precious kitty on. He also bought a small portable CD player with which to broadcast it. He then spent five hours playing it on a repeat across our hotel lawn, in the mistaken belief that he had somehow tapped into the soul of the Caribbean. After the sixth successive broadcast of 'Electric

Avenue', I marched across the grass to the verandah of his apartment. If I couldn't shut off Eddy, I reasoned, at least I could get a compensatory bottle of Banks. But there was a problem.

'You're too late, mate. The beer's all gone.'

'What, the *whole crate*?'

'Yup.'

'Who drank it?'

'I did.'

'*All* of it?'

'We're on tour, boyo. You've got to keep up.'

'Paul, it may have escaped your notice, but this is a cricket tour, not a rugby tour.'

'I'll need more money for the beer kitty, by the way. Right, let's go out, get pissed, and flirt with some honeys.'

*   *   *

We did indeed go out that night, all eleven of us, to St Lawrence's Gap, which is where the fleshpots of Barbados concentrate the most flesh per pot, as it were.

'You a cricket team, then?' said the cabbie. 'Who you playin'?'

'North Stars.'

'Whooooohooo! You gonna get some licks!!'

North Stars, according to the cabbie, hadn't lost a home game in two years. It was nice to know.

At the Gap, Tom, Matthew and I found a pleasant seafood restaurant on the beach. The other eight, eschewing food completely, selected the bar with the most pretty girls.

'Mmmm, women,' said Paul Daniels, sounding

uncannily like a Welsh Homer Simpson.

Eiran licked his lips lasciviously.

Two hours later we returned from the restaurant to find the eight of them huddled over their lager in a corner, giggling like schoolboys and saying things like 'No, you go on'—'No, *you* go on.' They still hadn't plucked up the courage to talk to anybody at all.

'Do you want me to go and talk to a *lady* for you?' I asked.

They nodded like six-year-olds.

I selected an attractive blonde woman who turned out, rather bizarrely, to be a horse-cloner (they exist, apparently) from the American Midwest. As she outlined the difficult birth pangs of the embryonic horse-cloning industry, there was a voice at my shoulder.

'Hello.'

It was Sean.

There was a voice at my other shoulder.

'Hell*eau*.'

It was Leslie Phillips. No—correction—it was Eiran.

I felt the curious sensation of being unable to breathe, which, I soon realized, was caused by horizontal pressure on my lungs exerted by a quite large person on one side and an even larger person on the other. I was being literally squeezed out of the conversation. Job done, I left them to it. Matthew, Tom and I hailed a taxi, and asked the driver to take us back to Sunset Crest. Even though it's a real place, it was embarrassing just having to mention its name. It sounded like a retirement home for toothpaste executives.

'So, you on holiday, then?' asked the driver.

‘No, we’re a cricket team, we’re playing North Stars tomorrow, and we’re gonna get some licks.’

‘How you know I was gonna say that?’

‘Intuition.’

‘Nice breeze up there though, at North Stars.’

Yes, the breeze of the ball whistling past our noses, I didn’t doubt.

I never asked how Eiran got on with the horse-cloner, but, if history is any guide, his inexplicably winning combination of huge spaniel eyes and Michael Bolton’s haircut usually tended to luck out. Paul’s new kitty-funded CD player, incidentally, broke down later that night and never worked again.

* * *

The next morning dawned blazing hot. It was going to be a perfect day. As we tried to eat our breakfast using a single shared whisk, Tom and I were greeted by the irrepressible, bounding figure of Paul Daniels. He was holding up a cricket shirt emblazoned with the team badge. He’d clearly been up for hours.

‘Look!’ he said. ‘Team cricket shirts! I’ve had eleven made, and eleven tour T-shirts. They’ll be ready by tomorrow!’

‘Brilliant,’ I said. They actually were very nice. Then a horrible thought struck me. ‘Paul, how did you pay for all this?’

‘Simple. I’ve had a whip-round. Next year’s subs! Isn’t that clever? I’ve already collected them off half the team. I told them it was OK with you.’

‘Paul! It is *not* OK with me! We *need* those subs, to buy kit and to hire pitches for next season.

Who's going to pay for all that?'

'Oh, you'll think of something.'

In fact I already knew exactly who would be paying for all that. Muggins here.

The minivan turned up and we piled aboard for the drive up to St Lucy, on the north tip of the island—home of the much-feared North Stars. As we pulled out of the hotel gates, Paul shouted to the driver to stop.

'The kitty's empty! We need more money for the kitty! We're out of beer!'

There was a mass chorus of grumbles. Several people pointed out loudly that he had drunk the last lot entirely by himself. This time it would be different, he insisted. Eventually, reluctantly, the ten of us coughed up a further tenner each, and Paul vanished into the supermarket across the road. He emerged a few minutes later, struggling under the weight of a huge brown cardboard box, which he heaved into the back of the van. As we chugged off once more towards our destination, somebody peeked inside. The box did not contain bottles of beer. It contained an enormous number of tins of pineapple chunks.

'Paul . . . what . . . ?'

'They're very good for you, pineapple chunks. Very healthy.'

We all stared at each other in goggle-eyed silence. Quite clearly, Paul Daniels was going insane.

*   *   *

For such a small island, the trip to St Lucy was a long one, meandering between the hedgerows of rolling British-style countryside. Tourist Barbados was left behind, as the bland suburban landscape of endless golf courses was replaced by sugar fields. The villages looked pleasant enough in the sunshine—what village doesn't?—but to be honest there is nothing quaint, attractive or inspiring about the architecture anywhere on Barbados. Suddenly, in the middle of nowhere, a large concrete sports stand reared up, topped by a substantial pavilion, and fringed by one or two friendly, waving palms. We had arrived. Our hosts, who were cheery and charming to a man, were there to meet us, as was the British High Commissioner, which was an unexpected honour. How had he even found out about the game? I wondered. 'It's my business to know about such things,' he replied suavely. Good old FCO. North Stars, it seemed, entertained a fair number of touring British sides, and invariably they 'gave them some licks'. I checked the plaques on the wall, to find out the name of the last touring side they'd 'given some licks' to. There it was, in cold print: Sussex. Jesus Christ.

My next surprise was the wicket, which was far from the vicious, rock-hard launch pad I'd expected to see in the Caribbean. Now I've scrutinized cricket pitches all over the world, from Ardley-with-Fewcott, where 'bounce' is a dirty word, to Tusmore House, where the molehills are so huge they're practically goathills, to the eggbox pitch at East Meon, which makes the lunar surface look like a billiard table, to Droxford's flatulent trampoline, to Charlton-on-Otmoor's homicidal strip of death. This resembled none of those. This was a straw-coloured spinner's wicket, pure and simple, like something from rural Pakistan. Not only could Geoff Boycott have stuck his car key into the cracks, he could probably have inserted his whole car. But this wicket didn't look like it was going to crumble during the day. It looked like it had been purpose-built, cracks and all, and fashioned to last.

'Do you have many spinners, then?' I asked the opposition captain, as nonchalantly as I could.

'All our bowlers are spinners,' he replied.

So much for all those helmets, chest guards, elbow guards and net sessions with a bowling machine. We only had one spinner, Paul's friend Dan, and I'd never seen him bowl.

I won the toss and opted to bat, just in case I'd been wrong about the cracks not widening during the day. On our way back to the pavilion I saw a teenage Bajan batsman practising, lashing balls into the chicken-wire fence with unbelievable precision and ferocity.

'That's Larry Babb,' said the North Stars skipper. 'We have high hopes of him making the national side. He scored 136 in eight overs last week.' I discreetly checked their scorebook. He wasn't lying. North Stars had made over 400 runs in a thirty-five-over match. Bloody hell.

A few minutes later I was back out again with Matthew to open the batting. There was indeed a pleasant sea breeze, which kept the heat down. North Stars did indeed have an all-spin attack, and accuracy was their shtick. Every ball turned, sure, but there was nothing off the stumps throughout the whole innings. You miss, they hit. Personally, I'm not keen on spinners opening the bowling. I think it takes away the fun. I rather enjoy the gladiatorial combat of someone you've never met before trying to injure you, but having to stay at least twenty-two yards away at all times. It's so much more gentlemanly than, say, rugby, when one never quite knows where your opponent's going to stick that roaming finger of his. Still, needs must. I pushed my third ball unconvincingly between square leg and midwicket for two runs. A few balls later I repeated the shot, shouted 'Yes!' and charged down the wicket. I arrived in Matthew's crease to find that it was still very much occupied by Matthew.

'Yes!' I shouted again.

'Sorry . . . what?'

I ran back to the other end, but of course I didn't quite make it. Here we go again, I thought. Once again I've been run out after completing a 43.9-yard dash.

'I'm terribly sorry,' said Matthew as I passed him on the way back to the pavilion. 'I was miles away.'

Yes, seven thousand bloody miles away.

After that, things didn't go too badly for a while. Matthew made 25, as did Sean O'Herlihy. Eiran got 29, while Greg—I'd calculated that the grassless pitch would suit his Australian style—made an impressive 30. But all of them were clean bowled shaping to hit out and up the scoring rate. Sean, in fact, was bowled by a one-fingered man—literally a finger-spinner. With the score at a pivotal 117–4, Paul Daniels came to the wicket. He was bound to be nervous, of course—we all were—but something clearly wasn't right with the Welsh wizard. He was literally bouncing up and down in the crease like a startled rabbit, and fending off the ball as if it had been dipped in myxomatosis concentrate. Paul hadn't really gone mad, of course. He was just under enormous pressure, nearly all of it self-imposed. He'd been used to being our saviour, back in the old days—our indestructible genius who could win us any game, dig us out of any hole. Now that he was over his illness, he thought it was his duty to mount that pedestal once again. He'd become a complete bag of nerves because he didn't know whether or not he was still up to the task. It didn't matter to us, of course, whether he attained his former glories or not. We were his friends. We only wanted what was best for him. And we wanted him to stop spending our money on fucking pineapple chunks.

A few balls later, Paul took a panicky heave and lost his middle stump. The psychological effect was palpable. Our remaining wickets went down for thirty runs between them. The North Star spinners reigned supreme: the umpires were like vets, putting a series of bamboozled batsmen to sleep. We finished on 151. It wasn't nearly enough. The British High Commissioner did his best to cheer us up. A few weeks previously, he pointed out, he'd come down by prior arrangement to watch the Royal Engineers bat at North Stars. He'd been an hour late for the start, by which time they were already all out. There'd been nothing for it but to keep batting. North Stars had duly obliged, so, by the time he'd finally pitched up, the Royal Engineers' score had reached 35–13.

Tea wasn't really tea, but a giant banquet of Bajan food, by the end of which we were all completely stuffed, especially Paul, who—still blaming himself for our batting collapse—had shut himself in the dressing room and gorged himself on tin after tin of pineapple chunks. The O'Herlihy brothers, meanwhile, were on the prowl for someone who might be able to sell them a little dope: after various failures in this regard the previous day, they were determined to nail down a supply of their favourite narcotic that would last them for the remainder of our three-day sojourn—say, about 7½ lb. They asked a member of the North Stars side if he knew of any suppliers.

'Sure,' he replied. 'You want our number seven or our number nine.'

(Note to any lawyers reading this: these numbers have been changed to protect the guilty.)

The British High Commissioner couldn't help overhearing the conversation. 'Make sure you don't ask the number six or the number eight,' he warned. 'They're policemen.'

Matthew, meanwhile, had made accidental contact with his own personal intoxicant. He was a reformed alcoholic, following a tempestuous artistic youth spent getting pissed in a New York garret, and hadn't touched a drop for fifteen years. The tea tables were laden with an odd-tasting fruit punch, which he began knocking back at an alarming speed.

'It's jolly good, isn't it, this fruit juice?' he announced. 'I haven't felt this good in years.'

On the way back out, Sean asked one of the home players what was in it.

'Just fruit juice,' came the reply. 'Fermented fruit juice.'

We took the field with Matthew reeling gently at midwicket. The rest of us weren't much better off: exhausted, hung-over, bloated with Bajan food, our jetlagged bodies under the impression it was the middle of the evening. On his way to the wicket, Aidan fell into conversation with Edwards, the North Stars opener.

'What you bowl, boy?' the older man asked.

'Swing,' Aidan replied.

'That's good,' came the retort. 'Cos I'm gonna swing you right out of da park.'

Aidan mustered all his strength and roared in with the new ball. His first delivery was indeed a perfect outswinger, which Edwards tried to drive through mid-off, and mistimed. The ball spooned gently to cover, where James O'Herlihy, uncurling himself like a fat tabby in front of the fire, reached up lazily to pluck it from the air. Only he didn't reach up far enough, and let it slip backwards through his fingers to the ground. Aidan was incandescent, with that burning inner rage that only fast bowlers who've just had a catch dropped can summon from the depths of their soul. James gave him a reassuring look as if to say, 'Hey, a chance on the first ball? The cat's among the pigeons now. By the law of averages, there'll be others.'

But there weren't. These weren't pigeons—they were vultures. Aidan's next five balls went screaming for four fours and a two. After six overs, North Stars were 54–0. Aidan was already trying to bowl too fast and haemorrhaging runs. Riaan's spell was more of a steady bleed. There was no seam movement at all unless the ball chanced to hit a crack, so I brought on Dan, our spinner, in place of Aidan. He normally played at a reasonable level, in the top division of the Thames Valley League; maybe he could winkle one of the batsmen out. Dan liked to bowl flat—very flat. The ball came back even flatter, on the way to the boundary. His first over went for 16. The hundred came up an over or two later, and Edwards retired to give the fearsome Larry Babb a go.

There's a scene in the film *Gallipoli* where the West Australian major is given the supremely pointless order to send his men over the top into an annihilating hail of machine-gun fire. 'Can't ask the men to do what I wouldn't do myself,' he mutters, straps on his revolver, and leads them off to their doom. Feeling much the same way, I took the ball from Riaan. I couldn't spin the ball for toffee, but I could toss it up and buy a wicket or perish in the attempt.

'You won't have any trouble with this bloke, mate,' Greg told Larry Babb from behind the stumps. 'He's rubbish.'

As the (albeit reluctant) donor of £1,000 towards his airfare and the only person keeping him from a lynch mob, you'd have thought Greg would have felt a modicum of gratitude towards me; but no, quite the reverse. He had taken profoundly against his benefactor, in the way that self-centred people always do when they think they have discerned a weakness in others. I glared at him in the way Sylvester glares at Tweety Pie, conjuring up a mental vision of his chirpy little frame headless and oven-roasted. As it happens, though, on this occasion he was dead right. I'd hate to give Greg's confidence-sapping remark any credit—rather, the problem was that I hadn't bowled a ball for four months—but I subsequently proceeded to deliver an entire over of full tosses. Bowling with all the menace of Bob the Builder, I supplied six gentle, guileless lobs, each one served with ice cream and a flake on top. It was the worst over I'd ever bowled, against the best batsman I'd ever bowled to. The idea had been to tempt Larry Babb into hitting the ball skyward, a concept with which he readily concurred. The trouble was, he hit the thing skyward wherever the hell he liked. One six cleared the main grandstand and was still rising as it passed the houses on the other side of the road. Even in first-class cricket I'd never seen a hit that big. All in all, I was lucky to get away with conceding just 23 off the over. I'd already given Tom the next over at the other end, on the same principle, and Babb continued with him where he'd left off with me. This time there were three monster sixes. It was men against boys; and the boys were a hell of a sight better than the men. By the end of Tom's over, North Stars had won the match. It was our biggest-ever defeat, and, it goes without saying, our quickest. It was also a timely kick up the arse: we had put no thought into this game, no preparation, no effort. We would have to buck our ideas up even to begin to compete at this level. We had indeed been 'given some licks'.

We weren't too down after the game, though. After all, it had been a fabulous experience just to play in the West Indies, and our hosts were wonderfully friendly and magnanimous in victory. Paul Daniels, still practically break-dancing on the spot, was all for hitting the clubs there and then, and largeing it until dawn, but he was made to wait. The British High Commissioner, bless him, came up with an idea to restore some of our lost honour: a 'boat race'—that is, a beer-drinking relay. Two teams of six line up with a full glass each, but no contestant can start glugging his pint until his predecessor has finished his, and placed his empty glass upside down on his own head to prove it. Oxford and Cambridge it wasn't, but, with our team dominated by several large O'Herlihys, North Stars were never at the races. Indeed, all six Captain Scott beer mugs were finished before the third Bajan was even halfway down his glass. After that we opted for the more reflective pleasures of sitting in the empty grandstand with a plate of chicken and rice and a dodgy fruit drink, chatting to the British High Commissioner and the North Stars players as the sun sank slowly towards the Caribbean. Eventually the sky blushed a rich shade of purple, the palms became picture-postcard silhouettes, the stars winked gorgeously through, and it was time to go home. We found Paul Daniels in the dressing room, curled into a ball on top of the kit, fast asleep.

* * *

The O'Herlihy brothers did, of course, have to go clubbing that night, because they were still in search of the elusive weed. They found it, too, in a sports bag full of big fat $100 wraps, in a dark corner of a nightclub on the west coast.

'Go on, open one,' said Sean. 'I'm not stupid.'

The owner of the sports bag opened one of the wraps for his benefit. It was indeed grade-A stuff, all present and correct. He resealed it and handed it over.

'Hold on,' said Sean. 'This wrap is slightly smaller than the others.'

'Impossible, man,' said the dealer. 'I weighed

them all out myself. They're all exactly the same.'

But Sean was right. His wrap was indeed fractionally smaller than the others.

'I'm telling you, man, they're all the same. If you don't believe me, take one of the others. Any one you like.'

'Thanks. I will.'

Sean put back the undersized wrap and selected one of the others. The dealer pocketed his $100 and vanished into the night. Sean opened the new wrap. It was full of straw.

Now *that* was clever.

'I can't believe it, man,' laughed the porter, back at the Europa Apartments. 'You fell for that? Why didn't you just ask me to get you some? Give me a hundred dollars, I'll bring you a great big bag in the morning.'

Sean handed over another $100. But the next morning the porter was nowhere to be seen. Sean asked at reception what time he was due to come in.

'That guy? He's off for a week now. He took off and said he ain't comin' back till next week.'

As a non-smoker myself, I was rather beginning to enjoy this game. Of course, I'm well aware that there was a dubious moral aspect to the whole escapade: Sean was openly spending money gleaned from the legal profession, an activity that many people find unethical, and which can cause considerable damage to users in the long term. But the harsh fact is that many people do practise law nowadays, and it would be practically impossible to stamp it out.

The next day, our last on Barbados, those of us who were in any state to get up went to inspect the

Test wicket at the Kensington Oval, which frankly would have disgraced a village pitch, then hired a yacht—the Limbo Lady—for a sunset cruise. When we got back to the hotel, it was clear from the gales of hysterical laughter sweeping across the lawns that the O'Herlihys had at last been successful in their quest. The North Stars' number seven, in fact, had come through with the goods. Dan, our ringer, in a tender and emotional moment, had unwisely confessed to having had a wheelchair-bound girlfriend, and to have once enjoyed a romantic picnic with her on the summit of Box Hill. The mental image of Dan turning to fetch the salt just as the wheelchair started to roll imperceptibly forward, and all that would have ensued, had combined with a hundred dollars' worth of the finest Bajan herb to produce an outbreak of literally uncontrollable laughter. They were in that state of being completely unable to stand, and unable to stop their sides aching as the air voided itself from their lungs. They sounded exactly like the audience for a very poor ITV sitcom.

All such fun has its downside, of course, and the following morning it was almost impossible to cajole the sorry-headed bunch out of the wreckage of their bedrooms and into the taxi for the airport. By the time we finally set off, we were running very late. Then, en route, Sean spotted a familiar figure sunning himself contentedly by the roadside.

'Look! It's the guy who fleeced me!'

It was indeed the drug dealer with the sports bag, lounging on a low wall, apparently all on his own.

'Stop the cab. I'm going to kill him!'

Sean would have, too. It took six of us to hold him down, while a stern lecture was collectively administered. We were late for the plane as it was. The last thing we needed was a roadside scuffle with a member of the Barbados criminal fraternity (who might possibly have been armed), and any of his mates who might have been hanging around, unseen, in the vicinity. We drove on, Sean still seething.

At Grantley Adams International Airport we checked our bags through to Buenos Aires via San Juan Puerto Rico and Miami, a nineteen-hour trip all told. But the air miles we'd been looking forward to were withheld from us: they could only have been allocated, it transpired, if the right advance paperwork had been completed in London. It was, apparently, a mistake by British Airways. Well I never. You don't say.

After a brief argument with the check-in clerk, who took away my whole book of tickets (including those for the Buenos Aires–Santiago leg) and wouldn't give them back until remonstrated with, Tom and I had to open the kitbag up for inspection by customs (it was our turn to carry it, according to the nice neat laminated rota he'd drawn up).

'Ho, you a cricket team?' asked the customs man.

'Yup.'

'Where d'you play, then?'

'North Stars.'

'You get some licks?'

'Yeah. We got some licks.'

'I play cricket too. My team went up to North Stars last month. Hoooo boy, we got some licks.'

'Yeah?'
'Yeah.'
Yeah, well. Bet they weren't as big as our licks.

8

Buenos Aires

Curiously, there are almost no flights between the black Caribbean countries and Latin South America. Even Guyana, which is on the South American mainland, and Trinidad, a mere handful of miles offshore, have next to no air links. Presumably the inhabitants of each place figure they've enough palm trees and beaches of their own to bother with anyone else's palm trees and beaches, thank you very much. So we were forced to fly 569 miles north to Puerto Rico, where we landed in driving rain, and from there to head a further 1,031 miles back in the wrong direction to Miami. We had three and a half hours to kill in San Juan's airport—just enough time, I reckoned, to drive into town and back for a Japanese-style tourist excursion. (Never trust anyone who tells you he's a 'traveller'. To be a tourist is the honourable thing.) A very appealing 'Doors of San Juan' tourist poster on the airport wall enticed half the team to come with me, although—as with all those 'Doors of Dublin' posters—such adverts really amount to an admission that there aren't any major attractions on show.

Both Puerto Rico and its capital city were founded by the delightfully named Juan Ponce de

Léon, who was with Columbus when he discovered the island in 1493. Curiously, Ponce named the country San Juan and the city Puerto Rico ('Rich Port'), the two names being mysteriously switched by some unknown scallywag at a later date. American troops pinched the lot from the Spanish in 1898, presumably on the grounds that they were hiding cannons of mass destruction. Quickly they went about their routine business of messing the place up, but in the 1950s came a change of heart. A seven-block-square area within what remained of San Juan's city walls was declared a historic zone, with tax advantages offered to anyone who restored (rather than demolished) one of Ponce's original buildings. As a result, some four hundred of these structures still survive—a carved wooden balcony here, an elegant pastel doorway there—although more often than not they are disfigured by cut-price shoe shops or slot-machine arcades with bright plastic signs. It is the rectangular Spanish street pattern, holding its shape despite the hilly ground underfoot, rather than the architecture, that helps San Juan retain a faint aura of its grand Hispanic past.

Pounding rain made our short stroll well-nigh impossible, so as night fell we repaired to a vaguely tropical-looking bar on a side street, with big electric fans and raffia-clad walls. Four customers, presumably regulars, perched on bar stools; the arrival of five British cricketers not only more than doubled the numbers present, but apparently established some kind of quorum. Solemnly, the Latino barman passed among the nine of us, handing out a variety of percussion instruments. Then he proceeded to the jukebox and switched it on, at deafening volume. The first number to blare out was 'Hotel California', and everything that followed was of a similarly hoary (but, in the circumstances, entirely appropriate) vintage. The entire bar set about a massive percussion jam, while huge old American automobiles cruised slowly through the filmic rain outside. It was brilliant.

'My God,' said Tom. 'We're in an advert!'

We were too. And it was a great ad to be in—much better than comparing washing powders, or driving round endless winding mountain roads in a new Audi because you've forgotten your Biro. Indeed, we became so carried away with the fun of it all that we never even considered the impossibility of finding a taxi back in such dreadful weather. The barman, when it finally crossed our minds, tried phoning for a cab, but there was a ninety-minute wait. There was nothing to do but take our chances in the spearing javelins of rain outside. Immediately it became clear that we had to get out of the city centre, where the streets were flooding fast, the traffic had become gridlocked, and every taxi was taken, and make our way out to the suburbs to find a cab coming in. Blindly, drenched to the skin, we ran east through the stair rods in the general direction of the airport, and found ourselves in the deserted docks. There, by a miracle, was a single lit-up taxi, the only vehicle on a lightless quayside highway. We piled in on top of each other, and made it to the airport with seconds to spare.

Two and a half hours later we were in Miami, still soaked but strolling through US immigration with considerable relief. Or rather nine of us were.

Matthew punctured the mood.

'Bad news, I'm afraid.'

'What is it?'

'Riaan and Aidan have been arrested again.'

*   *   *

There are times, really, when as a Briton one has to be glad of the old 'Her Britannic Majesty's Secretary of State requests and requires . . .' spiel in the UK passport. Personally, I never approved of getting rid of the lordly blue hardback ones. God knows what it must say in the South African passport: 'As a citizen of what was until recently the world's most reviled regime, please feel free to dick me around unto your heart's content, particularly in conjunction with the utter imbeciles who work for British Airways . . .' or words to that effect. BA, it turned out, in clearing up the blue/green-visa-waiver-form mess that had bedevilled Riaan and Aidan's outward journey, had not seen fit to do the same for the return leg. Not only were the pair in custody again, but this time they had 'previous', as a pair of persistent offenders. At least the sun wasn't beating into their plate-glass interrogation box as fatboy went to work again on his two favourite terrorists.

Thank heavens, then, for the reliable unpunctuality of American Airlines. Once again, by the time the mix-up had been sorted out and Riaan and Aidan had been released, our plane should have left. Once again it hadn't. Thank heavens, too, for the ludicrous paucity of staff on American Airlines flights: OK, it may (as with BA) have taken two hours for the drinks trolley to turn up, but, on the plus side, there was nobody about to lay down the law as to where one could or couldn't sleep. I spent a blissful night stretched out on the cabin floor with James O'Herlihy's feet resting on my head. We arrived in Buenos Aires in mid-morning on New Year's Eve, in (of course) driving rain. Not that we cared about a few raindrops, as long as the weather cleared in time for the game. It was New Year's Eve, we were in Buenos Aires, and we were thrilled to the core. The massive annual party the New Yorkers mount in Times Square is famous enough, as is the firework display on the Sydney Harbour Bridge, but what fabulous festivities might the Argentines put on? We already knew where to go. A *porteño* (as the inhabitants of Buenos Aires call themselves) on the plane down had told us to make for the *planetario* at midnight. The big open space before the city's planetarium would be heaving with people, he'd said. There'd be rock bands on a giant stage, and every bar and club would be jam-packed. We couldn't wait.

I spent the day checking out the city for somewhere to eat in the early part of the evening. Downtown Buenos Aires is a grand, dignified, dark metropolis, reminiscent in equal measure of Paris, Vienna and Gotham City. Tall nineteenth-century apartment blocks in carved stone hem the city's narrow avenues. Unfortunately its planners could hardly have legislated for the advent of the motor car, so increasingly these splendid old blocks are being torn down and replaced with concrete skyscrapers set further back to allow for road-widening. In one location, the Avenida 9 de Julio, an entire line of city blocks has been ripped up to create a multi-lane highway that bisects the city from east to west. Buenos Aires, both old and new, is quintessentially European. Among the sumptuous Viennese blocks are Mitteleuropean coffee houses and grandiose Burlington Arcade-style shop ping centres with wrought-iron-and-glass roofs. The Argentines themselves, in spite of the Falklands War, are relentlessly Anglophile. They enjoy polo and rugby. Many of their football teams have English names like 'Arsenal' (although I believe 'Sporting Moron' is a Spanish appellation, and not a reference to Millwall). The city contains a Harrods and a Claridge's Hotel. Even the Argentine skin colouring is pale white, far less obviously Latin than that of, say, the French or the Spanish.

I'd been to the city before, on a travel-journalism job, and had been furnished with a guide for the duration of my stay: Teva, a sweet, birdlike Argentinian lady of eighty-nine (as she proudly informed me). She spoke impeccable English, employing the exact intonations used by Celia Johnson in *Brief Encounter.* She had worshipped the Duke of Edinburgh since his youth ('*such* a handsome man, my dear'), and described the day of his marriage to Princess Elizabeth as the bitterest of her life. Sweet but entirely mad, I told myself. Argentina, Teva informed me, had the lowest proportion of non-whites of any South American country—just 2%. Contrast that with, say, Bolivia's majority of native Americans, or Brazil's huge black population.

'And do you know how we did it?' she said especially sweetly.

'Erm . . . no idea.'

‘We exterminated the Indians with machine guns, in a series of wars. The generals always put the black troops in the front ranks, so they’d all be killed too. Wasn’t that clever?’

I came within an ace—an *ace*—of slapping an eighty-nine-year-old woman. Only the realization that the blow would probably have killed her prevented me from doing so.

Such charming racial-extermination programmes, I should stress, are long past: the Pampas Indians met their hideous fates in the nineteenth century, at around the same time as the North American Indians were being wiped out en masse by US troops. The steady string of military dictators who have controlled Argentina since, terminating in the disastrous reign of General Galtieri, owe more to a historical tradition of *estancia*-owning rural strongmen taking charge of the country than to any predilection towards fascism on the part of its mainly urban citizens. Well, apart from all the sweet, birdlike old ladies, obviously.

Despite this stain on its character, nineteenth-century Buenos Aires is, in places, absolutely lovely. La Boca, the dockside neighbourhood built in the west of the city by dirt-poor Genovese immigrants, is simply stunning. Its houses are principally constructed from corrugated iron, but, because the builders could not afford any paint, they would filch leftover tins from the docks. The result is a riot of fishing-boat colours—yellows, blues, pinks, greens and reds—sometimes all competing for space on the walls of the same house. Later Boca-dwellers have added life-size papier-mâché caricatures of themselves, or of the famous, waving from balconies, beckoning you into perfectly preserved Victorian shopfronts or leaning sleepily on corrugated-iron windowsills. I spotted Juan and Eva Peron, Madonna (who played Evita on screen), a bruised-lipped figure who worryingly resembled Michael Portillo, and of course La Boca's favourite son, Diego Maradona. His original team, Boca Juniors, Buenos Aires's 'Italian' side, has been locked for a century in a bitter rivalry with River Plate (not Rio de la Plata, you'll notice), the city's 'English' side, from the posh northern suburbs. Boca's stadium, La Bombonera—'The Chocolate Box'—towers squarely above the narrow alleys of La Boca, where marching bands squeeze past street tango artists busking for cash. It is a place unlike any other.

Less extravagantly decorated but quietly pretty in its own way was San Telmo, the neighbourhood between La Boca and the centre. Its cobbled streets were thick with old bars, restaurants and antique shops. Here I found an incredible bargain: an original, huge, pre-war Argentinian cinema poster for *Gone With The Wind*, on sale for just forty quid. Forty quid! In London's film-poster shops, even brand-new ones start at £75; classic posters go for sums in the high three figures. This version of *Lo Que El Yento Se Llevo* was almost certainly worth a thousand. I felt a twinge of conscience as I shelled out £40 without informing the vendor what he might have asked me for it, but to be fair, almost everything in Buenos Aires was going for a song. Argentina was just coming out of a severe economic collapse, and the peso was in free fall. We could buy huge three-course steak dinners in elegant restaurants, with a fabulous bottle of Malbec thrown in, for a total bill of £3 a head. A cab ride from one side of the city to the other cost 50p. Brand-new CDs cost £2 each. Our four-star city-centre hotel was charging us just £9 per person. For a few wonderful days in our largely cut-price round-the-world odyssey, we could afford to lord it like Donald Trump. Well, Alan Sugar, anyway.

San Telmo was awash with first-rate drinking places. I chose the Bar Plaza Dorrego to kick off the evening, a turn-of-the-century classic with graffiti'd bar and tables, black-and-white floor tiles, ancient beer bottles lining the walls, and outdoor tables fringing the leafy square outside. But when I made my way back to the hotel (no one else, of course, had been arsed to explore the city at all) I discovered a mutiny in progress.

'Look,' said Aidan, 'I'm all for having a bit of fun on New Year's Eve. But you should have told us about the fancy dress.'

'Fancy *dress*?'

'Yeah. Paul said it was fancy dress.'

Matthew came up.

'Look, Harry, I think I might duck out of tonight, if that's all right. I haven't got a costume, and—'

'What the flying fuck is all this about fancy dress?'

'Well, Paul said—'

I strode off to confront the errant Mr Daniels.

'Don't you think it's a great idea?' he enthused. 'All of us, in fancy dress?'

'No I don't. And, anyway, we're going out in half an hour and nobody has a costume.'

'I have! Look—I brought mine from London!'

Gleefully he produced a full-sized Father Christmas outfit from his rucksack.

'Paul. You can wear that if you really must. But nobody else wants to wear a costume, or has a costume to wear. *Comprende*?'

The insurrection dissolved, we made the Plaza Dorrego for seven. The rain politely backed off as the last sunset of the year shone gold through the open bar windows, the clouds scattering in gorgeous disarray. Some of my team-mates, I admit, were visibly bewildered by my choice. Where were the giant video screens showing old footage of Wayne Rooney? Others nodded their quiet approval. Either way, it was New Year's Eve, we were going to have a good time, and none of us would have to dress as Cardinal Richelieu. At eight o'clock we strolled down the Calle Defensa to the Casa Esteban de Luca restaurant, a pleasant neighbourhood place—indeed, the only place I'd managed to find that was open. Our New Year's Eve banquet was all very nice, the food of a high standard, and the service impeccable. But there was one odd aspect to the proceedings: there was nobody else at all in the restaurant. The place was completely deserted. Where, we asked, were all the other diners?

'Well,' said the manager, 'of course they are not here *yet*.'

Rather mystified, we left the empty restaurant at eleven, and strolled out on to the deserted streets. Every other bar and restaurant seemed shuttered up. There was not a car in sight. San Telmo, obviously, was not the place to be on New Year's Eve. Eventually we located a prowling taxi, which radioed for support, and the two vehicles set off in convoy for the *planetario*, where the inhabitants of San Telmo were presumably already carousing.

But no. The *planetario* was deserted. Every restaurant and bar was shut. It began to drizzle again, morosely, and a low wind scudded across the huge expanse of grass. When quizzed, the taxi drivers merely shrugged their shoulders. Utterly bewildered, we asked to be taken to the Plaza de Mayo, the city's main square. Nothing. Nobody. How about the Plaza San Martin, the other big square in central Buenos Aires? Half the party cavilled at this: it was nearly twelve. They went off to bed in disgust, the evening a ruin. Only Tom, the O'Herlihy brothers and Paul Daniels—still dressed as Father Christmas—ploughed on with me to the Plaza San Martin and the Torre de los Ingleses, a tall, elegant tower donated to the city by the British government in 1910. From there a damp, grassy hill rose up to the north-west, affording an excellent prospect of the eerily deserted city. We made the summit as the tower clock struck twelve, popped open a bottle of champagne we'd brought from the restaurant, and prepared to have our own unilateral mini-celebration. Then, with a rush and a whoosh, a hail of fireworks went off about a quarter of a mile away, behind the trees on the furthest side of the park. We knocked back our drinks and ran.

The fireworks, it transpired, were being let off by one man, a private citizen standing alone in the middle of an empty street. On a balcony high above, a family party was taking place, and kids and grannies were crowding at the rail to watch the rockets burst. With incredible excitement, the toddlers on the balcony realized that their family fireworks had actually summoned forth Father Christmas and his band of helpers.

In halting Spanish, we explained to the man that we were English tourists, and did he know of any public New Year celebrations taking place in the city?

'No,' he said. 'But you can come to our party if you like.'

The poor man really had no choice. His kids were going crazy for Santa. As we ascended in the lift, he explained that he was a colonel in the Argentine army. He had fought as a young lieutenant in the Falklands, where most of his friends had been killed and he had been taken prisoner by 2 Para. He had, he said, been treated so well and with such dignity by his captors that he had formed a lasting admiration for the British military and the British nation. It would be an honour, he said, to have six Brits at his party. His father, he pointed out just as the lift clanged to a stop, was a retired general who'd helped mastermind his country's campaign from the mainland, and had a rather different opinion of the British, but that didn't matter a jot.

The lift doors opened straight on to the apartment.

'I have brought you', announced our host, 'six British guests.'

The old general rose slowly to his feet in dignified outrage, and beckoned to his wife to do the same. Everyone froze. Then, without a word, the pair stalked stiffly out of the party and retired to bed.

The minute they'd gone, there was a relieved exhalation all round and the atmosphere relaxed. The little children ran across to Father Christmas. The colonels (of whom there proved to be a surprising number at the party) jovially poured us all drinks. Eiran and James O'Herlihy noticed an acoustic guitar in the corner, and started to sing and play (they're actually not bad at all). The party started to go with a swing. New Year's Eve in Buenos Aires, it seemed, was not to be a washout after all. After a while, one of the colonels' wives, an exceptionally well-preserved brunette in her mid-forties, cornered Paul Daniels in an unlit doorway and—bizarrely—put her hand up the front of his costume; then she began to stroke his chest in a seductive manner. What was it about Argentines and Father Christmas?

'Please, what is your hotel and your room number?' she breathed huskily into his ear. Paul drunkenly blubbed out the information.

'I shall be there tomorrow night,' she whispered.

'Er . . . righto.'

I'd heard of the Welsh incursions into Argentina, but this was ridiculous. Paul lurched off around the party 'wahay'ing and hissing to the rest of us that he'd scored. Personally, I did not feel this was good news. What if he got caught? The prospect of Daniels strapped to a metal bed frame in a basement cell at Argentine army headquarters, being tortured with an electric cattle prod, was not one that augured well for the future of the tour. Especially as he'd probably organize a whip-round among his captors, to buy them some up-to-date torture equipment. It was not without a degree of relief on my part that things began to wind up around 2 a.m. I got in fast with the thank-you-for-having-us speech. Our host looked utterly bemused.

'Yes, the party is over,' he said. 'But . . . surely the evening is just beginning?'

The party was not closing down, we realized: it was simply relocating to a nearby bar. All of us—kids, grannies, the lot—set off down the street, cricketers shaking our heads wonderingly at the back.

'Hey, are yous lot English?' called a voice behind us, in a perfect Geordie accent. We turned round. A young man stood on the empty, rain-slicked pavement. He was, it turned out, a Newcastle University student called Seb, of mixed Chilean–Argentine parentage, who was home for the holidays. He was, at last, able to furnish answers to the mystery of the vanishing New Year's Eve.

'Us *porteños* divvent normally gan out for the evening till eleven or twelve, but New Year's Eve is different. We like to spend it with us families, like, then gan out afterwards, from two o'clock at the earliest. In a couple of hours' time this place'll be buzzin'. I'll take yers to the Kilkenny, only it's not open yet.'

He gestured to a huge Irish pub on the other side of the road, locked and deserted, its windows dark. It was 2.10 a.m. And it wasn't open yet?

We followed the gaggle of colonels through the doors of another bar, the John John—a JFK theme pub, somewhat bizarrely—that had just thrown open its doors for business. The only other customers were two young girls.

'Mmm . . . *ladies*,' came the suave tones of

Terry-Thomas, a.k.a. Eiran O'Herlihy, at my shoulder.

'And you'd like me to go and talk to them, I suppose?'

Mentally, I donned the broad-brimmed hat and purple leather coat again. The girls turned out to be Cynthia and Ingrid, a lawyer and a sports teacher respectively.

'Hello,' came a voice at my elbow, almost immediately.

'Hell*eau*,' came its companion.

I felt the old, familiar sensation that accordions experience every day of their working lives, and left them to it.

At four o'clock we said goodbye to the colonels, who took their wives and kids off to bed (I had to stand on the white fringe of Daniels's red cloak to prevent him going with them) and we transferred to the Kilkenny, with Seb, Cynthia and Ingrid in tow. By this time we'd been joined by the other six members of our team, who'd been roused from their beds by urgent phone calls. The Kilkenny, so unpromisingly dark and shuttered just two hours before, was absolutely heaving. It was an enormous place, and there must have been a good thousand people or more in there. The music was ear-splitting (most of it apparently laid on by Guns 'n' Roses), and the bar staff were whizzing forth drinks at breakneck speed. Barely-clad Argentinian girls gyrated on the dance floor, sporting risqué English tattoos immediately above their low-slung belts. 'Show me the money,' read one (at the front). 'Insert coin here,' read another (at the back), right above a visible centimetre of shapely bum-cleavage. Normally I wouldn't go within a hundred yards of a bogus Irish bar, unless it was actually within the borders of the Irish Republic, but the Kilkenny was clearly the number-one place to be on New Year's Eve. Also, let's not forget, we'd been drinking steadily for nine hours now: frankly, in the state we were in, anywhere would have seemed like the number-one place to be. Immediately, the single players made a cavalry charge into the massed ranks of women on the dance floor, while the attached players pogoed violently (and rather tragically) with each other in a corner. Well, it seemed like great fun at the time. Riaan, though, who was unquestionably the staunchest single man among us, also happened to be a six-foot-three-inch blond, qualities which made him an unwilling magnet for the collected womanhood of Buenos Aires. Wherever he went, at least three girls hung from his arms, beseeching him to make free with their favours. Moral discomfort contorted his features. He had the look of a monk who'd just parachuted into a nudist colony.

Also successful with the opposite sex (for the second time that evening) was Paul Daniels, who had wisely stuffed the Santa costume into his rucksack and changed into civvies. He racked up the first point of our sexual league table by entwining himself around a pretty young Argentine who spoke next to no English. The progress of this romantic attachment was unfortunately brought to an abrupt halt, however: the minute he put his rucksack containing his Father Christmas outfit down to snog her, a thief grabbed it and ran off into the night. What *was* it about Argentines and Father Christmas?

By 10 a.m. the music was still pounding, the Kilkenny was still heaving, and all of us were utterly, hopelessly, irredeemably drunk. Even Riaan, his moral composure finally overwhelmed, was wrapped around a girl in a corner seat. Tom and I decided to call it a night, and emerged into the bright sunshine of an Argentinian New Year's Day. Daniels staggered out after us, almost literally blind drunk, followed by his new girlfriend.

'Hotel?' she asked, hopefully, in her best broken English.

' 'S very kind, but I've got one, thank you,' slurred Paul. ' 'S nice.'

And with that he turned and lurched off in the wrong direction, leaving her standing alone and bewildered in the street.

* * *

I surfaced at about one o'clock and managed to rouse Tom. Both of us felt as if a road gang were drilling our brains out. It was the single worst hangover of my life. I thought I was going to throw up, every step I took. We tried a few other people's rooms, but the results were no better. The door to Eiran's room was opened by both Cynthia *and* Ingrid. *That figures*, I thought. In the room shared by Riaan and Paul Daniels, the Welshman was out cold. The young South African, meanwhile, was in a state of moral shock that far outweighed any physical ill effects.

'I can't believe what I did,' he moaned. 'I've been unfaithful to my girlfriend. I'm utterly worthless.'

'No you haven't,' we reassured him. 'You got very drunk and kissed a stranger. That's all. Just forget about it.'

'I've been tempted by Satan. The Devil sent her to tempt me, and I failed that test.'

'Riaan, the Devil does not go about dispatching strange women to tempt nice Christian boys to misbehave. Do you seriously think the door is going to fly open and some sex-crazed woman sent by Satan is going to barge in and tie you to the bed?'

'I've got to ring my girlfriend and tell her what I did, and beg her forgiveness.'

'What? No, Riaan, that would be a very bad idea. What you have to do is forgive *yourself* and never do it again.'

'You don't understand. I can't live a lie for the rest of my life!'

Tom and I left him to his private agonies, and located a *parrilla* that was open for lunch. A giant doorstep steak and chips, we thought, might top up a few missing carbohydrates or two. Afterwards we took a train out to Tigre, which is the Argentinian equivalent of Henley-on-Thames. We'd known Argentina was Anglophile, but Tigre was ridiculous. Red phone boxes, rowing eights on the river, nice little houses with lawns sloping down to the water, a Victorian Gothic clubhouse with a striped awning and the words 'Buenos Aires Rowing Club, 1878' carved (in English) into the stone façade, brightly painted pleasureboats, families milling about eating ice-cream cones—it was a perfect facsimile of a lovely summer's day out in Berkshire. OK, so the river water was suspiciously chocolate brown (these were the estuary channels of the Paraná, not the upper reaches of the Thames), and some of the trees overhanging the dappled waters were suspiciously spiky and tropical-looking, but the overall impression was that we'd wandered on to a film set. A more delightfully relaxing spot to take two thundering hangovers for a day out would be hard to imagine.

We returned to Buenos Aires after nightfall, just as a drama was enacting itself at our hotel. Paul Daniels, having finally surfaced, had taken himself off to the headquarters of the Buenos Aires Police to demand a full-scale criminal investigation into the theft of his Father Christmas costume. The fact that he spoke not a word of Spanish, and the local police not a single word of English, made this an extremely long and no doubt highly entertaining encounter. But while he was over at police HQ making dramatic pronouncements like 'El costuma de Santa Claus . . . est volare!' to the exasperated inspectors, the libidinous colonel's wife was arriving at the team hotel, done up to the nines and determined to improve her acquaintance of the previous evening. She made her way straight up to Daniels's room in the lift, wearing only a strappy little dress and high heels. Arriving outside the room, she flung open the door to reveal a sleeping figure curled in its bed. 'I want you!' she announced lasciviously, and began to advance. But it was not, of course, Paul Daniels beneath the sheets: it was Riaan, who had retired early, to confront mentally the challenges that Satan had in store for him. Would the Devil send another temptress to lead him off the straight and narrow? As his room door flew open, the young South

African's screams could be heard echoing throughout the hotel corridors.

* * *

The day of the game dawned blazing hot and sunny, and the team bus ferried us, our kit, Seb, Cynthia and Ingrid to the moneyed northern suburbs where the Argentinian version of the Hurlingham Club was situated. A substantial two-storey Victorian brick building set amid perfect emerald lawns, it was at its most impressive inside, where it resembled a spacious, extravagant old public school. QV herself scowled down, gilt-framed, upon an elegant world of wood panelling and parquet flooring, dotted with original grandfather clocks and mottled photos of ancient teams with improbable moustaches. The marvellously austere billiard room contained a veritable palisade of century-old cues, together with a yellowed poster that offered to explain to bewildered billiards players the newfangled rules of 'Russian Pool, or Indian Pool, or "Slosh"'. Technically, the Hurlingham Club was closed for the Christmas and New Year period, its corridors deserted, but our presence there had been negotiated as a special favour by the wonderful duo who run Argentinian cricket, Grant Dugmore and Lucy Mulcahy. It was they who, not knowing us from Adam, had gone out of their way to arrange hotel, fixture, transportation, the lot: Dugmore had even picked us up from the airport personally. A South African, he was no mean cricketer himself, having once been on the books of Western Province. The Argentinian league (which featured such gloriously named sides as St Albans and Old Georgians) was also in Yuletide abeyance, he told us, but he had put together a one-off Buenos Aires XI for the game. Who was in it? I wondered.

'Well, most of them—seven or eight—are from the national side.'

This was not good news. Argentina had recently distinguished itself at the ICC Trophy, defeating Holland, and had come close to qualifying for the World Cup.

'Then there's me,' he went on, 'then a couple of cricket coaches attached to the ACA, club pros, one each from England and Australia.'

Marvellous. Another whole country to pit ourselves against, leavened with three professional cricketers. But we were determined to have a go, and to put the disaster of North Stars behind us. We'd beaten an entire nation before, after all. Albeit on a Tuesday. And we weren't jetlagged—we'd actually travelled back slightly eastward, to within three hours of UK time. We were just very, very hung-over.

I won the toss and decided to bowl. The wicket was firm and bouncy, but the outfield—still very soggy from the recent rain—would make scoring difficult. With luck, it might dry out to our advantage during the day. We watched some of the Argentines practise. They were fit and athletic, with gold bracelets, neck charms, long hair held in check by hairbands—well, you've seen the Argentinian national football side. Imagine Captain Jack Sparrow from *Pirates of the Caribbean*, times eight.

'Argentinian men do not love women,' sniffed

Cynthia. 'They love only themselves.'

'Themselves in mirror,' added Ingrid.

The Argentinian batsmen were certainly proficient, but they had reckoned without Riaan having had the fear of God put into him. The big South African bowled his massive heart out, and ripped the top of the home side's batting to pieces. Aidan, at the other end, wasn't having quite so much luck: as Paterlini, the Buenos Aires opener, whistled a sweet off drive straight past him to the boundary, Aidan applauded.

'Good shot,' he said.

'Go fetch your sheet,' replied Paterlini, lip curled, in full Falklands-avenging mode. 'Engleeshman.'

'What did you say?' said Aidan, squaring up. I wasn't sure whether the 'sheet' or the 'Engleeshman' had offended him most, but I hurried forward to prevent a full-scale diplomatic incident anyway. Tempers placated, we resumed.

The fifth Argentinian wicket went down on 50, which brought Grant Dugmore to the crease. Paul Daniels called the whole team together for a huddle. Wasn't this my job? I wondered.

'Listen, you lot,' he said. 'This is their best player. He's probably going to give us one chance at best. It might be a tricky chance, but we have to take it. Do you understand? When he gives us that one chance, *we have to take it*.'

A few balls later, Aidan bowled Dugmore one of his cunning slower balls, which he obligingly skied to midwicket. There, underneath the rapidly falling cherry, was Daniels himself, circling the descent like a drunk trying to focus on a clock tower. Finally he got himself in line, and pouched the chance with both hands. Then, with a massive *clack*, the ball bounced off his rigid plastic finger-guard, squeezed out of his hands, and fell to the floor. We held our heads.

Paul had been prophetic, at least. An hour later, with the score on 99–5 and Dugmore advancing on 50, we had cause to reflect on his prescience. But we were not done yet. Everybody weighed in with a wicket or two, especially Dan, our spinner, who snaffled Dugmore on 49, whereupon the Argentinian tail folded suddenly. Both the professional overseas coaches were dismissed for 0. Buenos Aires were skittled for 120, which gave us a fighting chance. Sean and I went in to the lovely old red-and-cream dressing room to pad up, and to psych ourselves up for the task of meeting the Argentinian fast bowlers head-on.

I'd faced fast*ish* bowling in my life before, of course, but the only real fast bowling—by professional standards—that I'd ever encountered was in 1999, when the editor of the Test-match programme asked me to go into an outdoor net for twenty minutes against Darren Gough. 'The village batsman v. the pro' was the idea. The day selected was the Monday after the group stages of the World Cup, when England were expected to have secured their place in the quarter-finals by easing past Zimbabwe, and were to spend a day at the Oval, relaxing in the company of the press. Unfortunately, though, it was Zimbabwe who had eased past England, and our stars who were having to explain to the tabloid assault pack why they had gone out of a World Cup on home territory at the first hurdle. Gough, in particular, was in a foul mood, and refused to speak to me or even acknowledge my nervous attempt at a handshake.

'This the journalist?' he asked the PR, curtly.

'I'm not a journalist,' I said, truthfully but unconvincingly.

He did not reply.

I went into the net. A couple of England players—Dean Headley, Alec Stewart—rolled along to watch. Gough ran in with that familiar pumping run, his arm windmilled, the ball shot forth like a bullet from a gun, bit into the wicket, and leaped. I had just enough time to get in behind it, hopefully with bat straight, left elbow high and head steady. It seemed amazingly quick. The ball cannoned into the middle of the bat and plopped back harmlessly on to the turf. Gough turned his back contemptuously and ran in again. Same ball, same result. The third ball, though, was different. This one was dug in a bit shorter, spearing upward towards my throat. I tried to get the bat higher, in the fraction of a second available for adjustment. The ball whacked into my right thumb with a tremendous, crushing impact. I pulled off my glove. The plastic thumb-guard came out, split into two pieces. My thumbnail, too, was split lengthways in two, and bright crimson blood eased in a steady drip-drip through the break.

'Steady on, Darren,' said Alec Stewart under his breath. 'He's only an amateur.'

'Sorry, mate,' offered Gough shortly, the first time he had spoken to me.

'Do you want to stop?' asked the PR.

No, no, I insisted. I was going on with this.

After that, in fact, Darren Gough was sweetness and light for the rest of the day. He certainly bowled nothing remotely as fast as that again. I was stupidly proud of the fact that I wasn't bowled, nor did I nick one, for the rest of the session. This was foolish pride, however, for a number of reasons. First, the surface was immaculate. Secondly, I didn't dare hit the thing in anger, in case Darren's new sunny mood evaporated once more. Thirdly, and most importantly, every time I played a defensive shot and didn't *exactly* middle the ball it would fly off horizontally in the direction of third or fourth slip at 70 m.p.h. In a village game, of course, there'd be no third or fourth slip, and those semi-middled soft-handed defensives would have fallen harmlessly to one side. But I was uncomfortably aware that in a real game, a first-class game, Darren Gough would—in truth—have dismissed me over and over again.

I couldn't help reflecting on this as we made our way to the crease at the Hurlingham Club, to be greeted by a cordon of four slips and a gully, all placed nearly twenty yards back from the stumps. Even more pressing was the now-searing afternoon heat, touching 100°, which was making me sweat buckets inside my unfamiliar helmet: hot salt water was funnelling through my hair, trickling down my forehead, and pooling in my eyes, making them sting. Facing Darren Gough, or the bowling machine at Lord's, I'd airily put a helmet on at the crease. I'd never actually tried to walk wearing one, let alone run. Here the thing clanked noisily with every step, every movement I made, however slight. My vision was restricted to a narrow, glaring letterbox of light, made intermittently out of focus by the film of hot sweat. The bowler's nickname was 'Shaggy', and as I took guard the Argentines geed him up, clapping and yapping and jabbering at each other in Spanish.

'Vamos, Shaggy!'

'Hola, Shaggy-baby!'

'Go, Shags!'

Shaggy scythed in, a long, loping run-up. The ball thumped into the deck. It was what I expected—just short of a length, seaming away towards the slips—but just a touch too wide. Leaving it would have been the safe option, but I opted for a tad more aggression. It sat up nicely, and I cut it behind point, where it pulled up for a single in the sodden grass. Not a bad start. Sean came to the crease. A few immaculate backward defensives later, a ball bit deeper into the turf crust, diverted sharply, and flew horizontally at speed to fourth slip, where Grant Dugmore dived to hold a fabulous catch. 1–1.

Eiran came in next, and together we put on twenty-five or so runs, but all the work was his. The difference from our net session at Lord's could not have been more pronounced. Unlike the bowling machine, Shaggy and his fellow opener wouldn't let me settle, mixing up the away-seamers with foot-crunching inswingers and the like. At such speeds, it was all I could do to adjust in time without fending the ball to the hungry slips. Eiran, though, was a revelation. Batting helmetless, he seemed to relish the succession of deliveries rearing up towards his face; ducking inside them, he would swat them contemptuously away behind square. Our total began to mount. My own luck, though, could not last: finally a ball flashed horizontally to the far end of the slip cordon, where a dark-haired figure swooped through the air to hold the catch. Dugmore again.

Matthew and Aidan kept Eiran company briefly,

until, with our score on 62–4, disaster struck. Through sheer exhaustion Eiran misjudged a quick away-seamer, and once again the slips did their work. His dismissal brought Paul Daniels to the crease. Daniels was—if anything—even more nervous than he had been in Barbados; jumpy, jittery and unable to settle. This time we really needed him to stick around, to contribute something, but it was clear that his nerves were utterly shot. A few balls later he was gobbled up at third slip. Tom came and went just as quickly, and before long we were reeling at 77–7, still forty-four runs short of a winning total.

We found a new hero in the shape of James O'Herlihy, who took over where his brother had left off. Dan contributed four runs to a partnership of 17, while Riaan added six out of the next seven. Both fell to the slips, who had now held seven victims between them, Dugmore pouching no fewer than four. By the time Greg came out to join James at the wicket, we needed 14 to win with one wicket remaining. Gradually the score advanced: 107 . . . 109 . . . 112 . . . 113. Puffing fatly for breath in the heat, James rested on his bat handle. The Argentines brought Shaggy back.

'Vamos, Shaggy!'

'Hola, Shaggy-baby!'

'Go, Shags!'

James took guard. Shaggy roared in off his full run-up. It was an in-seamer, quick, beautiful. It kept hideously low, the first bad bounce of the day. James's middle stump lay flattened in the dust. We had lost by seven runs.

* * *

Our momentous encounter at an end, and the earlier exhortation to 'Go fetch your sheet' notwithstanding, the Argentines proved as delightful as their Caribbean counterparts. They produced cases of beer all round, and plenty of free dope for the O'Herlihy brothers; we held a jolly, impromptu party on the beautiful sunlit Hurlingham lawns. It is often the way: the craziest, angriest cricketers on the field are often the most sweet-natured off it. Conversely, the nicest, most charming players (rather like avuncular TV presenters) are usually the ones to watch when the whites are off. Dear old George, one of our favourite Charlton-on-Otmoor players from many years ago, was one such. A charming old rural buffer who seemingly wouldn't hurt a fly, he vanished from the team rather suddenly one year. He had, it seemed, made himself blind drunk, lain in wait for his wife at a bus shelter, attempted to murder her (unsuccessfully) with a pair of kitchen scissors, and then run into a nearby field and given himself up to a combine harvester, under the misapprehension that the large red object before him was in fact God.

Our party at the Hurlingham proceeded apace with another 'boat race', in which the Argentines were duly trounced, but the event was spoiled slightly for me by the arrival of an unexpected guest: a journalist from the *Buenos Aires Herald*, the city's English newspaper, named David Parsons. A stiff old gentleman with a liver-spotted bald head and hooded eyes, he took me aside to interview me for a good hour or so about our tour, what we thought of Buenos Aires, and so on. I blathered aimlessly in reply, rather wishing I could get back to the party, while Eiran splashed happily in the swimming pool at our feet. There was something odd about the man, his curious Anglo-Argentine accent (which put me in mind of the infamous Teva), and the interest he was taking in Eiran's aquatic cavortings. In fact, when we finally saw his published piece, it consisted only of a single paragraph: a diary story, wondering whether the members of the Hurlingham Club would be happy to discover that someone with 'tinted skin' had been using the club pool during the Christmas break. It was an unpleasant realization to discover that my instincts regarding Mr Parsons had been correct. I still don't believe, by and large, that Argentina is a racist country; but then perhaps it's worth mentioning that one of the most popular chocolate bars on sale there is called a 'Rhodesia'.

For me, the near-complete absence of racism is one of the things that makes cricket such a wonderful sport. The all-time great players, for instance, have earned international reverence in equal measure. White cricket fans would be as excited to meet Vivian Richards as black fans would be to meet Sachin Tendulkar, as Asian fans would be to meet Shane Warne. I can't think of another sport where this attitude would so comprehensively apply. In a quarter of a century of playing village cricket, I've only once encountered racist opposition at an English ground: that was at a village in Sussex, a gorgeous chocolate-box vision of a ground, where the local side had sadly been colonized by a family bearing bulldog tattoos and the like. We turned up one year with a South African and a black opening bowler.

'Fuckin' South Africans. Don't want no fuckin' South African c**ts here,' said the family patriarch to no one in particular. Was he an old Communist, I wondered, unable to tear himself away from an apartheid-era view of the world? Then, come the second over, our black bowler took over.

'Fuckin' coons. Don't want no fuckin' black bastards here,' he muttered.

We obliged him by not returning the following year. He was, we were informed by one of his embarrassed team-mates, a local police constable by profession.

* * *

On our last full day on the South American continent, Tom and Paul obligingly joined me on a short flight across the estuary of the River Plate to Montevideo, in Uruguay, a city I needed to visit in order to research a novel I was writing. The place was fascinating: a tatty and run-down metropolis with rusty 1950s cars cruising up and down, like Buenos Aires's Midwestern cousin. A jutting finger of land ends in the old port, where the *Mercado del Puerto* clusters about a decaying English clock beneath an ornate cast-iron roof: here we found *parrilladas* by the score, endless lines of charcoal barbecues, hundreds of yards long in all, heaving with monster sausages, rack ribs and giant slab steaks. All one had to do was take a pew, summon a few beers, and before long you'd be facing more meat than any human being could eat, together with a total bill for a quid. After lunch we visited the fort, then the skyscraper-fronted beach, all fourteen miles of it, where impossibly good-looking women posed in thong bikinis while their boyfriends played beach football. At first glance it resembled the famous beachfronts of Copacabana or Ipanema in Rio, but up close there was one huge, weird difference: the water. The waves that furled on to the beach were not Atlantic sea water, but fresh water from the River Plate. It was like swimming in hot, brown tea—an extremely peculiar sensation indeed.

Back in Buenos Aires for our last night, we went dining in Las Canitas, a warm, lit-up street of open-air brasseries and restaurants, and had a rather belated but wonderful thought. If a really good bottle of Malbec—worth, say, £20 in London—cost just £1 here, then what the hell could we get for £20? We decided to find out. The results were, well, incredible. Mouth-watering, delicious, such adjectives cannot do justice to the honeyed nectar—three bottles of it—that we poured down our throats that night. In fact I was still necking a fourth bottle at the airport the next day, my *Gone with the Wind* poster rolled gingerly in the other hand, as we prepared to board our connecting flight to Santiago.

By now I was beginning to view airport check-ins with trepidation, wondering what new tricks the distant gremlins at British Airways had up their sleeves. Needless to say, they and their One World pals did not disappoint. This time it was Tom's turn to suffer. The check-in clerk at Bridgetown who had tried unsuccessfully to take away my Buenos Aires–Santiago ticket had, it turned out, successfully sequestered Tom's. The Buenos Aires airport staff were unequivocal: Tom could not board the flight, even thought he had the receipt, even though it was not his mistake. He would have to pay for the whole round-the-world ticket again, in full. It was more money than we had between us. The plane was due to leave in under two hours. There were no alternatives. We were in despair. Tom, it appeared, would have to spent the rest of his life in Argentina. Well, I suppose there are worse fates.

But there *was* one tiny chink of light. One of the check-in girls busy explaining the impossibility of our situation was exceptionally pretty. There was only one thing for it: we sent for Eiran. Big puppy eyes, Michael Bolton hair . . . they like that sort of thing in Argentina, don't they? If only we still had the Father Christmas costume. After an hour and a half of smooching, cajoling, complimenting and hard bargaining, he had worn her down. If Tom stumped up the £177 single fare to Santiago, he could board the plane. We scrabbled together our cash. The boarding gate had already shut, so she radioed ahead to clear the way. A mad dash followed, as we raced after her through the airport. For what seemed like the umpteenth time on the trip, we made it to our seats with seconds to spare. Eiran planted a huge smacker on the girl's lips just before the plane door was heaved shut, and we lifted off into the setting sun towards Santiago.

9

Down Under

On a packed Saturday night at Santiago's international airport, we did our best to locate the queue for the Auckland flight—the only flight, you'll remember, said by British Airways to be crossing the Pacific that day. But we couldn't find it. The only queue we could find was the massive great line for the Santiago-to-Sydney jumbo. Eventually we got to the front.

'Excuse me, is this the flight to Auckland?'

'Well, it stops in Auckland, at 0425, but nobody ever gets off there. Most people prefer to fly on to Sydney.'

You don't say. Well strike me down.

We were, it turned out, the only eleven people booked to get off the plane in the middle of a damp New Zealand night. Even here, on the other side of the world, the tendrils of British Airways' utter uselessness had reached out to strangle us. The supposedly non-existent flight to Sydney was not only here but heaving with happy punters. Perhaps we might yet change things? Perhaps we might still get to catch the last day of the Sydney Test, which was shaping up for a thrilling England win? We explained our situation and asked to be allowed to fly straight to Sydney instead.

'Well, your luggage can fly straight to Sydney, but you can't. The booking conditions of your ticket stipulate that you can't change your seats out of Auckland until you're actually in Auckland.'

'So we'll have to leave our luggage on board, get off at four-thirty in the morning, and beg to be allowed back into our seats?'

'Yes.'

I could almost see Sheila's mocking face, grinning at me from 7,248 miles away. There was nothing for it but to spin the BA roulette wheel of incompetence one more time, and see where the silver ball landed. It had to be worth a try. The only slight consolations were that we would be well rested by Auckland—the eight-hour jetlag would see to that, for Auckland's small hours corresponded to Chile's lunchtime—and that in Lan-Chile we had finally found a plush, comfortable carrier with a surfeit of extremely hospitable staff, who weren't mysteriously dressed in uniforms cut from someone's granny's curtains. Lan-Chile were punctual too—none of that stacked-up-over-Heathrow-for-three-hours nonsense—so we were able to touch down at Auckland Airport bang on time, in (you've guessed it) sheeting rain.

Almost as the wheels touched tarmac, we hared our way to the British Airways transfer desk. We didn't have much time: our flight shut its doors again at 4.50 a.m. As rapidly as we could, we blurted out our story to the whey-faced *apparatchik* behind the desk and asked for our tickets to be altered so that we could reboard.

'I'm sorry, but this counter doesn't open until 5 a.m.'

'Yes, but the flight closes at ten to five. If you don't help us, we'll miss it.'

'As I believe I just said, this counter doesn't open until 5 a.m.'

'Then how are we supposed to board a flight that shuts at ten to five?'

He gave us an especially smug look.

'You should have thought of that yesterday, shouldn't you?'

'Is there anyone else who can help us?'

'You are at the correct counter. But, as I have already indicated, it doesn't open until 5 a.m. Now, if you'll excuse me . . .'

It took the most enormous effort of will to refrain from reknotting the man's tie, thereby altering his neck hole from a size 16 to something about sixteen sizes smaller. Disconsolately, we made our way through the deserted baggage hall, to be greeted by the sight of our luggage (which had supposedly stayed on the plane) spinning mockingly about the carousel. So, if we had managed to reboard the flight to Sydney, we'd have arrived there without any luggage. The cloud in this silver lining, of course, was that we'd now have to cart it round Auckland with us for the day.

The last hurdle to be surmounted was immigration, where a weensy problem arose. Dope had been as ludicrously cheap as everything else in Buenos Aires, and the O'Herlihy brothers had over-indulged with their usual gusto. The whole team had held one of them upside down and shaken him before boarding the flight, to ensure that no leftover supplies still lurked in inside pockets or similar places of refuge. Unfortunately, we had reckoned without his habit of stuffing handfuls of the stuff straight into his coat pockets. The linings must have been shot through with dried strands of weed, for, the moment he went near New Zealand passport control, every sniffer dog in the place went berserk—yapping, barking, licking, straining to get near him.

'I'm, er—I'm very popular with dogs,' he explained sheepishly to the phalanx of burly handlers gathered around him. 'Put me anywhere near a dog, this always happens.'

Personally, it was his Pepsodent smile as he said this that I found the least convincing. By some miracle, he was eventually released by the authorities, presumably because—unlike their Miami counterparts—they could find no sadistic pleasure in keeping him there. The rest of us, meanwhile, took a bus to downtown Auckland, a space-age confection of concrete, glass and steel masts when viewed from a distance, but up close a drab, featureless world of closed red-brick shopping centres. The bus dropped us immediately outside a polyester-uniform store called Neat 'n' Trim, which seemed to me to sum up everything wrong about New Zealand. Not that it isn't a fine country, and not that the sight of Mount Cook on a sunny day isn't enough to take a man's breath away, but having to press your body against a polyester-uniform display to avoid gusting rain sweeping through an empty shopping centre at 6 a.m. does tend to take the gloss off the *Lord of the Rings* side of things. A shop up the road, even more excruciatingly, was called Shampoo 'n' Stuff.

Here, on this lonely corner, we said our goodbyes to Aidan, as he began his gigantic solo odyssey around northern Asia. His big frame shook with emotion.

'Win it for me, boys,' he urged.

'We'll burst every sinew.'

'Just watch us go, Aidan.'

'We'll do our damnedest with ten men, mate. Who knows, maybe the Aussies will lend us their star player?'

Later, I cornered Greg on this very point.

'Greg, when we get to Sydney, can you give your mates in Perth a call, and see if they can provide us with a decent spare player in Aidan's place?'

'Sure, I could make that call.'

'Good. Let me know what they say.'

'I mean, I could make that call, if there's a quid pro quo.'

'What do you mean?'

'Well, I've put in a lot of work, organizing this match against my old team, and I've come a long way to play in it.'

'Like most of us, yes.'

'Well, if you're asking me to do any *more* organizing, like trying to find a twelfth man, then it's only fair that I be rewarded.'

'*Rewarded?* Rewarded with what?'

'I should captain the side.'

I reflected on this for a picosecond or two.

'You know what, Greg? You can fuck off. We'll play with ten.'

* * *

Our damp day in Auckland came up trumps in the end. Tom, Dan, Matthew and I took the ferry to Devonport, where we roused the staff of the Esplanade Hotel (a stately Victorian pile) for breakfast. This was actually our third breakfast of the day, as by now it was the middle of the afternoon in Buenos Aires, but it was far and away the best. In fact I'd go so far as to say it was the best breakfast I've ever had: a delicious, warm crayfish omelette, the fresh crayfish swathed in melted butter and hollandaise sauce within, the whole topped with toasted caraway seeds and chopped parsley, with a glass of Buck's Fizz on the side. If you're ever in Devonport ... After breakfast we went round the corner to Bryan Jackson's museum. Jackson is a maniac who is congenitally unable to throw anything away: his cavernous museum contains every ancient household object you can think of, from spark plugs and house bricks to the ceramic insulators from telephone poles. More specifically, he has also preserved such gems as the front page of the newspaper from the day the *Titanic* sank, which I suppose must make Mr Jackson about 127 years old. As we dawdled around the displays, Andrew Caddick was busy annihilating the Australian batting in front of a baying crowd of England fans in Sydney, but, hey, we had ceramic telephone insulators to look at. After that we went down to the stone pier and watched Tom do impressions of a storm-tossed Meryl Streep in *The French Lieutenant's Woman*. It was that sort of day.

We finally landed in Sydney just as rain set in for the evening, our fifth consecutive rain-soaked arrival. Sydney was only a rest stop really, preparatory to the more serious business awaiting us in Perth, but Greg, who was within touching distance of home territory, was determined to show us the ropes. We went out for a group meal that night in Potts Point. Just as I was perusing my menu, I felt two hands lasciviously massage my shoulders.

'Well *hello*,' said the campest voice in world

history. 'And what can I get *you* gentlemen?'

When the waiter had taken our orders, we rounded on Greg.

'So, what happened to "No poofs in Oz" then, Greg?'

'Well yeah, of course, there are a few poofs in *Sydney*—everybody knows that. But that's just *Sydney*. There aren't any anywhere else. There aren't any poofs in *Perth*, that's for sure. Just you wait and see.'

Back at the hotel, Matthew got the phone book out. It was time, after half a century of waiting, to track down his errant father. As he flicked through to the right page, his brow furrowed.

'What is it?' I asked.

'It's just . . . there aren't many Radfords in London. Or New York for that matter. But there are'—he gulped—'rather a lot in Sydney.'

'Good luck,' I said, and left him to it.

*   *   *

With a day to spare to sample the glories of New South Wales, we decided to compensate ourselves for missing out on the Test by hiring a car and following England to Bowral, a small upcountry ground where they were playing a one-day game against the Don Bradman XI. With the international one-dayers coming up, it was the England players' chance to stake a claim for inclusion in the side. Bowral is where Bradman was brought up and first played cricket, and it is hard not to conclude that but for this happy accident it would be a forgotten town. If Bowral was a person, it would be Thora Hird. It is a place of retirement homes, medical centres and doctors' surgeries: in Bowral, death seems ever-present. Also, despite its leafy hedges, Bowral is a town of flies. Everyone in this part of Australia, it appears, has their own personal fly. It's not yours to keep, you understand: you just get to borrow it until the next funeral.

The game, it transpired, was a sell-out, and what's more the police weren't letting anyone without a ticket within a hundred yards of the ground. A humiliating hour and a half followed, wheedling at every passing fan in the hope of spare tickets, but eventually we had bought the requisite number. We were in, and we soon found a good position, right by the boundary rope, in the sunshine. England batted first, but despite their Sydney heroics it was clear from the start that in the one-day game they were out of their depth. Ronnie Irani, in particular, looked nervous and out of touch. Perhaps he'd been put off after being introduced by the local announcer as 'Ronnie Irony'. Mind you, a similar sort of introduction hadn't seemed to bother 'Oasis Shah'. Only when Adam Hollioake came in did matters pick up. Suddenly the Australian bowlers looked ordinary, as Hollioake clattered them effortlessly about the park, on his way to a superb unbeaten 50. It will come as no surprise to be reminded, therefore, that it was Irani and not Hollioake who was given the all-rounder's berth for the subsequent internationals, with unhappy results.

At the tea interval, the crowd swarmed good-humouredly over the pitch, across the wicket and even into the pavilion, hunting for autographs. Matthew queued to get Steve Waugh's signature for his son Cosmo, and Paul Daniels queued to obtain it for himself. Paul's like that—the type of big, beaming, bouncing chump who can happily queue up in a line of kids to have his bat signed. Perhaps it's because he's a Welsh boyo. Being excruciatingly English, I can't do anything of the sort. I'm always reminded of a line (inexplicably cut) from the film *Monty Python and the Holy Grail*, where King Arthur, having received his divinely appointed quest, sheepishly asks for God's autograph. 'Er . . . it's for my sister,' he says.

So I waited outside, and watched as a kilted bagpipe band marched on, trouncing various Scottish reels in the process.

'Are you real Scotsmen, or Australian Scotsmen?' I asked one of the pipers politely, in a break between numbers.

'We're real fucking Scotsmen,' he growled back angrily, in the broadest of Aussie accents.

Served me right, I suppose.

After tea England put up a modicum of resistance, but the game was over from the minute Mark Waugh strode to the crease. Waugh was imperious, utterly destroying the English bowling as he advanced to a quite superb unbeaten century. Cutting, pulling, driving—never have I seen a batsman so in command at the top level. It will come as no surprise to be reminded, therefore, that Mark Waugh was pointedly omitted for the subsequent internationals. Where *would* selectors be without these trial games?

By the end of the match the temperature had plummeted, as it is wont to do upcountry, and we were shivering in our shorts. Suddenly it was like spring in Oxfordshire (and the Captain Scott XI *has* had more than one game snowed off in its time). We willed England to let themselves be put to sleep quickly, then piled off to the pub in the car. The pub we chose from our guidebook, the Surveyor-General in nearby Berrima, claimed to be Australia's oldest, dating from 1831. I'm not sure what Britain's oldest pub is, but I imagine it's a genteel sort of place, half-timbered perhaps, with coach parties of old ladies sipping G&Ts on cardboard coasters, at little oak tables. The Surveyor-General's Arms was altogether, well . . . *rougher*.

'Are you drunk?' demanded the barman as we walked through the door. ' 'Cos if you are, you can fuck off.'

Matthew, who was in the lead, chose to reply in the singular: 'Actually, I haven't touched an alcoholic drink in fifteen years.' (This wasn't strictly true—viz. the fruit punch in Barbados—but we'll let it pass.)

'Fifteen fucking *years*? Jeez. Are you from Melbourne?'

We sat down for a quiet drink, surrounded by large anti-violence signs. The only other inhabitants of the bar, a group of men at the far end of the room, were clearly working their way up to a major fight. Eventually there came the sound of crunching glass and flying 'fuck's.

'I think we should leave,' said Tom.

'Yes, let's,' said Matthew.

'I'm off,' said Eiran, quivering with fear.

'Come on, you lot,' I remonstrated. 'They're fighting each other, not us.'

It was no good. All of them went to finish their drinks in the car, leaving me sat at the table alone.

The punch-up at the end of the bar was brief, spectacular and good-humoured, and the participants shook hands with each other afterwards, before trooping past my table one by one and out into the car park. As they passed by, they offered their apologies.

'Er . . . sorry about that, mate.'

'Hope we didn't disturb your drink or nothin', mate.'

'Sorry, mate . . . er, g'day.'

Really, their manners were impeccable.

*   *   *

I sat next to Matthew on the plane to Perth, watching the endless, featureless brown of Australia roll out beneath us for hour after hour. Finally I ventured to ask the question that had been politely queuing in my head since we'd left Sydney.

'So . . . your dad. Did you have any luck trying to find him?'

'I didn't try.'

'You didn't *try*?'

'I don't know . . . some things are better left as they are. I mean, I've come all this way—it was one of the main reasons for coming all this way—but when it came to it, I just couldn't go through with it. I just sat there for an hour, staring at the open phone book. I just couldn't do it.'

'I'm sorry.'

'That's all right. The funny thing is, it doesn't bother me any more, now that I've been to Sydney.'

And that was the end of the search for Matthew's dad.

*   *   *

Perth, not to put too fine a point on it, makes Auckland seem like rock 'n' roll central. It could well be the most suburban place on earth. Imagine the population of Weybridge relocated to the architecture of Kuala Lumpur. Space-age skyscrapers claw into a flawless blue sky, while, at their base, Alan and Jean from Godalming are getting an excellent deal on incontinence pants. Well, I say 'a flawless blue sky'—it was, of course, raining when we touched down, but the raindrops didn't last.

To our immense fascination, Greg's dad was there to meet us—a small, dapper, ex-RAF man in colossal shorts, sporting a Kitchener moustache.

'Where are you from, then?' he asked Sean O'Herlihy breezily.

'I'm half Irish, half Malaysian.'

'Oh yes? I went to Malaysia once. Didn't like the food, didn't like the people.'

I could see the sinews in Sean's neck tighten. He could have ripped Greg's dad in half in a split second. And probably should have. But he kept his cool somehow. Then the old man dropped his bombshell.

'Good to see you, son. I got the money you sent, and I've bought the Mitsubishi you wanted. It's a fine vehicle. White. I've parked her up at your house.'

We literally goggled. Greg had used my subsidy, at least in part, to buy a new car. And here was his dad bragging about it. I could have kicked up an almighty fuss, but I didn't. Greg could go hang when we got back to London, but for now it was more important to keep the team together. And I'd never see my money again either way. So, reluctantly, I let it go.

'I say, that Nelson Mandela's a black bastard, isn't he?' announced Greg's dad, by way of general conversation.

If only I had a rifle, thought nine of us in unison.

We ended up going for a drink on Cottesloe Beach, but we didn't stay long. The day had a nasty taste to it. The Americans, who were limbering up to invade Iraq (despite all noises to the contrary), had stationed a massive aircraft carrier right off the beach, and every open-fronted bar was packed with shaven-headed US servicemen. We felt like the biggest terrorist target in the world.

'You know what?' said Greg, who'd knocked back a few beers by now. 'This is the best bloody beach ever. One day my kids'll grow up here. You know why it's the best bloody beach ever?'

He was warming to his theme now, as he never had before in Britain.

'No Abos. Abos should be shot like vermin.'

We left him to it, headed back to our hotel, and went to bed.

* * *

I phoned Cie before turning in, to tell him of our near-miss in Buenos Aires.

'Hey, man,' he said, commiserating. 'You're going to win in Perth, I know it.'

That was it. We were doomed.

Even the normally reliable Cie couldn't cheer me up. I spent the entire night wide awake, assailed by überjetlag and disturbed by the day's events. Matthew—with whom I was sharing this particular room—slumbered soundly enough, no doubt dreaming dreams of absent parents. In fact he snored so loudly that the sound put me in mind of going over the top at Arras. So as not to wake him, I retreated to the bathroom, passing the interminable hours in a pristine white space that put me in mind of Perth as a whole: clean, comfortable and characterless. When day broke we were due to face Greg's old side. Would they all be like Greg, I wondered: a team of eleven exceptionally short men with cork-fringed hats and green-and-gold hair, all 'g'day'ing furiously in unison? It didn't bear thinking about.

In the event I need not have worried. They turned out to be eleven of the loveliest, kindest, most charming people you could ever hope to meet anywhere. Their ground was leafy and pleasant. Of course we could borrow an eleventh man to replace Aidan, they reassured us, and of course they'd give us someone who could bowl. The only two unsurprising discoveries were (a) that we'd be playing in well over 100° and (b) that the home side were hideously good at cricket. They were, it transpired, a Grade side boasting a number of elevens. The team facing us was split down the middle between Grade B and Grade A players, Grade A being the level roughly equivalent to bog-standard English county cricket. Where did English village cricket pitch up on this particular scale? I wondered. Was there a Grade Z? We were going to have our work cut out, that was for sure. And, just to make things harder, we would begin playing at an hour that—according to our body clocks—was approaching midnight.

I won the toss, inspected the rolled red earth of Western Australia, and realized that—not for the first time—I didn't have a clue what to do; so I opted to chase. The game was to be cut up into quarters anyway, because it would be too tough for one side to field for forty overs in such heat.

'Er, Harry,' asked Greg, sidling up to me. 'Can I ask a favour?'

'What is it?'

'Can you not call me Greg in front of these guys? They know me as Johnny.'

I didn't ask.

The game began. Riaan, sweating, indefatigable, opened the bowling in harness with our new team-mate, Mark Arnold, their former opening bowler who'd recently retired through old age (i.e. he was about a decade younger than I was). From the way Riaan's first couple of deliveries were sent screaming into the baked outfield I thought we would end up facing a total in excess of 300, but thereafter he tightened up magnificently. He and Arnold were superb, we gave it all we had in the field, and after twelve overs the opposition was limping along at 23–2. Then I made a captaincy mistake: I held back Riaan's last two overs for the finale and replaced him with James O'Herlihy's gentle swing. In fact it was the older Arnold, not Riaan, who was tiring, and the next six overs were plundered for fifty runs, the severely jetlagged O'Herlihy (who'd been out on the lash, of course) spraying the ball around like an Alsatian marking his territory. I brought on the even more geriatric, inoffensive part-time bowling of me.

'You'll have fun here, boys,' announced Greg to the batsmen. 'This one's shit.'

The batsman, Collins, strode confidently down the wicket to loft my first delivery into the next state, missed it—rather to my surprise—and was neatly stumped by Greg. I'd love to think it was a brilliant piece of psychology on his part, but I'm afraid that he really had meant it. Had it hurt him, I wondered, to whip off those bails?

The first quarter closed with the Aussies on 75–3 off twenty overs. We were utterly bushwhacked, but it was time to turn round and head out to bat. Again I donned the gladiatorial armour of stomach padding, elbow padding and the rest. And the helmet, of course. The bloody helmet. Clank, clank. By the start of our innings the temperature had climbed to 105°. I'd barely got halfway to the wicket before a waterfall of sweat had salted my eyeballs like a tin of anchovies. As in Buenos Aires, I could see the line of slips and gullies twenty yards back from the bat, stood like a blurry firing squad, silhouetted in a white rectangle of light, presaging my upcoming doom. 'Come on, Thompson,' I told myself. 'This time you have to find something extra. This time you have to dig deep for the team and stick around. It's your job. It's what you do. In fact it's all you do. Never mind that this bloke normally bowls at first-class cricketers and that you can't actually see anything. Never mind that your body thinks it's two in the morning and you haven't slept for thirty-six hours. Just show some guts.' I'd actually started the trip, I remembered, hoping to get round the world in eighty runs. It might even make a good book title, I'd thought. The way I was headed, I'd be lucky to get round in eight. 'So come on. Show some *defiance*. Remember David Steele.' The cricketer, not the politician.

I once watched a programme on TV about the 1972 Ashes series, when an Australian line-up of huge, hairy, muscular men headed by Dennis Lillee and Rodney Marsh had pulverized an England team of small, dapper, Brylcreemed men like John Edrich and Brian Luckhurst. My then girlfriend, who'd been 'persuaded' into watching the show with me, exclaimed (rather wittily I thought), 'My God—we've put out a team of headmasters!' And so we had. Frankly, it would not have been a surprise to see Edrich and Luckhurst walk to their inevitable fates sporting pipes and cardigans. Clanking out to open the batting in 105° at Perth, that was how I felt—like a headmaster, facing eleven large, hairy Aussies.

The opening bowler, a rangy youth by the look of it (it was hard to tell), began his extremely long run-up. The fielders geed him up as he ran, clapping and yelling.

'Let's go, Shaggy!'

'C'mon, Shaggy-baby!'

'Go, Shags!'

I've heard of *déjà vu*, but this was ridiculous. Couldn't they even have dreamed up another name?

A gleaming, crimson leather sphere shot past my nose at 80 m.p.h. and was taken high above his shoulder by the keeper, with a satisfying *thwack*. At least I'm fairly sure that's what happened. It wasn't easy to tell via Anchovyvision(TM). Another ball followed, just short of a length, probing for the outside edge. In my current state of incapacitation I was utterly incapable of connecting with anything. It too whistled past my nose. *Just don't bowl at the stumps*, I thought. I felt like a drunk trying unsuccessfully to land a punch on a static adversary. Finally the umpire called, 'Over.' Somehow, someway, I'd survived six balls of the stuff. Through the greasy letterbox I watched Dan—who'd chosen to step into the firing line with me today—negotiate an equally perilous maiden over. It was my turn again. There was nothing for it. Who cared if my head was split in two? The helmet had to go.

I stopped the game, pulled off my gloves, and yanked off the wretched thing. Suddenly the world came into focus—like switching from an elderly VHS to DVD widescreen with surround sound. Suddenly I could hear. Suddenly I could *see*. Suddenly I felt a whole lot more confident.

'C'mon, Shags!'

'Let's have this bastard, Shaggy!'

The ball speared into the rock-hard ground just short of a length and spat. I saw it every inch of the way, got in line, left elbow high, textbook technique. I had to play it, or lose forty-two years of dodgy NHS dental work. I heard it fizz into the middle of the bat, where it connected with an almighty thud.

Except it wasn't quite the middle of the bat. It was a millimetre or two to the right of the middle. The ball didn't fall harmlessly to the ground. It flew horizontally, Darren Gough-style, to the far end of the slip cordon, where it was effortlessly pouched. I was out for a duck. Around the world in 0.8 runs, anyone?

After that things went from bad to worse. Matthew came in—not a bad batsman, remember:

a county senior and MCC player—and suffered an identical fate before the over was out. Sean hung around a bit, but eventually went the same way for one run. By the time Shaggy finished his opening spell he had taken three wickets and conceded just one run. We had pitted ourselves against a proper fast bowler on a bouncy Perth trampoline, and we had been found wanting. He had run through our upper order like a chicken through a bag of millet. We just had to hope that the Grade B bowlers would be more to our liking, or it would be all over bar the clucking. A Sri Lankan spinner came on next, so Dan (who was still there) decided to take risks and attack, bludgeoning twenty-five useful runs before he too was snaffled by the bowler. Daniels, looking as jittery as ever, came to the crease just before the twenty-over mark, and against all odds succeeded in surviving until the break. We limped to the halfway point, somewhat bruised and battered, at 62–5.

The second half of their innings saw the Australians trying to push up the rate against Dan and myself. Dare I say it, we didn't do a bad job. Dan found the bouncy track to his liking, and at one point I heard one batsman mutter to the other in midwicket confabulation, 'He's bowlin' darts, mate!' Except, being Australian, he pronounced it 'daarts'. For the rest of the trip, Dan was to be renamed 'Jocky'. He finished his spell with 0-35, myself with 2–27—a reasonable menopausal flourish for an old fart who'd semi-retired from bowling a year or two before the trip. The trouble was, we hadn't taken enough wickets. When it came to the slog of the last few overs, the Aussies had men to lose: they piled on the runs, and finished with 171–6. We needed a further 110 to win. We'd have to bat almost twice as well as we had in our first quarter.

The Aussies, however, not to mention ourselves, had reckoned without Paul Daniels. Whether it was the psychological boost of the interval, arriving to save him after those first few nervous strokes, or whether the ghost of his former talent had simply seized him by the scruff of the neck, a change slowly manifested itself. Gradually, the Welsh wizard began to take charge of the bowling. With Mark Arnold, our borrowed bowler, holding up the other end, Paul started to pummel the Australian attack to all corners. Small children and furry animals fled for cover as he peppered the pavilion. In what seemed like a flash he passed 50, and the pair had added seventy runs when Arnold was needlessly run out. Riaan kept Paul company for a while, then Eiran—going in low down on account of extreme alcoholic exhaustion—kept up the good work. Daniels, though, was simply magnificent. Slowly he began to close on the opposition's total. When Eiran finally perished with two overs still to play, we were twelve runs short of victory with two wickets in hand. Paul had the bowling. There was only one thing the Australians could do.

'Go, Shaggy!'

'C'mon, Shaggy-baby!'

'Let's go, Shags!'

Restored to the attack, the opening bowler came in off his full run-up, and let loose a pearler. Daniels's middle stump went cartwheeling. Paul stood motionless, shoulders slumped, looking for all the world as if he would break down in tears.

His effort had been so heroic, so magnificent—but he had fallen just short. Exhausted, beaten, jetlagged and distraught, he trailed back to the pavilion for 72. Tom, the last man, did his best, but two runs and three balls later he was run out in a futile attempt to give James O'Herlihy the strike.

We had lost by nine runs.

We had failed to 'win it for Aidan'.

Of course, we easily won the boat race.

* * *

With a day and a half to kill in Perth, most of the team were shattered, flattened, and unable to budge from the side of the hotel pool. Matthew and I, though, set our sights further afield and took the boat out to Rottnest Island, a popular day trip for the city's inhabitants. Rottnest is famous for its clear blue water and its scenery, but I found it a stark, glaring place. Thankfully there was a shortage of visible *Rotts* (the Dutch explorer Willem de Vlamingh named the island 'Rat's-nest' because it appeared to be overrun with kingsize rodents), but instead we found bluetongues, large, ugly, slow-moving lizards that looked like throwbacks to the Cretaceous era. The place was flat, with brackish salt lakes inland, the most prominent of which was called Baghdad. Given the presence of the aforementioned huge US warship offshore, this was disturbing. Could they possibly be that stupid? We hurried past, taking no chances. Eventually we settled on the beach at Parakeet Bay, where I went swimming while Matthew sat broiling like the ultimate preposterous Englishman in hat, long-sleeved shirt, long-sleeved trousers and stout shoes. The problem with Rottnest, we decided, like that of the Western Australian coast itself, was that it was so flat and featureless. Behind the beach was no hinterland and precious little vegetation, just a parched, lifeless, low-lying wilderness. We'd asked in our hotel if there were any places of interest around Perth, and among their recommendations had been a wave-shaped rock in the desert, 150 miles away. This rather said it all: Perth, it seemed, was the kind of place where one made a 300-mile round trip to see an interesting-shaped rock. Or didn't, in our case.

On our way back, we returned via Perth's sister city, Fremantle, and were shocked to discover a real, unexpected, slumbering gem. Fremantle was absolutely beautiful, if disconcertingly deserted in the late-afternoon sun. It's a perfectly preserved Wild West town, a frontier city of spindly wrought-iron colonnades and wooden balconies, where at any minute you fully expect to see a figure come flying out of the Orient Family Hotel and Quality Swan Brewery, accompanied by a splintered swing door and a snatch of tinkling piano, and land on its back in the road. There are even horse-drawn carts in the streets. This, again, is the legacy of Empire. Look closer at the buildings: the names picked out permanently in pastel paint on carved stone speak of a time when architecture married civic pride to technological optimism: the Adelaide Steamship Co.; the P&O Buildings. Fremantle was a purpose-built modern city, constructed partly as a statement of Victorian commercial bullishness. Of course, for the Victorians, modern meant elegant, beautiful and intricately decorated. Perth, up the road, is also a modern, confident city, but its lines are antiseptic, its skyscrapers novelty-shaped, the results strangely characterless. It has no soul.

On our last half-day we journeyed out to the West Australian vineyards for lunch, but it was a hard slog to derive enjoyment from the trip. We found a nice restaurant in the end, all its tables resolutely corralled indoors, with the blinds drawn (barbecues apart, Western Australians don't seem to dine alfresco), and, yes, the waiters *were* camp. But the journey out there had been depressing. For mile after mile we had driven on geometric roads across a featureless plain dotted only with concrete warehouses, huge steel drums and flapping polythene. One area of this wasteland was even named 'Herne Hill'. There were no old buildings, only that familiar industrial-estate feeling. Western Australia, I concluded, should feel like cowboy country, but (Fremantle apart) it doesn't. It's pioneer territory all right, opened up by settlers, its natives massacred in the approved Argentinian manner, but the job appears to have been carried out by a coach party from Letchworth. Come to think of it, it probably was.

10

Singapore

The journey from Perth to Singapore is actually shorter than the journey from Sydney to Perth, being a mere four hours forty minutes long, a duration which to us Scotties—inured as we were by now to the *longueurs* of international air travel—felt like a short walk to the newsagents. Incredibly, like our Australian internal flight, it passed uneventfully, with no disasters, cock-ups, arrests, lost luggage, missing tickets or anything else of that ilk, presumably because the highly experienced and rather camp team from Qantas were in control of the arrangements. Nevertheless, by the time we touched down in Singapore we were still drained from our Australian exertions, still resolutely jetlagged, and, in one or two cases, edging towards fractiousness. Tom, in particular, was a trifle tetchy, and spoiling for a fight. Things came to a head in the sticky tropical miasma of the Singapore airport taxi rank. Like a good Samaritan, I'd loaded his luggage on to a trolley from the carousel when he'd been held up in immigration, and was now transferring it to a communal taxi boot—no easy feat, I can tell you, when one hand is gingerly clutching a *Gone With the Wind* poster furled inside several badly Sellotaped-together toilet rolls. Tom, meanwhile, wandered off in a different direction, to the other end of the rank.

'Over here, Tom!' I shouted. 'Your luggage is in this cab!'

'Well, take, it out again,' he said irritably. 'I'm fed up with being crammed in with four other people all the time. I want my own cab.'

'Tom, it's at the bottom of the boot. Get your own cab, and collect your luggage later.'

'No!' he demanded. 'I want my suitcase here right away!'

Laboriously, the taxi boot had to be unpacked and Tom's cases extracted. I carried them the length of the rank and deposited them at his feet.

'There,' I said. 'Only trying to be helpful.'

'Well don't,' he said peevishly, and summoned a taxi with a lordly, beckoning hand.

'Yessir!' said the driver smartly, engaged reverse gear, and roared up, driving right over Tom's suitcase in the process. It lay pancaked in the road. I cracked up.

'That's not funny,' said Tom.

'Yes it is,' I retorted.

Gingerly, he lifted the lid of the squashed case. Inside was Tom's favourite pillow from my spare bedroom, as expected, but it was framed by about fifteen rolls of Muji designer toilet paper. I didn't even know Muji *made* toilet paper. Oh, and a pair of neatly polished shoes. In a linen shoe bag. Completely squashed. I cracked up again.

Better to draw a veil over Tom's subsequent tantrum. Suffice to say that if you've ever seen Gene Wilder go ape in *The Producers* you'll get the idea.

*   *   *

We found Aidan right enough in Singapore, safe and sound and raring to go. The dripping fast bowler we'd left so lumpen-throatedly in that sodden Auckland dawn had arrived in Singapore a day or two before us, and had passed his time on the Malaysian side of the border, being cosseted like a long-lost puppy by various O'Herlihy relatives. He looked tanned, fit and determined to grip a shiny cricket ball in his hand once more. Frankly, playing cricket was all any of us would have time to do in Singapore, as—thanks to the vagaries of the One World airline schedule—we only had thirty-six hours on the ground in the city. Could there be a more majestic continent than Asia, rolling out from the minarets of Istanbul to the temples of Angkor Wat, stretching from the steppes of Mongolia, through the jungles of Burma to the mighty peaks of the Himalayas? Er, probably not. And we'd be there for a day and a half, to play a game of cricket in a Singapore suburb. Well, I did say from the start that this was a daft idea.

Our original plan—to play against the famous Singapore Cricket Club on their city-centre *padang* ground, an oasis of green amid the towering skyscrapers—had had to be abandoned. Only a few months previously the Bali nightclub bomb had horrifically killed the majority of an SCC touring party, so now was hardly the time for us to turn up in metaphorical party hats and streamers. The SCC had kindly passed us on to the Ceylon Sports Club, the Sri Lankan expat team, who would be playing us instead. Not only had I made contact, I'd checked them out on the web as well: the CSC were, of course, a far better side than their English counterparts. They were the champions of Singapore, no less. Some of their leading batsmen averaged over 100. We had the usual mountain to climb.

Or did we? As a people-carrier drove us out to the CSC the following morning, less than twelve hours after we'd touched down in the city, a call came through on the team mobile. It was the captain of the Ceylon Sports Club, and he had bad news. The game was off. Eleven faces did not so much fall as plummet through the floor.

'I am truly sorry,' he said, 'but it has been raining heavily for many days here in Singapore. The pitch is literally under water—many inches deep. It is like a paddy field.'

This was a disaster indeed. I remonstrated, as the others strained to listen.

'But we had a deal,' I said. 'You agreed that we'd play come what may, whatever the weather, even if the game had to be called off after one ball. The whole point of our trip is that we play cricket in every continent.'

'I am afraid it is too late for that. I have sent the team home. There is no way of calling them back.'

I began to get desperate.

'Then . . . then we could play a one-ball game against just *you*. You could bat for one ball, we'll field, and we'll declare it a draw!'

Ten heads nodded hopefully in the people-carrier.

'Even one ball would destroy our wicket. The pitch is literally a lake.'

'So . . . why don't we use your artificial wicket?'

'There is no artificial wicket at the Ceylon Sports Ground.'

'But . . . but I saw it on your website.'

'I am afraid you are mistaken. There is no artificial wicket at the Ceylon Sports Ground. I am sorry, there is nothing more I can do. Goodbye.'

And with that he put the phone down. We ordered our cab into reverse, heading back to the team hotel. This was a catastrophe. What on earth could we do? Turn up at a local radio station, perhaps, and advertise our plight to the tiny island nation? The blessed irony of the whole thing was that we were now two-thirds of the way round the world, and Singapore was the first place where we hadn't touched down in pissing rain. This realization gave me a sudden—suspicious—thought. I posed the cabbie a question.

'Excuse me, but has it been raining much in Singapore these last few days?'

'Here? In Singapore? No rain here for many days, sir. Very dry.'

'Really? How interesting. Would you turn around again, please. We're heading back to the Ceylon Sports Club.'

The cabbie, who was clearly coming to the conclusion that we were all quite mad, did as we'd asked, and before long we pitched up at the CSC.

At first the place seemed deserted. Changing rooms, showers, bar—all were locked up. We walked out on to the cricket field. It was utterly, completely, bone dry. The earth was rock hard. There, in the middle of the oval, lay a gleaming artificial wicket. The only problem was the grass in the outfield, which was a good twelve inches long. Nobody had been arsed to mow it for weeks. Finally we located the captain, working alone behind a desk in his office. To say that he looked startled when eleven burly cricketers burst in (well, eight or nine burly cricketers and two or three weedy ones) would be an understatement. I put on my best QC voice.

'So, the pitch is under water, is it? Like a paddy field, you said.'

He quailed.

'It . . . er . . . it must have dried quite quickly during the night. I did not have a chance to look this morning.'

'And the artificial wicket?' I said. 'What about

that? Was that built by pixies during the night?'

'I . . . I . . . er . . . '

Sean took the situation into his own large and capable lawyer's hands. He leaned over the desk and grasped the CSC captain (who was not a big man) by the throat.

'Now you listen to me,' he explained carefully. 'Here's what we're going to do. We have to be at the airport at 3.15 tomorrow afternoon, which means we're going to have to leave here at two. That gives us just enough time for a thirty-five-over match starting at 8.30 a.m. You are going to have the full Ceylon Sports Club side here for 8 a.m. No excuses. We're going to leave our kit here, ready for the match. We'll be back here in the morning. If the full CSC side isn't here, ready and changed by eight, we're going to burn down the pavilion. Is that clear?'

'Yes,' croaked the captain. 'That is very clear indeed. Thank you.'

'Good,' said Sean, releasing the man's shirt and tie. 'We'll see you tomorrow morning.'

We stepped out of the air-conditioned closeness of the captain's office into the streaming trafficky stickiness of Singapore.

'I know this part of the world,' said Sean. 'There isn't a cat in hell's chance that their team will be here at eight o'clock tomorrow morning.'

'Oh, I don't know,' I replied, still secretly impressed by his display. I had seen the light of fear in the captain's eyes.

* * *

I spent the rest of the day trawling the sights (such

as they were) with Tom, who seemed to have completely recovered from his hissy fit of the night before, thanks no doubt to liberal soothing applications of Muji toilet paper. We stopped off for Singapore Slings at the newly restored Raffles Hotel, the highlight of the city's somewhat scratchy colonial heritage. I took his photo beneath the street sign for Cad's Alley, and resisted the temptation to post copies there and then to both his rival love interests. After that we immersed ourselves in the faceless shopping arcades of Orchard Road, ultimately settling on an admittedly rather fine and substantial branch of HMV, where I purchased a Brazilian version of 'Hit the Road Jack'. An afternoon in Orchard Road is rather like the run-up to Christmas, only without the good will to all men. We did our best to join in with the commercial spirit of the place, but a certain amount of enthusiasm was lacking. All in all, perhaps because of that morning's whiff of skulduggery, Singapore was the least popular destination among the Captain Scott tourists. Matthew declared it the least appetizing place he'd ever been to. He had a point: why anyone would choose the place for a holiday was beyond us. Singapore is a huge, permanently sweaty anthill, its crowds swarming to their own hidden purpose, its streets more Chinatown than China in their gaudily dressed internationalism, its salesmen relentlessly rude to visitors for all their shouted bargains. We retreated to another colonial oasis: Sean took us all for dinner on the silent balcony of the Singapore Cricket Club, overlooking the deserted pitch, the bar dotted with old photos of mullet-haired seventies celebrities who'd hit town, many years ago, for the Singapore Sixes. But the ghosts of the Bali bomb were drifting through the evening breezes, which made for an unsettling experience.

Trivial though our own concerns were by comparison, it was hard for us not to wonder what the morning would bring. We'd had matches cancelled on us at short notice many times before, of course. University College, Oxford, pulled out on the day of the game no less than seven years running, the seventh and final time with the excuse that 'burglars had made off with the heavy roller'. Who were these burglars? Geoff Capes and Giant Haystacks? The Earl of Leicester cancelled our visit to Holkham Hall during the foot-and-mouth outbreak, lest we import the disease to Norfolk from its well-known breeding grounds in central London. When Princess Diana died, we had two games planned for the following weekend: on the Saturday the opposition insisted we play, because it was 'what she would have wanted'. On the Sunday the opposition insisted on scratching, because it was 'what she would have wanted'. It was hard to imagine, as the poor woman gasped her last breath, that she would have harboured any strong views on the subject, but such are the whims and fancies of cricket-fixture secretaries.

As it turned out, despite Sean's doubts, we need not have worried. His hands-around-the-throat technique had been just the tonic. We arrived at the Ceylon Sports Club just before 8 a.m. to a scene of astonishing industry: eleven neatly dressed CSC cricketers were ready to meet us in sharply pressed whites, all smiles and handshakes as if nothing untoward had happened. The stumps were being driven into the baked earth. The dressing rooms and showers had been opened up, and our kit was lined up neatly ready for us. Only the outfield remained a problem, the grass long enough to hide an entire regiment of Vietcong. No matter. It would just have to be a low-scoring game. A very, very low-scoring game.

Determined not to let everybody down with the bat as I had in the previous two games, I padded up and headed off to the nets for a practice session. Intrigued, the CSC's star player, an Indian Under-19 international named Dharmichand, followed me down there. Dharmichand, I learned on the way over, had recently returned from skittling the England Under-19 side, numbering Ian Bell among his victims ('So what?' I hear you say. But bear with me). A spinner-batsman, he held the staggering record of bagging five-wicket hauls in nine consecutive innings. Please could he bowl at me? he wanted to know. *Dharmichand, old son, you're in for a shock*, I thought. Sure, I said. Time for you to live and learn a bit.

The young Indian magician's first ball turned in to me almost at right angles. I'd never faced anything like it before. The next delivery looked exactly the same as it left his hand, but it shot across me at right angles in the opposite direction. For the third ball, I determined to thrust my front leg as far forward as I possibly could, to get right to the pitch of the ball and negate any spin. But it didn't spin. It shot vertically upward and hit me on the chin. By now it was a moot point as to who was the more bamboozled—me or him. Me, because I was utterly incapable of reading the mysteries of his whirling fingers, or him, because none of his stratagems to outwit me were working—I was just too inept to fall for them. Ian Bell might have been suckered by his tricks, but I was too stupid to open the box. A crowd of CSC players was beginning to build, and beginning to marvel at the presence of an opposition batsman quite so ill-qualified to resist their secret weapon. I swear I could see a glint in the captain's eye.

But this epic duel would have to wait, for it was time to toss up. I won, and opted to bowl. Some of those watching CSC eyes had looked bleary: for once, with the breakfast-time start, jetlag would work in our favour. We might just catch them cold. And this time we were really, *really* fired up. Aidan in particular looked muscly, fit and bursting to bowl. Dharmichand, it transpired, was the Ceylon Sports Club's opening batsman as well as their star bowler, and he strolled out nonchalantly to the crease. Almost immediately, however, he lost his partner, snaffled by Aidan like a poodle by a Rottweiler. 5–1. The number three was altogether more cautious, runless, strokeless, determined just to see off our new-ball bowlers, while Dharmichand accumulated. After twelve overs the home side had crawled to 21–1, of which Dharmichand had 20 and the new man 0. This, it was becoming increasingly clear, was to be no ordinary cricket match. The bounce was horrifically low, so there were only two ways to get runs: by pushing the ball into the long grass and snatching a quick single while the fielders tried to find it, or by leaping down the wicket like a madman, getting to the pitch, and driving the ball over the bowler's head. That option, I thought, might mean catches and stumpings, so I decided to invite it. I packed the mid-off/mid-on areas with four fielders and brought on our two slowest bowlers, Dan and myself.

'Here we go,' announced Greg to the home batsman as I took the ball. 'It's party time. We've lost it now.' *For fuck's sake, Greg,* I thought, *will you just shut your trap for once?*

As it was, the ploy worked to perfection. Straight away Dharmichand danced down the wicket towards me in search of a lofted off drive, got an inside edge to a slow off-cutter, and succeeded only in flicking the ball up to Riaan at square leg. A few balls later the number three tried the same shot, and Greg was forced to pull off an excellent stumping. Again, his inadvertent psychology was paying dividends. Each new batsman that came in tried chicken-headedly to attack the slow stuff, invariably with fatal results. Within just six overs, the CSC collapsed from 21–1 to 44–8, Dan snaffling four of the newcomers to my three. Too late, the last three bats—with half an innings still to play—reverted to the accumulation method. I brought back Aidan and Riaan, who blasted them out in successive balls. The Ceylon Sports Club, champions of Singapore, were all out for just 58 runs in twenty-five overs. It looked like a walkover for us, but it wouldn't be, of course. 58 on this outfield was worth triple that under normal conditions. Dharmichand's 20 would have been worth a half-century anywhere else.

Sure enough, the Indian was to be one of the CSC's new-ball bowlers, and was allocated the second over. The sight of my utter confusion in the nets had indeed been too tempting for the home captain to resist. But this, I thought, might prove to be a fatal mistake on his part, for a batsman has to be good enough (or, strictly speaking, bad enough) relative to the bowler for the ball to find the edge of the bat. As long as I could get in the way somehow, sheer non-comprehension was as valuable a weapon as any against such a top-drawer opponent. *Come on, Thompson,* I thought. *All the wiles of the mystic East won't get past your true British pig-ignorance.* After I had played out an opening maiden from the other bowler, Sean—who hadn't been down at the nets—was to face Dharmichand's first ball. I walked down and warned him about the colossal amount of turn that the Indian seemed to be able to extract from any surface.

'Sure,' he said, 'I'll keep a lookout.'

The first ball was an off-side wide, barely on the edge of the mat, so Sean shouldered arms to let it pass. Except that it suddenly deviated at right angles and flattened his leg stump.

'Jesus,' he said.

Forget Shane Warne's famous ball to Andrew Strauss: that had nothing on *this*. Sean stood there open-mouthed in sheer astonishment, before trailing back to the pavilion.

Riaan was in next. Facing the same alternatives as the CSC had faced earlier, long-grass accumulation or a golf swing over the top to a packed field, we agreed that the former course was the more sensible. I managed to get myself down to Dharmichand's end, and thoroughly outwitted the poor fellow. I was hit on the nose, on the bum, and right in the box. I certainly never laid bat on ball. Never can he have outclassed an opponent so thoroughly. It was like watching a chess grandmaster lay out a series of brilliant opening gambits in a failed attempt to entrap a ten-year-old novice. It wasn't pretty to watch, of course, and pretty soon our team-mates were getting restless at the pair of us. Riaan eventually cracked, and to mighty cheers hoiked a huge six over long on. The next ball, he tried to repeat the shot, and perished in the deep.

Paul Daniels was next to the crease, and he too came prepared to engage in a defensive display. The innings resumed at a snail's pace. Finally Dharmichand's spell came to an end. He had taken one wicket for four runs. So far so good. After fourteen overs, we were 23–2 and well on course. Then, horribly, dreadfully, the wheels came off.

In a master stroke of captaincy, the Sri Lankans put on a mediocre bowler who had me beaten all ends up in no time. Then Paul Daniels ran himself out, forgetting that even the most powerful cover drive would travel no more than three yards from the wicket. It was a time for the ship to be steadied, a time for calm heads. Unfortunately the heads of our incoming batsmen were as calm as raspberry trifle in an earthquake. The same collective suicide instinct overwhelmed the Captain Scott middle order as had engulfed their CSC counterparts. One after another, Matthew, Eiran and Tom came forward and essayed wild swipes, airy, head-in-the-clouds stuff that saw them perish for a combined four runs. We had collapsed from 23–2 to 36–7, and not one of our batsmen had made it into double figures. It was like watching the old Captain Scott. Dharmichand's 20 was beginning in hindsight to look more like a century.

James and Aidan were next at the crease and—at last—were prepared to listen to the entreaties of their captain, on bended knee, begging them to take their time and show a little patience. There was, after all, half our innings still remaining to play with. The Geoffrey Boycott playing style might not be pretty to watch, but it certainly has its uses. I actually met the great man once, and—short of something polite to say—told him that he'd been the favourite batsman of my childhood (not true: it had been Barry Richards).

'You know why that was, don't you?' said Geoffrey.

'Er . . . why?'

'It's because I was *very good.*'

I scrutinized his face carefully for signs of humour, irony, sarcasm, anything really. There were none. He had really meant it. What price some of that dogged self-belief now? Gradually, agonizingly, James and Aidan began to accumulate, in the style of the Yorkshire Zen master. Inch by inch, the score began to mount. Slowly, the temperature and the humidity began to rise in tandem as well, the latter touching 100%, until all of us were completely soaked in sweat. The two batsmen especially, having to keep out a succession of balls that shot along the ground towards their ankles, most of their finest shots coming to naught in the long grass, were virtually drenched to the skin. Determination infused each and every one of us. Finally, Aidan and James crawled into double figures off successive balls. Their partnership was worth twenty-one precious runs. We were two short of victory with two overs remaining. Aidan, unable to resist, went for a big winning hit and was promptly caught. He returned to the pavilion in despair.

Dan strode out to the wicket, and survived the rest of the over. A snatched bye off the last ball brought the scores level. We needed one to win off one over, with Dan on strike. He hit his first ball like a rocket, straight off the middle of the bat. It jammed in a clump of grass a yard away, disturbing a Japanese soldier who'd been hiding there since 1945. His second ball was hit with equal timing and ferocity, but could get no further. His third ball, however, neatly bisected the point and cover fieldsmen and disappeared into a small thicket between them. As the two scrambled to retrieve it, Dan and James hared towards each other's respective ends. The ball came whizzing in and broke the stumps: too late. We had won. We had beaten the champions of Singapore by two wickets, with three balls to spare.

There was no boat race. Still clad in our sweat-soaked cricket kit, we were already on our way to the airport.

* * *

It is hard to describe the collective feeling of elation that washed over us as we made that trip. We had stuck together to overcome opponents who, on paper, should have made absolute mincemeat of an English village team. We had finally won a match on our round-the-world tour. And, in a funny way, justice had been done. Such was our sense of exultation that we were even prepared to forgive British Airways their latest atrocity. Yes, good old British Airways. Where would we be without them, sending us off on wild-goose chases all around the world? We had scurried to the airport to catch a Cathay Pacific flight to Hong Kong, 2,582 miles and four hours in completely the wrong direction, because—Sheila from British Airways had assured me—there were no direct flights at all from Singapore to South Africa, our next destination. Hong Kong that day, she'd said, was our only option. No other flight on no other day would work for us. And there, of course, on the departures board, that very evening, was a direct Qantas flight—a One World Carrier, no less—departing from Singapore to Johannesburg.

Ha ha ha, British Airways, we laughed. Aren't they priceless? What's an extra few thousand miles when you're travelling round the world? What's an extra eight hours in the air, and three hours or so more in an airport departure lounge? These were mere bagatelles, we told ourselves, for seasoned travellers such as ourselves to deal with.

We didn't care.

We had beaten the champions of Singapore.

11

Cape Town

We arrived in Cape Town at lunchtime in—I think you've guessed it now—driving rain, after an exhausting journey of just over twenty-four hours from South-East Asia. But, no matter how worn out and jetlagged you are (and we'd added another six hours to that particular tally), there's something about Cape Town's sheer majesty that is guaranteed to lift the spirits. Even in cloud the setting is stupendous, for the cloud sits in a grey sheet atop Table Mountain (it's called the Tablecloth locally) and surfs mysteriously over the edge, its wisps and swirls evaporating into thin air as it does so. We were berthed in the town centre, right beneath the enfolding arms of Table Mountain's protective wall, in a friendly old pile called the Metropole, where most of the team promptly crawled off to bed. Ever the tourist, however, I couldn't help noticing that—majestic cloud formations or no—it was sunny right offshore. It was time for a boat trip, so I dragooned Tom into accompanying me to Robben Island, the long-time prison of (among others) Nelson Mandela. As the boat headed north into Table Bay, it became clear that the cloud and rain existed only as an isolated blanket over the mountain and the city: the rest of Cape Province basked in glaring sunshine. As we watched, the Tablecloth slid suffocatingly down the mountainside and swamped Cape Town's streets in its grey shroud, the buildings disappearing from view in a swirling mound of vapour.

Robben Island had been a prison camp ever since the earliest days of the VOC, the Dutch East India Company, which incarcerated anyone who fell foul of its globalist corporate aims (there's nothing new under the sun). By the time of the apartheid era it was used to house any black person criminal enough to voice the suggestion that there might be anything in this equality lark.

Today former inmates escort visitors on a tour that takes in the whole island, from the cell blocks and watchtowers to the lime quarry where Nelson & Co. were forced to slave. Mandela—on account of his status, one presumes—was accorded the 'privilege' of a minuscule solitary-confinement cell, where cat-swinging would not have been a potential pastime. The other prisoners were wedged in inhuman numbers into a barracks block with concentration-camp-style bunk beds and barred windows. Bizarrely, someone had gone out of his way to decorate the end walls with colourful life-sized cartoons: two Yuletide bells and a large orange Father Christmas, the latter bearing a sack branded with a big US dollar sign. This was curious indeed. Was this inmate satire? An attempt by the authorities to bring Christmas cheer to their charges? Or a means of taunting them vis-à-vis the inevitable historical triumph of global capitalism, from the VOC all the way through to McDonalds? Nobody, it seemed, could solve the mystery.

The following day, Tom, Matthew and I decided to hire a car. I'd never actually seen Tom drive before. Not having a car, he was usually a passenger in my beaten-up old Granada on the way to matches, and a real granny of a passenger at that. He would cluck, tut and make various other poultry noises from the back seat if the speedometer so much as touched 71 m.p.h. on the motorway. But put him behind the wheel and he turned into Ayrton Senna on cocaine, tailgating, weaving across lanes, and shouting 'Get out of the way, you c***!' at anyone in his path. So he *did* have hidden depths after all. It certainly made for a fascinating day's drive. We set out to explore some of Cape Province's Dutch colonial legacy, starting with the gorgeous winery at Vergelegen to the south-east of the city. The journey there was a sobering one, past mile after mile of dirt-poor townships splattered haphazardly across Cape Flats. It put me in mind of passing a really horrific motorway accident on the opposite carriageway, followed by a seemingly never-ending queue of trapped cars lined up behind it, and wondering what on earth all those people are going to do to get out of there. The N2 between Cape Town and Somerset West is only twenty-eight miles long, but when you're watching human misery unfold for almost the entire duration it tends to concentrate the mind.

Vergelegen, when we finally found it, was a tiny jewel of almost implausible perfection. In fact it was so lovely that, after Cape Flats, it was hard not to feel cross for a while. To put matters in perspective, I suppose one should remember that when the estate was built by Governor Willem Adriaan van der Stel, in 1700, this was more or less empty country. There were no black townships, indeed precious few black people hereabouts, to disturb old Riaan van der Stel's gleaming white world. His creamy, gabled homestead is flanked on one side by an idyllic rose garden, and on the other by the original Chinese camphor trees planted by Riaan himself. Then along came several million Africans and, of course, the British to turf the Afrikaners out. The list of Vergelegen's subsequent proprietors is an almost Wodehousian microcosm of South African history: the British handed it first to Sir Lionel and Lady Florence

Phillips, then even more amusingly to Charles 'Punch' Barlow and his wife, Cynthia. (If 'Punch' Barlow didn't have a pipe rammed into a firmly set jaw then I'm a Dutchman. Cynthia probably did too.) Today the winery is run by Anglo-American Farms Ltd, as if that needed saying. Our lunch there was suitably delicious. We felt suitably guilty.

After lunch we drove north to Hermon and Tulbagh, up the Breede River valley. This was an altogether more barren world than the coastal strip, the spaces between towns bereft of humanity, the stark rocks enlivened only by the occasional unintentionally humorous road sign, 'Pasop vir bobbejane'—'Beware of baboons'—being my favourite. For hundreds of miles we saw barely a living soul, animal or human. We certainly didn't see any black people. This was the Afrikaners' world, an implausible colonial society carved from an arid wilderness as the British pushed in behind them and stole all the best land. Hermon was little more than an extravagantly baroque renaissance hotel with a petrol pump opposite, which required a whole hour of our time to locate its owner. Tulbagh, when we finally got there, was a perfect eighteenth-century Cape Dutch village of ornate, gabled white houses. It was to here, apparently, that the early Boer settlers would trek from the wilderness when their children needed baptizing. The loveliest street, Church Street, was so perfectly preserved that every building had been declared a national monument. Tulbagh was utterly deserted. Clearly, it had maintained its architectural integrity because no one had been mad enough to build a house there for two hundred years. This sweet, lovely Dutch hamlet in the middle of a semi-desert was, frankly, the work of utter maniacs. We had come a long way to see it. It being a very small hamlet, our visit was over in minutes. We left feeling slightly bewildered.

Finally we made our way back to Cape Town via the coast road, to drink in the famous postcard view of Table Mountain for mile after unchanging mile. We stopped once, on the perfect, white-sand beach that runs alongside the road, to dip our toes in the sea and remind ourselves that Cape Town's water really *is* that cold. Far too cold to paddle in, let alone swim in—cold enough to send spasms of shock shooting up the unwary European leg. Maybe that's why no one ever escaped from Robben Island—because they would have frozen into a solid block during the swim home. Any comparable beach in any comparable latitude anywhere else in the world would be crowded with bathers, its coast road lined with restaurants and bars; but the strand north of Cape Town, for all its wild beauty, is eerily deserted. The Agulhas current has seen to that. Cape Town, in so many varied respects, is the ultimate flawed paradise.

* * *

The day of our final match, against our old adversaries Rygersdal 3rd XI, dawned—yet again—implausibly sunny and bright. I had reasonably high hopes of getting something from this game, as the old Captain Scott side had perished here by a mere three wickets, but one look at the state of the Scott players at the breakfast table changed all that. Most of them couldn't recollect anything of the night before. Aidan and Dan, in particular, could not recall how they'd come to have their heads shaved to the skull, although the comparison with Dr Evil and Mini-Me was immediate and fetching. Dan was hideously aware that in a week's time, on his return to London, he was due to attend a meeting with the Home Secretary. His only vague recollection of the night before, however, was his attempt to copulate with the tap-hole of an eighty-eight-gallon wine barrel while doing an impression of the Proclaimers. Pour all those hours of jetlag into the mix (well, nearly twenty-four all told) and one could tell instantly that this was not a side best equipped to take on Cape Town's third finest.

Matthew, Tom and I were in slightly better nick, for we had retired like feeble old men at a mere two o'clock that morning; we had even joined the party late, following a sedate dinner at a dodgy Italian restaurant in Seapoint, foolishly chosen from the pages of Lonely Planet. I hasten to say that this was the only city guide I had managed to find back in London. Lonely Planet guides are all very well when it comes to general information—buses to the torture museum, opening hours of local skating rinks, etc.—but are best avoided when it comes to selecting hotels and restaurants. The hotels they recommend will inevitably be heading down the plughole at speed on account of the endless supply of drunken Australian backpackers walking through the door clutching Lonely Planet guides. The restaurants selected are invariably cheesy curry houses and pizza places miles out in the suburbs, which just happen to be 50p cheaper than their city-centre counterparts.

There's a studenty inverted snobbery at work here. You'll see sentences like 'San Intereste is Peru's steel rivet capital. Although there's not a great deal to see or do there, it's a great place to hang out if you've got a couple of months to spare'—in other words, if you just happen to be a student, or the Duke of Argyll (and that's assuming that the idea of 'hanging out' in a dreary industrial city for most of the summer would fire the Duke of Argyll's imagination. Maybe if he was allowed to wear his kilt). But I mustn't be too hard on Lonely Planet, for they had given us the Metropole Hotel, which was currently full of ex-drunken English cricketers forlornly eating hearty breakfasts like condemned men. Copious amounts of eggs, bacon, sausages, mushrooms and tomato were consumed. The taxis came. We set off for Rygersdal.

We were greeted on arrival by the opposition captain, Richard Horton, a hefty, jovial sort, who whisked us through the club car park with indecent haste. The reason, it transpired, was that five members of their previous touring opponents, Durham University, had been mugged at gunpoint on turning up at the self-same car park. Things were rapidly changing, it seemed, in this area of Cape Town. In the absence of gun-toting muggers, however, I was a little more worried by the calibre of the touring opposition. Durham University? Wasn't that a little stiff for Rygersdal 3rds? Horton was full of apologies, meanwhile, explaining that he had been forced to field a weakened side today. His opening bat and opening bowler were missing, as both had been playing in a day– nighter at Newlands the previous evening. *Newlands?* I thought. Who *were* these missing stars?

‘Charl Willoughby and Herschelle Gibbs.’

What, Charl Willoughby of Leicestershire and South Africa? Herschelle Gibbs the South African international, one of the finest opening bats in the world?

The same.

‘Excuse me, this *is* Rygersdal 3rds we’re playing today, isn’t it?’

‘No . . . Rygersdal 1sts.’

Ah. Well, that would explain it then.

I *had* told them that we were just a village side. Honestly, you have to believe me. Just like I’d told every other bloody fixtures organizer around the world. I don’t know why they’d all ignored me. Maybe there’s something irresistibly enjoyable about seeing a team of (mainly) Englishmen having their faces rubbed in the dust. Which is what was about to happen to us, unless we pulled our socks up and played as never before.

Rygersdal won the toss and chose to bat—which was no surprise, as the wicket was harder and shinier than Aidan’s head, the outfield was harder and shinier than Dan’s, and the temperature was already soaring to volcanic levels. Groaning at my useless inability to forecast a coin toss, the Scotties stumbled blinking into the sunlight. Riaan and Aidan, at least, were determined to do the business on home soil, especially Aidan, who’d taken only two wickets on tour so far. How we needed him today, and he didn’t disappoint. He removed the number-one and number-three batsmen with fine late outswingers, both nicked to the keeper. His second, later, spell was to be even more spectacular. Riaan, meanwhile, didn’t get a wicket but was splendidly economical throughout.

Aidan's second success, though, had brought the aforementioned Richard Horton to the wicket, who turned out to be a superbly destructive batsman in the Colin Milburn mould (i.e. none too thin). He dispatched Aidan's best efforts to all corners with muscular efficiency, then did much the same for Dan and for James O'Herlihy. The Rygersdal score began to advance hideously, as Horton himself advanced on a century. Once again I felt I had no choice but to bring myself on.

'Oh, you'll enjoy *this*,' said Greg loudly. 'This bloke's *shit*.' The last word was uttered with particular venom, even for Greg.

'Can it, Greg,' I said.

Horton halted me in my run-up, and turned to address the little keeper.

'You know what? Here at Rygersdal we don't like blokes who sledge their own side. Especially their own skipper.'

Well said, sir, I thought. There were some 'hear hear's in the field. Greg looked suitably deflated.

Shortly afterwards, Horton shaped to drive one of my more innocuous deliveries out of the ground, then stopped and defended it at the last minute, exhaled, and made a face as if to say, *you nearly had me there*. I was as sure as hell I hadn't, but I let it pass as a fluke. Then he did it again. This became a pattern: whoever was bowling at the other end was treated imperiously, but I was treated with mystifying respect, almost always at the last second. I can only suppose that this was intended to teach Greg a lesson, for Horton was an extremely nice man. Certainly it seemed to have confused his team-mates, three of whom proffered up their unguarded stumps to me almost as if they were expecting the ball to do something devilish.

By the time Riaan and Aidan came back for their second spells, the Rygersdal score had passed the 200–6 mark and Horton was well into three figures. Slowly they turned the screw again. At last we reached the final over. Horton launched a huge mow against Aidan and was stumped (how Greg managed to stand up to someone of Aidan's pace I've no idea). In came the number nine, who was out lbw first ball. Then, off the last ball of the innings, the number ten lost his middle stump. Aidan had five wickets, and a hat trick to boot, and was sweatily exultant. Greg had taken four dismissals behind the stumps, bringing his tour total to an excellent twelve—not that anybody rushed to congratulate him. Rygersdal had scored 222–9 from their forty overs. Topping that was going to be a very tall order indeed.

I was painfully aware that this would be my own last opportunity to register any sort of score with the bat. Along with Riaan and Tom, I had failed to get into double figures once all tour. If I could even help see off the opening pair, that would be something, and might set up an easier time for those who followed. Our starts had not been very impressive of late—23–2, 4–3, 29–6—and it is, of course, extremely difficult to win a game of cricket without a decent start to one's innings. The fast bowlers were limbering up and the usual line-up of predatory slips was forming as I waddled out to the wicket, padded up like the Michelin man's English cousin. Matthew had volunteered to accompany me into the firing line this time, which was brave of him, following on the back of two ducks. As it was, he was superb, especially off the back foot, just like the old Matthew, while I just did my best to stay with him. The heat seemed as ferocious and the bowling every bit as swift as at Perth, but somehow, just for once, I managed to avoid nibbling at any away-swingers and giving the hungry cuckoos in the slips anything to feed on. We had taken the score to 36 after nine overs, and had seen off the opening bowlers, when I relaxed and foolishly lost my off bail. I'd like to say that I'd finally made it out of single figures, but I hadn't. Around the world in eighty runs? No—just eighteen.

Eiran came and went in a trice, but his brother James, who was proving a real revelation on this tour, batted stylishly and with calm efficiency against some high-quality bowling. When Matthew fell at last, Sean O'Herlihy took his place with equal poise. At the halfway stage we had reached an impressive 96–3. It was, in fact, an excellent platform to launch what inevitably came next: our middle-order collapse. What is it about cricket teams that their middles must collapse, like overcooked soufflés? Psychologically speaking, one can only presume that middle-order batsmen are prey to a combination of impatience to get at the bowling, and overconfidence at the apparent ease with which the earlier batsmen have mastered it. Certainly that's what happens at village level. Whether at international level the likes of, say, Andrew Flintoff ever observe the upper order successfully negotiate a spell from Glenn McGrath and loudly declare, 'This bloke's rubbish—let me at him' is open to doubt. Anyway, suffice it to say that, from a very respectable 96–3 at the halfway stage, we had subsided to a very hopeless 117–7 just seven overs later, still more than 100 adrift with only three wickets in hand, and staring defeat in the face.

Greg stuck around for a bit, but when Aidan and Tom came together at the wicket, 80 was required off the last ten overs, with only Riaan waiting in the pavilion. By an amazing coincidence, eighty runs was approximately double what the three of them, put together, had managed all tour. Even more amazingly, they set about the previously rock-solid bowling as if it were mere chaff. Aidan and Riaan, to be fair, are excellent batsmen at village and league level, with centuries under their belt, but, as I had so amply demonstrated, such achievements are as naught when it comes to the real thing. Tom, not to be outdone, was making a mockery of his own recent form, his tour batting average to date being a princely 1. (I was going to say that he had stood his tour batting average on its head, but then it would still have been 1.) He dispatched a series of elegant on drives to the boundary in fine style, while Aidan thumped the ball to all corners rather more vigorously. Aidan perished in the deep with the score on 182, after a stand of 39, but Riaan came in and blasted no fewer than three huge sixes back over the bowler's head and out of the ground. The last over began with us just twelve runs short of victory, and Riaan on strike. Richard Horton took off his main bowler and paced out his run up: he was going to finish matters himself.

Looking back now on that final over, it is hard to imagine how someone so very, very good at batting could be so utterly, completely useless at bowling. Certainly the man was a sportsman, and he was giving us every chance. His first ball, a gentle, looping off-spinner, trickled directly to the feet of first slip. His second was in danger of braining the square-leg umpire. Two wides. Ten to win. Confidence grew in the pavilion. The third ball, however, flew even higher than the other two. If there'd been any low cloud we'd have lost sight of it completely. Perhaps Riaan did. At any rate, it sailed way over his head, disturbing a flock of migrating swallows, described an ungraceful parabola, and landed directly on the bails. The South Africans rushed to mob their delighted skipper. Riaan and Tom trudged disconsolately towards the pavilion. It should, of course, have been a no ball, but no one on the field of play, umpires included, seemed to have noticed the fact. Still, given Horton's extraordinary choice of bowler for the final over, it would have been churlish to deny him his moment of triumph. We had lost—once again—by just nine runs. We were knackered, sweaty and beaten (no sado-masochism jokes, please), but we were proud and happy to have done so well.

So many people had been so nice to us around the world, so kind and hospitable, especially at Curtin University/ Victoria Park in Perth, that it seems invidious to single out any one of our many hosts for special praise. But the Rygersdal team and their captain deserve that special praise. We could not have been more royally entertained. Utterly unfazed by their heavy defeat in the boat race, the South Africans simply insisted on having another go, and another go, until barely anyone on either team could stand up. (Mind you, they had managed to get five of the Durham University team so drunk that they'd been sick into oil drums the previous weekend.) A magnificent barbecue—or *braai*, as they stubbornly insist on referring to it down there—was held on the outfield, as great shafts of orange sunlight angled down between the hard-edged black corners of the massif silhouetted above us. It was a truly amazing location for an impromptu party. I couldn't help feeling, though, that there was a slight difference between the Cape Town party spirit on display here and the party spirit we'd encountered at the waterfront on New Year's Eve 1995–6. Then the sense of optimism had been palpable, a sense of rebirth, a sense of excitement at the possibilities ahead; now there was more of an eve-of-Waterloo, deck-of-the-Titanic feeling in the air. Let's have as much fun as possible while we still can.

'They say we should leave,' said Richard Horton, strolling up behind me, drink in hand, as I admired the view, 'but how can we ever leave our mountain?'

* * *

Staggering back through our hotel lobby at 2 a.m., drunk and exhausted, I was more than a little surprised to be hailed by one of the two girls sitting behind reception, an attractive blonde eighteen-year-old.

'Hi . . . what are you doing right now?'

'Er . . . I'm going to bed.'

'Do you want to take me out for a drink instead?'

'Well . . . I . . . haven't you got to look after reception?'

'Oh, I don't work here. My parents are friends of the owner. I live in the hotel. My name's Sam.'

'Oh, right . . . um . . . OK then. Sam.'

Why not? I thought. No harm done, was there, in allowing myself to be picked up by a random woman. After all, it didn't happen every day. And, by the look of open-mouthed incredulity on the face of Tom, who was halfway up the stairs, there'd be a certain social cachet attached to the encounter.

Sam took me to a city-centre bar called Manhattan, which was still going strong in the small hours. It took my keen eyes a mere half-hour or so to establish that she was (a) a regular and (b) the only woman in the room. Manhattan was a gay bar. This was fine of course, no problem, not that I'd ever been to a gay bar before; but I have to concede that, when she disappeared to the lavatory for an extended period, by the time I'd been chatted up by my seventh man I was childishly grateful to see her return. In fact we shared an extremely pleasant, sociable evening. Eventually I crawled into bed at 4 a.m.

'Well?' said Tom, from the other side of the room.

'Well nothing. I've just been on an ordinary, everyday night out . . . to a gay bar.'

The following morning, of course, everyone was agog to find out the identity of the mystery woman who had been so desperate as to choose me for a drinking companion. Eiran seemed especially keen to discover who she was.

'She lives in the hotel,' I explained. 'I'll introduce you later today.'

There's only one way this is going to end up, I thought.

*   *   *

Our last significant tourist pilgrimage was down to Boulders beach—so named because of the large quantity of giant boulders that litter the sands—near Simon's Town on the eastern side of the Cape of Good Hope. Here a few of the warmer waters of the Indian Ocean seem to have sneaked in past the Atlantic's guard, become trapped between the rocks, and then succumbed to a good broiling from the sun, for Boulders beach is the only place in Cape Town where it is possible to swim without a seven-inch-thick wetsuit. It is also, bizarrely, home to a substantial colony of penguins. You would think that penguins, given their preference for summering in the Subantarctic would seek out colder water for their holidays, but no, just like humans, they crowd on to the beaches where the water is warmest. This leads to the extraordinary spectacle of penguins and swimsuited humans splashing about side by side, or sitting on the boulders gawping stupidly at one another. They are short, fat creatures who exist entirely on a diet of pilchards (that's the penguins, not the humans, although by the look of some of the latter the same description might apply). These, in fact, were bona-fide African penguins (they used to be called jackass penguins, but presumably that was deemed racist towards jackasses).

I'd visited Boulders beach a decade previously, on the last Captain Scott South African tour, and the whole thing had been somewhat informally organized. Now, increased visitor numbers had led to the place becoming rather more regimented.

There were painted wooden boardwalks everywhere, and all the best stretches of open sand had been designated 'penguins only' beaches—as if, in a bizarre parody of apartheid, preferential treatment had been reserved not for whites or blacks but for black-*and*-whites. This was a slight pity, as we'd brought a bat and ball in the car, and quite fancied a final game of beach cricket in the sun; but the penguins had bagged all the best bits of beach.

Penguins stopped play. Sounds familiar.

This, I thought, is where I came in.

*   *   *

The taxis pulled up outside the Metropole for the last time. Those of us who were leaving piled our luggage into the boot. It was a sad moment. Then, gingerly, I placed the precious *Gone with the Wind* poster in its makeshift cardboard tube across the back shelf of the car for its last, risky journey. The cabbie, a tall, rubicund black guy, promptly picked it up and tried to squeeze it into the boot, down one side of the suitcases.

'No!' I said. 'Not there. It's fragile.'

' "Fragile"?' he said, mystified. Clearly he didn't speak much English.

'Delicate. Easy to break. Handle with care,' I said, racking my brain for suitable phrases. I took the tube from him, patted it in what I hoped was a suitably fragile manner, and replaced it on the back shelf. He picked it up again.

'It go in lot better like this!' he smiled earnestly, and snapped it clean in two over his knee. The two halves came completely apart, and he wedged them back in the boot beside the cases. Horror-stricken, I extracted the poster from the remains of its packaging, the cabbie still beaming hopefully. Rhett Butler and Scarlett O'Hara had been literally ripped apart by a dirty great tear that split the poster from top to bottom. Later I would take it to a vintage-poster restoration service in London, to see if anything could be done. The man behind the counter shook his head.

'Well, there are two options. You could have it fixed so's you wouldn't see at a cursory glance, but it wouldn't bear close inspection. That'd cost a hundred quid.'

'And how much would the poster be worth, with that sort of mend?'

'About a hundred quid.'

'What's the second option?'

'An invisible mend. A real professional job. I'd send it off to a specialist. Only a professional would ever know it'd been torn. That'd cost a thousand quid.'

'And how much would it be worth then?'

'About a thousand quid.'

I felt like I was living a Roald Dahl short story.

* * *

Not all the Scotties were catching the final plane out of Cape Town. Aidan, of course, was heading to East London to marry his childhood sweetheart, but we would see him again. The same could not be said for Riaan, who had sadly played his last game for us. He was returning to his one-horse dorp in the north of the country, where the men do God's work and wear very long beards (a bit like

Tehran, only a tad more fanatical); there were emotional goodbyes all round. For three weeks we had travelled the world as a unit, and had rather got used to the lifestyle and the camaraderie. Now the party was about to split in two. Sean and James O'Herlihy had changed their air tickets somehow, in order to attend Aidan's wedding, and planned to stay on in South Africa for the Cricket World Cup.

'I'm sticking around as well,' said Eiran, 'for a month or two at least.'

'Oh, are you staying for the World Cup as well?' I asked.

'No, I'm, er . . . moving in with Sam.'

'*Moving in?* As in cohabiting?'

'Er . . . yeah.'

Blimey, I thought. *That must be some sort of world record.*

12

Heathrow

The rain was, of course, lashing down at Heathrow, near horizontally. The temperature was a degree or two above freezing. By tacit agreement, we quietly abandoned our plan to play a scratch game in a local park. After all, we'd 'done' Europe. And there were only six of us. Standing there in the arrivals hall, watching those big, fat kitbags lurch on to the carousel for the last time, we felt strangely empty—as if a part of our lives had been stolen. It was as if we'd been aboard a joyous, whirling fairground ride, and all of a sudden we'd been told to get off. The lights had dimmed. Tom's laminated kit-carrying rota had reached its end, its lustre faded. Part of me wanted to grab one of the kitbags, run round to departures, buy another round-the-world air ticket, and climb back on board for a second go. Of course, what we'd just done was profoundly idiotic in every respect, but that didn't stop it feeling like some sort of weird achievement. The fact that we'd lost nearly all our games didn't matter a jot: our Caribbean debacle aside, we knew we hadn't let ourselves down. Personally speaking, the fact that I'd been found so severely wanting with the bat didn't bother me either: I'd done my best, which was to come rock bottom of the tour batting averages, and that was fair enough. One has to accept one's limitations. Besides, thanks in part to a bit of South African generosity, I'd mysteriously come top of the tour bowling averages instead, which would suit this old has-been just fine.

Off we all went, then, to our former lives. Dan, shaven-headed, went off to brief the Home Secretary. Paul, his last drop of hyperactive energy spent, headed off home to Islington. Tom only came back to my flat for long enough to pick up his stuff: his wife had finally decided to have him back. Now, at the time of writing, they have a baby daughter. We would not see Matthew on the cricket field for another year, as his domestic circumstances finally closed in on him. At last, unable to stand living with a cricket ban, he got a divorce.

None of us ever saw Greg again.

13

Oxford

It is a gloomy Sunday afternoon in Oxford, four months later. The Captain Scott XI is playing its second game of the season, on a billiard table of a wicket at Balliol College, and drifting inexorably to defeat. Our total of 240 off forty overs is being easily overhauled: the home side have scored 186–2 from thirty overs, and look to be in no trouble at all. Part of the reason is that Aidan has pulled up with a torn muscle. Part of the reason is that Riaan isn't with us any more. But most of the reason is a quiet, unspoken inertia that has settled on our side like house dust. Playing cricket on a gloomy day in Oxford just doesn't have the glamour of, say, cavorting beneath Table Mountain, or joining battle at the Hurlingham Club in Buenos Aires. It's curiously hard to motivate yourself when the sun isn't beating down, the palm trees aren't waving in the breeze, and there isn't a plane at the end of the runway, waiting to whisk you away. Failed Test cricketers must feel much the same when they're sent back to Leicestershire or (especially) Glamorgan.

Then, suddenly, Eiran's mobile rings, by the side of the pitch. Sam, whom he has dragged all the way from Cape Town for the start of the season, answers it. Cie is dead. He'd been playing in London for his Sunday side, the Railway Taverners, having turned out for us the day before. The previous evening, in fact, he had complained of feeling unwell. He had died suddenly at the crease, bat in hand. He had scored 89 not out, and was closing in on a century, when he had clubbed a ball to the long-leg boundary, spun round on his heel, and collapsed to the floor. At first the other players had assumed that he'd merely lost his balance, until they'd realized that he was not moving. He had, it transpired, suffered a massive heart attack, and was almost certainly dead before he hit the ground. All those sausage sandwiches had finally come home to roost. The loss of this lovely, generous, friendly, popular and eternally youthful-seeming man utterly stunned each and every one of us. Bewildered, we wandered about the outfield in small, shocked, miserable groups. It felt as if the heart had been ripped out of our own team. The Balliol side, who were very kind about it, asked us what we would like to do. Abandon the game, or carry on? Nobody really knew the answer. We were in what-he-would-have-wanted territory.

'I know what Cie would have wanted us to do,' said Eiran. 'He would have wanted us to keep playing. And to turn the game around, and win. Then he would have wanted us to do the same in every other game this year—to go through a whole season unbeaten.'

It seemed a wild idea, a virtual impossibility; but nobody was going to vote against it. We went back to the game, and went at Balliol with renewed vigour, like men possessed. Forty-five minutes later the home side were all out for 230, and we had won by ten runs.

Two hundred cricketers came to Cie's funeral, most of them from the amazing assortment of teams he'd turned out for in his short life. A memorial tournament was held, and both ourselves and the Railway Taverners ordered pitchside benches with his name on them. Ours had 'Modo Egredior' carved beneath. We raised the money by putting up a collection box in the Grape Street Wine Bar. Despite our high proportion of poverty-stricken cricketers, the Scotties contributed over £500. The Taverners did likewise. The Rain Men (being the rump of the old Scott side) contributed a measly £20.

Come September, we completed our other little memorial to him, by going through the entire season unbeaten. Fate, or good fortune, had come to our aid more than once: we'd been plummeting to defeat at Minster Lovell, for instance, when it had poured with rain. Elsewhere, there had been acts of kindness: the captain of Stansfield had generously thrown his wicket away on reaching his century, almost certainly on purpose, with victory there for the taking. But there had been terrific performances too. At the end of the season we'd visited Laxton Park in Northamptonshire, a side who (in the days when they'd been able to boast a brace of county players) had stuffed us many times. Here Eiran had smashed the club record for a single innings, scoring 163 not out. We'd all turned out in memorial cricket shirts with Cie's smiling face embroidered at the chest: as Eiran hit the winning runs, he leaped in the air for joy and kissed his little Cie badge. We had done it.

Laxton Park declined to play us again the following season, because, as the fixtures secretary explained down his long nose, they 'didn't like the manner of Eiran's celebrations'. How very, very

British of them. How very, very traditional. How very, very shit. How easy it is, I thought, to employ the famously British virtues of good manners, modesty and self-effacement as a mask for jealousy, mean-spiritedness and defeatism. As a nation, an empire, we've been duty-bound to export the former, and where we have done so we have deserved credit; but all too often we have been just as guilty of the latter. What, in the end, was Captain Robert Falcon Scott really about? Joking apart, what did his example really mean? Was it about retaining an unemotional grip on protocol in minus 70° Celsius? Or was it about doing his damnedest, win or lose, and having his friends by his side at the end?

Postscript

My girlfriend, Lisa, and I are sitting in a windowless office in a west-London hospital. It is a clammy day at the beginning of May, but even in this stuffy room the air seems to be rushing past my ears. I have just been told the reason for the mysterious pains in my right side, the high temperatures and the outbreaks of breathlessness which have kept me away from pre-season nets. It seems that by some unexpected mischance I—who have never smoked a single cigarette in my life—have managed to contract advanced, inoperable lung cancer. Two fist-sized tumours are growing at the entry to my right lung, which has collapsed and become infected. Undoubtedly I have been running around with this condition for years, as it slowly grew in its ugliness—around Cape Town, around Buenos Aires, around all those beautiful places. I am due to go into hospital on the following Monday as a matter of urgency, to begin chemotherapy. My former lifestyle—work, sport, the lot—is about to come to an end. Within a month, although I do not know it yet, I will be living in a hospital bed, hooked up by tubes to a drain on the wall. One of my ribs will have been removed, as will the staggering volume of two litres of pus from my collapsed right lung. My temperature will be 105°. My blood pressure will be 60/45, equivalent (I am told) to that of a man bleeding to death in a car crash. My life will have become a daily battle not just with cancer, but with *Staphylococcus aureus*, better known to the uninitiated (like myself) as the 'SA' bit in 'MRSA'.

I have a day to fill between being told that I have cancer and the start of this debilitating treatment. By coincidence, it is the day of the first cricket game of the season, against Corpus Christi College, Oxford. I have already dropped out of the side because of feeling unwell, but no replacement has been found as yet, and I'm travelling up to the game anyway, as all the kit is in the back of my car. The thought of playing crosses my mind, but I stuff it well to the back. Perhaps, perhaps, if there is an emergency, I tell myself, I will be needed. I'd be mad to play, of course, but I know this could well be the last time I ever pick up a bat. News of my predicament has spread throughout the team, and everyone is full of sympathy when I arrive. Everyone who is there, that is: there is no sign of the three O'Herlihys, who are late as usual.

With only seven players present, the Captain Scott side has little option but to bat: a pity, as heavy rain during the week has turned the wicket into a green-topped mudbath, a bowler's paradise. Corpus have come mob-handed, with one or two Blues bowlers from other colleges. The resulting debacle is all too predictable. Our thinned-out top order plays defiantly, but is unable to withstand the barrage of seam and swing for long: after an hour we are 41–6. The opposition players talk loudly and confidently about beer matches. The sole not-out batsman, Buster by name, is a fifteen-year-old schoolboy. I ascertain the location of the O'Herlihys. They are stuck in heavy traffic on the M40, at least an hour away. The choice is simple: either I go out to bat or the innings must be declared closed at 41 all out. So, of course, I put my pads on and limp out to the wicket. I have the same conversation with Buster that I had with the tramp, a decade or so before Buster was born.

'Do you know how to do a forward defensive?'

'Sure thing.'

'Right—you and I have got an hour to last. And neither of us are going to get out.'

I have supreme confidence in Buster. As we know, there's no harder batsman to dislodge than a fifteen-year-old schoolboy.

In the event, we don't just rely on forward defensives. We play the odd shot or two as well. But every run is agony. After every single I have to lean on my bat handle and gasp desperately for breath. My right lung is splitting. I could ask for a runner, of course, but I want to do this myself. I don't want to get beaten. It has become childish but importantly symbolic for me not to lose. The ball mustn't even beat the bat.

After an hour or so we have doubled the score to 82–6 when I see a familiar battered car pull up and disgorge its three large, hairy occupants. An over later and Sean is there, suited and booted on the boundary. I beckon him on to replace me. We meet halfway.

'Why,' I ask him, 'must you *always* be so fucking late?'

And then he puts his arms round me, and I realize that my knees have buckled and my legs have given way, because there just isn't any energy left in the tank, and for a moment he has to take my weight. I realize too that my face is wet with tears, and I realize that I love this stupid bunch of deadbeats with all my heart, and that I am going to miss them so very, very much.

The Captain Scott innings finishes on 145–8 from forty overs. In reply, Corpus Christi are 120 all out. We win by twenty-five runs.

After twenty-seven years, I have another, harder, battle to fight now, and I must leave the Scotties to it. If you'll forgive the crap cricketing metaphor, I can see the line of slips waiting for me, twenty yards back. I haven't the licence to make a single mistake; my only chance is to carry my bat through to the end. And of course I won't be wearing a helmet. I want to see exactly where I'm going. It's a tough task, but perhaps it's not completely impossible.

After all, we did once beat a country. On a Tuesday.

Afterword

Harry died in my arms on 7 November 2005. We had married earlier that day.

Facing a physically superior foe was never something he was afraid of, and during his illness he felt as confident as always that he could outwit it with the power of his extraordinary mind if he tried hard enough; but sadly this particular cancer—which was one of the most aggressive of its type that his oncologist had ever seen—didn't play by the rules.

The treatment was impossibly gruelling, but this exceptional man was focused, cheerful and brave to the last. Unfortunately the severe lung infection that had squatted inside him ever since the appearance of a lung abscess early on in his treatment had threatened to overwhelm him all along, and in early November, his body weakened by rounds of chemo and radical radiotherapy, it suddenly took a final and fatal hold.

He did actually play cricket a couple more times after the episode at the end of this book. However, on the last time—a beautifully sunny day in June—he managed to dislodge his permanent chest drain in the process of 'a little light fielding', and, as he had to have another section of rib removed in order to put the drain back, we figured that enough was enough.

We travelled extensively during the summer, visiting seven countries despite his illness, and Harry also managed to catch some live Ashes action at Lord's and the Oval. The England cricket team might have thought they were winning the Ashes for themselves, but we knew they were doing it for Harry.

Eight days before Harry died we attended the Captain Scott XI's annual cricket dinner, and he presented all the awards and gave just as irreverent and rousing a speech as usual. Five days later he went through the copy-editor's final set of queries on this book.

He was borne to his grave in Brompton Cemetery by a squad of Scotties, following a magnificent address given by Sean. As we all tottered away, I heard an unmistakable *glunk!*—someone had tossed in a cricket ball. I smiled for the first time in days. A few people looked shocked, but Harry would have liked that. Besides, it would go with the cricket bat I had placed in his hands.

Lisa Thompson
December 2005